THE TEACHING
PORTFOLIO

THE TEACHING PORTFOLIO

A Practical Guide to Improved Performance and Promotion/Tenure Decisions

Fourth Edition

Peter Seldin, J. Elizabeth Miller,
Clement A. Seldin

Foreword by Wilbert J. McKeachie

JOSSEY-BASS
A Wiley Imprint
www.josseybass.com

Published by Jossey-Bass
A Wiley Imprint
989 Market Street, San Francisco, CA 94103-1741—www.josseybass.com

Jossey-Bass books and products are available through most bookstores. To contact Jossey-Bass directly
call our Customer Care Department within the U.S. at 800-956-7739, outside the U.S. at 317-572-3986,
or fax 317-572-4002.

Jossey-Bass also publishes its books in a variety of electronic formats. Some content that appears in
print may not be available in electronic books.

Library of Congress Cataloging-in-Publication Data

Seldin, Peter.
    The teaching portfolio : a practical guide to improved performance and promotion/tenure
decisions. — 4th ed. / Peter Seldin, J. Elizabeth Miller, Clement A. Seldin ; foreword by Wilbert
J. McKeachie.
        p.   cm.
    Includes bibliographical references and index.
    ISBN 978-0-470-53809-8 (pbk.)
        1. College teachers—Rating of—United States.   2. College teaching—United States—
Evaluation.   3. Portfolios in education—United States.   4. Portfolios in education—United
States—Case studies.   I. Miller, J. Elizabeth, 1958-   II. Seldin, Clement A., 1948-   III. Title.
LB2333.S46   2010
378.1'224—dc22

                                                                              2010014411

Printed in the United States of America
FOURTH EDITION
PB Printing   10 9 8 7 6 5 4 3 2 1

The Jossey-Bass
Higher and Adult Education Series

Contents

FOREWORD

Almost twenty years ago, in 1991, I wrote the Foreword for the first edition of Peter Seldin's seminal book, *The Teaching Portfolio.* I said then that the portfolio offered a promising solution to the problem faced by professors to supply persuasive documentation of their teaching effectiveness. The reason for my genuine optimism, I said, was that the teaching portfolio provided tangible concrete evidence needed by those responsible for personnel decisions, and at the same time, it provided a useful structure to stimulate critical self-analysis and improvement in teaching.

In the time since I looked into my crystal ball and wrote those prophetic words, use of the teaching portfolio concept has been adopted by several thousand colleges and universities throughout the United States and by countless other institutions around the world. And in the process, *The Teaching Portfolio* has become the most widely used and all-time best seller in the teaching portfolio field.

I thought the first edition of the book was great. Then the second and third editions each added some helpful new suggestions. Now, in this fourth edition, Peter Seldin has been joined by coauthors J. Elizabeth Miller and Clement Seldin. Each brings a wealth of hands-on experience with the teaching portfolio. Together, these three authors have written a remarkably useful book. They have mastered the art of simplification, used straightforward language, and provided suggestions that are practical and easily implemented.

Especially noteworthy new features of this edition are:

- The detailed guides for preparing a portfolio for promotion and tenure as differentiated from a portfolio for improvement

- The specific suggestions on how to find a mentor to help in developing the portfolio
- The detailed nuts-and-bolts chapter on preparing a portfolio
- The expanded section on electronic portfolios and a new section on clinical educator portfolios
- The time-tested strategies for getting started with portfolios.
- The pragmatic answers to questions commonly raised about developing and using portfolios

The Teaching Portfolio, Fourth Edition covers just about everything you should know about portfolios. It includes models of successful use; provides a field-tested, widely used template; offers sample teaching portfolios; and gives immediately useful advice. Seldin, Miller, and Seldin have extensive portfolio involvement as researchers, practitioners, and mentors to faculty who are preparing portfolios. This broad-based experience has enabled them to gain new perspectives and insights, as well as refine and modify what has already been learned about portfolios. The new edition puts much of this wisdom into practice.

I believe that college teaching has improved since I began teaching in 1946. One of the major factors contributing to this improvement is the development of the teaching portfolio.

University of Michigan   WILBERT J. MCKEACHIE

Preface to the Fourth Edition

Not long ago, an academic friend ran into us at a national conference and asked us how she could *really* convince others that she was an effective teacher. Student rating scores, she said, were an obvious way to measure teaching effectiveness: the higher the rating, the greater the effectiveness. We told our friend that it was an obvious (and necessary) way, but that it struck us that student rating numbers were hardly a complete basis for determining teaching effectiveness and that they needed to be augmented by data from an array of other sources. We also pointed out that student rating numbers did not provide information on *what* a professor did, *why* he or she did it, or *how* he or she did it. And these numbers did not present a rationale for pedagogical choices made, expectations realized, or circumstances that promoted or inhibited teaching success.

Our friend pondered what we had told her. Okay, she said, if using student rating numbers alone is a flawed approach to measuring teaching effectiveness, is there a better way? We said there is. It is the teaching portfolio. Our friend was not familiar with the concept and asked how she could learn more about it. *The Teaching Portfolio, Fourth Edition,* we told her, is a book that will be helpful. It covers just about everything you should know about portfolios; gives models of successful use; provides a field-tested, widely used template; and provides sample teaching portfolios and practical materials.

Why a New Edition?

Since 2004, when the third edition of *The Teaching Portfolio* was published, we have collectively visited more than one hundred colleges and universities and talked with countless faculty and administrators about the portfolio and its place in the evaluation and development of teaching. We have also had the distinct pleasure of working one-on-one as mentors to hundreds of faculty members as they prepared their personal teaching portfolios.

During that period, we picked up new ideas, gained new perspectives, and refined and modified what was already known about portfolios. This new edition of *The Teaching Portfolio* puts many of these into print.

Like the first, second, and third editions, this one keeps the focus on self-reflection and documenting teaching performance. But in this edition, considerable substance has been added:

- A new detailed table of contents for portfolios prepared for personnel decisions and for portfolios prepared for improvement purposes
- A new section of nearly one hundred prompt questions to guide the preparation of each part of the portfolio
- An expanded section on the key factors to consider in choosing portfolio items
- A new section on the important items to be sure to include in the portfolio appendix
- An expanded section on the specific topics of conversation needed between the professor and department chair on portfolio expectations
- A more detailed section on how to gain institutional acceptance of the portfolio concept
- An expanded section on electronic portfolios and a new section on clinical educator portfolios
- An expanded section on how to prepare a portfolio without a mentor
- A new section on how to evaluate portfolios for tenure/promotion decisions, including a field-tested form for doing so

How This Book Is Organized

The Teaching Portfolio, Fourth Edition has three parts.

Part One presents the what, why, and how to develop teaching portfolios. It outlines an extensively tested step-by-step approach to create a portfolio, discusses how to prepare it for tenure decisions or for improvement in performance, and offers an array of field-tested suggestions for improving portfolios.

Chapter One discusses the teaching portfolio concept: what it is, how it includes the scope and quality of a professor's teaching performance, how it is based on structured reflection and thoughtfully selected information on teaching activities and provides solid evidence of their effectiveness, and how it differs from other approaches to evaluate and improve teaching. It also provides a detailed table of contents.

Chapter Two describes the many possibilities from which faculty members can select portfolio items relevant to their academic situation, discusses the factors to consider in choosing items, outlines the three main categories of the narrative, provides suggestions as to the length of each category, and sets out more than one hundred prompt questions to guide the preparation of each part of the portfolio.

Chapter Three outlines the necessary topics of conversation between the department chair and professor on portfolio expectations and specifics of what and how teaching performance is to be reported, provides helpful guidelines for getting started with portfolios, and spells out ten field-tested ways to gain institutional acceptance of the teaching portfolio concept. It offers practical advice and takes a hard look at what works and what does not.

Chapter Four examines in important detail the key sequence of steps in creating a teaching portfolio. It then discusses the need to begin the process by deciding the purpose in preparing it and the audience that will read it, outlines how to describe an approach to teaching and select portfolio items that illustrate teaching style and offer evidence of effectiveness, and offers helpful suggestions on how to present the entire portfolio in a unified container.

Chapter Five examines the key role of the mentor, describes the collaborative approach to developing a polished portfolio, recognizes that sometimes no able mentors are available, and provides important self-assessment questions that can serve as a helpful checklist for those who are preparing a portfolio without a mentor's advice.

Chapter Six presents a list of specific, field-tested suggestions to faculty as they prepare their portfolios (with or without a mentor). Among others, the detailed recommendations include housing the portfolio in a binder with tabs; cross-referencing the narrative to the appendix; explaining the evidence; bringing the teaching philosophy statement to life; limiting the number of student or colleague comments; and using graphs, charts, italics, and boldface to enhance reader interest.

Chapter Seven discusses how to evaluate teaching portfolios for personnel decisions, what should be evaluated, and how it should be done. It discusses the key requirements of practicality, relevance, and acceptability; outlines common pitfalls in the evaluation of portfolios; provides practical advice in the form of a twenty-point general checklist of items to consider; and includes specific criteria and suggested evidence that can be used to evaluate teaching from portfolios.

Chapter Eight offers pragmatic answers to questions commonly raised about developing and using teaching portfolios. It discusses how a portfolio differs from the usual end-of-year faculty report to administrators, how much time it takes to produce a portfolio, who "owns" it, why no two portfolios look alike, why models and mentors are so important, and why an elegant portfolio cannot disguise weak performance in teaching.

Chapter Nine discusses electronic teaching portfolios; describes how technology allows portfolio developers to collect and organize the contents in many formats, including audio, video, graphical, and text; examines the use of hypertext links to organize the material; and outlines the strengths and weaknesses of electronic portfolios.

Chapter Ten examines the clinical educator portfolio and describes how it differs from the traditional teaching portfolio. It discusses individual instruction, direct patient care, board certification, how working with adult learners affects teaching methods, and the need for clinical educators to document different types of teaching—for example, bedside, didactic, and simulation.

Part Two, new to this edition, contains profiles of campus use of the teaching portfolio. It describes how four very different colleges and universities have implemented portfolios, what worked and what did not, purposes, tough decisions, and key strategies.

It also includes a personal report by a university provost on what he looks for in reviewing portfolios submitted for tenure and promotion purposes.

Chapters Eleven to Fourteen contain profiles of campus practice and provide detailed yet concise accounts of what four campuses are doing with teaching portfolios: Loyola University Maryland, University of Massachusetts Amherst, Elgin Community College (Illinois), and Florida Gulf Coast University. The settings and practices are diverse by design, reflecting the broad individual differences in institutions. The intent is not to present the best of current practice (though many positive examples can be seen in the profiles) but rather to demonstrate how teaching portfolio use depends on context and purpose, as well as the mission and culture of an institution.

Chapter Twelve presents a personal report by the provost at Florida Gulf Coast University on what he looks for in reviewing portfolios submitted for tenure and promotion, what separates strong from weak portfolios, and the kinds of evidence that are most persuasive. It includes the practical but surprising recommendations that he, an "end user," makes to faculty who are preparing their portfolios for personnel decisions.

Part Three is also new to this edition and contains the actual teaching portfolios of twenty-one faculty members from an array of disciplines and a wide range of institutions. None of these portfolios appeared in earlier editions of this book.

Chapters Sixteen through Thirty-Six contain the sample portfolios, all developed under the guidance of a skilled portfolio mentor. These documents reflect the advice and strategies presented in Part One. Because each portfolio is an individual document, varying importance has been assigned by different authors to different items. Some faculty discuss an item at length, while others dismiss it with just a sentence or two or omit it altogether. This is as it should be. Although there is a general template for teaching portfolios, much of what goes into them is determined by special factors such as purpose, career point, academic discipline, and personal preferences of the individual faculty members who prepare them. Together the sample portfolios are rich sources of ideas to professors in all disciplines.

CONCLUSION

The Teaching Portfolio, Fourth Edition offers the kind of ready-to-use, hands-on information that is required to foster the most effective use of portfolios. This new edition identifies key issues, red-flag warnings, successful strategies, and benchmarks for success. It is written for faculty members, department chairs, members of promotion and tenure committees, and graduate students planning careers as faculty members. The language is straightforward and nontechnical.

In 1991, the first edition of *The Teaching Portfolio* was published. Since then, the book has gained tenure as perhaps the most widely used and all-time best seller in the teaching portfolio field. We are humbled by this overwhelming show of trust and approach this latest edition determined to build on the solid foundation that made the first three editions such highly regarded tools for self-reflection and for documenting teaching effectiveness.

Pleasantville, New York   PETER SELDIN

DeKalb, Illinois   J. ELIZABETH MILLER

Amherst, Massachusetts   CLEMENT A. SELDIN

June 2010

ABOUT THE AUTHORS

Peter Seldin is Distinguished Professor of Management Emeritus at Pace University in Pleasantville, New York. A behavioral scientist, educator, author, and specialist in evaluation and development of faculty and administrative performance, he has been a consultant on higher education issues to more than 350 colleges and universities throughout the United States and in forty-five other countries around the world.

A well-known speaker at national and international conferences, Seldin has presented programs at more than thirty American Council on Education national workshops for division and department chairs and deans designed to enhance department leadership. He has contributed numerous articles on the teaching profession, student ratings, educational practice, and academic culture to such publications as *The New York Times*, the *Chronicle of Higher Education*, and *Change* magazine.

The more recent of his sixteen books are *The Academic Portfolio* (2009, with J. Elizabeth Miller), *Evaluating Faculty Performance* (2006, with associates), *The Teaching Portfolio* (2004), *The Administrative Portfolio* (2002, with Mary Lou Higgerson), and *Changing Practices in Evaluating Teaching* (1999, with associates).

Among recent honors, Seldin was named by the World Bank as a Visiting Scholar to Indonesia. In addition, he was elected a Fellow of the College of Preceptors in London, England. This special honor is given to a small number of faculty and administrators who are judged to have made an "outstanding contribution to higher education on the international level."

J. Elizabeth Miller is associate professor of child and family studies at Northern Illinois University (NIU) in DeKalb. She teaches courses in family theory and human development and mentors graduate students in undergraduate teaching. She has been honored four times with excellence-in-teaching awards.

Miller is the founding director of NIU's teaching assistant training program, which has served more than eight hundred teaching assistants. She is the outgoing chair of the Women's Caucus of the American Association for Higher Education and has served on the board of the National Council of Family Relations.

A presenter at numerous national and international conferences, her research interests focus on the interplay between feminist teaching and learner-centered instruction, as well as the improvement of college teaching. She has extensive experience mentoring faculty members and graduate students as they prepare their teaching and academic portfolios.

She is the coauthor of two well-received books, *The Academic Portfolio* (2009, with Peter Seldin) and *Exploring Family Theories* (2009, with associates) and has published journal articles and book chapters in faculty evaluation, work and family in higher education, religion and family, and mentoring graduate students.

Clement A. Seldin is professor of education at the University of Massachusetts Amherst, where he teaches undergraduate and graduate courses on the social foundations of American education. He has provided service to both his institution and profession as director for field-based graduate programs, director of internships, and member of regional research and editorial boards. He has been honored with many teaching awards, including the prestigious University of Massachusetts Distinguished Teaching Award.

Clement Seldin's research agenda focuses on contemporary problems in American education. He has examined several controversial and timely issues that have a direct impact on the lives of teachers and students. In addition, he has specialized in faculty development in higher education, with emphasis on teaching and academic portfolios.

He has contributed over thirty articles to national education journals and presented over forty research papers at regional and national conferences. Seldin has also served on research

teams for the Schools of Education Project, a comprehen-
sive multiyear research study of the nation's twelve hundred
schools of education, directed by Arthur Levine of Columbia
University. This major study resulted in three significant reports:
Educating Leaders (2005), *Educating Teachers* (2006), and *Educating
Researchers* (2007).

ABOUT THE CONTRIBUTORS

Peter G. Anderson is a professor of pathology, director of pathology undergraduate education, and preclerkship curriculum coordinator at the University of Alabama at Birmingham School of Medicine. He recently received the Alpha Omega Alpha Medical Honor Society Robert J. Glaser Distinguished Teacher Award and is active in national and international medical education organizations.

Nancy V. Baker is a Regents Professor and head of the Government Department at New Mexico State University, Las Cruces. The recipient of multiple teaching awards, including the university's highest recognition, she publishes extensively on law in the executive branch, including two scholarly books on the office of the U.S. attorney general.

Marc Jonathan Blitz is associate professor in the Law School at Oklahoma City University. He teaches and writes on constitutional law and on law and technology, and also teaches national security law, administrative law, evidence, and law of alternative dispute resolution. He was voted 2007 Professor of the Year by the Law School's merit scholars, was a Priddy Fellow, and has made significant use of visual technology, including interactive diagrams, animation software, and virtual world platforms, in his teaching.

Wiebke J. Boeing is assistant professor in the Department of Fish, Wildlife and Conservation Ecology at New Mexico State University, Las Cruces. She teaches classes in natural resource management, and her research focuses on the ecology of aquatic food webs.

Michael D. Brown is associate teaching professor at Brigham Young University, an affiliate of the Church of Jesus Christ of Latter-day Saints. A recipient of his college's Teaching Excellence Award, he is a member of the Physiology and Developmental Biology Department and BYU's interdisciplinary Neuroscience Center.

Michaela Burkardt is associate professor of physics at New Mexico State University, Las Cruces. She currently provides faculty development for STEM (science, technology, engineering, and mathematics) faculty through the university's Teaching Academy.

Kristine De Welde is an assistant professor of sociology at Florida Gulf Coast University, where she teaches courses on gender, family, methods, the sociology of food, and Hurricane Katrina. Selected for inclusion in *Who's Who Among America's Teachers,* she has published and presented extensively on pedagogy and service-learning.

Esther L. Devall is professor of family and consumer sciences at New Mexico State University, Las Cruces. She has received college, university, and national recognition for her teaching excellence and has been awarded almost $10 million in state and federal grants.

Monica A. Devanas is the director of faculty development and assessment programs at the Center for Teaching Advancement and Assessment Research at Rutgers University. She has been teaching microbiology for twenty-five years and is active in issues of science education and programs for retention of women in science and in National Science Foundation–funded grants to enhance science education both at Rutgers and in precollege populations.

Amanda Evans is assistant professor of social work at Florida Gulf Coast University. She has published and presented widely on issues related to neurobiology, trauma, and violence. She has twenty-five years of experience in health, mental health, and management. As a medical social worker for the first fifteen years of her career, Evans practiced in trauma, emergency, and cardiac settings. She is a certified mediator and serves as a consultant on issues related to organizational behavior and conflict.

Donna Price Henry is dean of the College of Arts and Sciences and professor of Biological Sciences at Florida Gulf Coast University. She is currently leading the construction of three academic buildings with instructional, research, performance, and office space. Henry has been instrumental in undergraduate curriculum innovation through integration of service-learning and undergraduate research projects.

Amy E. Hughes is an assistant professor of theater history and criticism at Brooklyn College, City University of New York, where she serves on the executive board for the Roberta S. Matthews Center for Teaching. She has published and presented on many topics related to teaching, including communication-intensive courses, role play, and pedagogical transparency.

Stephanie Jensen-Moulton is assistant professor of musicology at Brooklyn College, City University of New York. She has published articles on women in hip-hop, the nineteenth-century pianist "Blind Tom" Wiggins, and feminist pedagogy and is currently researching cultural intersections of opera and disability.

Richard R. Johnson is a professor of political science and chair of the same department at Oklahoma City University. He has served as a Priddy Fellow and a Fellow of the Faculty Teaching Academy at Oklahoma City University. He has been actively involved with civic engagement, arts integration, portfolios, and learning communities regionally and locally.

Aaron Kozbelt is associate professor of psychology at Brooklyn College of the City University of New York. He is the head of the CUNY doctoral subprogram in psychology—Cognition, Brain, and Behavior—and publishes widely on the psychology of creativity, aesthetics, the arts, and humor.

Vicki D. Lachman is clinical associate professor and track coordinator for the Innovation and Intra/Entrepreneurship in Advanced Nursing Practice in the College of Nursing and Health Professions at Drexel University. She is nationally known for her presentations and writing in clinical and applied ethics, especially in the area of moral courage.

Margaret Loring is an English instructor at Doña Ana Community College in New Mexico, where she has taught developmental and college level classes for fourteen years.

Mathew L. Ouellett is director of the Center for Teaching at the University of Massachusetts Amherst, where he is also a lecturer in the School of Education. He is editor of the well-received *Teaching Inclusively: Resources for Course, Department and Institutional Change in Higher Education* (New Forums Press) and is active in higher education organizations such as the Professional and Organizational Development Network in Higher Education.

Peter Rennert-Ariev is an associate professor of curriculum and instruction and chair of the Education Specialties Department at Loyola University Maryland. His scholarship focuses on teacher education, professional development, and assessment. He recently received the Outstanding New Scholar Award from the School of Education, University of Maryland at College Park.

Martha S. Rosenthal is a professor of biological sciences at Florida Gulf Coast University. The recipient of a number of teaching awards, she teaches courses on human physiology, neuroscience, human sexuality, and drugs and society. Her textbook on human sexuality will be published by Houghton Mifflin/Cengage Learning.

Richard Schnackenberg is assistant professor of mathematics and chair of the Department of Chemistry and Mathematics at Florida Gulf Coast University. While actively teaching for forty-four years, he spent twenty years in the world of professional theater.

David E. Smith is associate professor of chemistry at New Mexico State University in Las Cruces. He teaches courses in general chemistry and physical chemistry, as well as distance education courses for dual-enrollment high school students.

Annalise Sorrentino is an associate professor of pediatrics in the Division of Pediatric Emergency Medicine at the University of Alabama-Birmingham (UAB) and has been the recipient of numerous academic and teaching awards. She graduated from the University of Missouri–Kansas City School of Medicine and completed her pediatric residency and emergency medicine fellowship at UAB.

Kimberly Tarver is a professor of physical therapist assistant at Elgin Community College. She serves on the college's Multicultural and Global Initiatives Committee and is committed to on-campus initiatives relating to the teaching portfolio, multicultural curriculum transformation, and other learner-centered strategies for student success. She contributes to regional agencies that support suicide prevention and underprivileged children and their families.

Ronald B. Toll is provost and vice president for academic affairs and professor of marine sciences at Florida Gulf Coast University. Previously he held numerous academic administrative positions at several institutions. A recognized leader in advancing learning outcomes, his interests include academic building design that supports pedagogical flexibility and faculty career development.

Mary Pelak Walch is an assistant professor in the Department of Communication and Philosophy at Florida Gulf Coast University. Her teaching and research interests are in the areas of media ecology, rhetorical criticism, and communication pedagogy.

Heather A. Walsh-Haney is an assistant professor of forensic anthropology within the Criminal Forensics Studies program at Florida Gulf Coast University. As a member of the U.S. Public Health Services' Disaster Mortuary Operational Response Team, she has helped in the identification of victims from the World Trade Center and Hurricanes Katrina and Wilma. She brings these practitioner-based experiences into her undergraduate and graduate courses.

THE TEACHING
PORTFOLIO

THE WHAT, WHY, AND HOW OF TEACHING PORTFOLIOS

Part One discusses the teaching portfolio concept: what it is, what might go into it, why the contents depend on the purpose for which it is to be used, how it is based on structured reflection, why collaboration is important, why expectations must be discussed with the department chair, and how electronic portfolios and clinical educator portfolios differ from traditional teaching portfolios.

CHAPTER ONE

AN INTRODUCTION TO THE TEACHING PORTFOLIO

An important and welcome change is taking place on college and university campuses: teaching is being taken more seriously. Interest has mushroomed rapidly in recent years, burrowing into all areas of the country. Institutions are moving from lip-service endorsements of the importance of teaching to concerted and sustained efforts to evaluate and reward it. As for faculty, they are being held accountable as never before to provide solid evidence of the quality and effectiveness of their instruction.

The familiar professorial paradox is crumbling on many campuses. Traditionally, college professors were hired to teach but rewarded for research. Although this is still true in many institutions, especially those with strong graduate schools, it has been largely swept away on campuses stressing undergraduate education. Today, teaching may still be in second place in the race with research, but the gap is slowly closing.

What is behind this new emphasis on teaching? The growing number of students and parents facing rapidly escalating tuition bills has led to pointed questions about the quality of teaching and played a part. So have the rapid changes in educational technology, which have forever altered concepts of teaching and learning. But perhaps the most compelling force behind the demands for teaching accountability is the unrelenting budgetary squeeze that legislatures and institutional governing boards face. It has pressed colleges and universities hard to take a much closer look at each professor's teaching effectiveness.

Unfortunately, factual information on teaching performance is often skimpy at best. The typical curriculum vitae lists publications, research grants, publications, and conference presentations but says almost nothing about teaching. It offers little factual information about what the person does as a teacher, why he or she does it in that way, or how well he or she does it. Evaluating teaching performance in the absence of factual information is very difficult. Rewarding it is also very difficult, as is improving it.

Is there a way for colleges and universities to respond simultaneously to the movement to take teaching seriously and to the pressures to improve systems of teaching accountability? The answer is yes. A solution can be found by turning to the teaching portfolio, an approach increasingly recognized and respected. Although reliable numbers are hard to come by, estimates are that as many as twenty-five hundred colleges and universities in the United States and Canada (where it is called a teaching dossier) are using or experimenting with portfolios—a stunning jump from the ten institutions thought to be using portfolios in 1990.

WHAT IS A TEACHING PORTFOLIO?

A teaching portfolio is a factual description of a professor's teaching strengths and accomplishments. It includes documents and materials that collectively suggest the scope and quality of a professor's teaching performance. The portfolio is to teaching what lists of publications, grants, and honors are to research and scholarship. As such, it allows faculty members to display their teaching accomplishments for examination by others. And in the process, it contributes to both sounder tenure and promotion decisions and the professional development of individual faculty members. As a result, it provides a strong signal that teaching is an institutional priority.

The teaching portfolio is not an exhaustive compilation of all the documents and materials that bear on teaching performance. Instead, it culls from the record selected information on teaching activities and solid evidence of their effectiveness. Just as in a curriculum vitae, all claims in the portfolio should be supported by firm empirical evidence. Selectivity is important because the portfolio should not be considered a huge repository of indiscriminate documentation. Rather, it should be seen as a judicious, critical, purposeful analysis of performance, evidence, and goals.

The portfolio permits faculty to describe the unique circumstances of their courses and general approaches to teaching, explain their use of specific strategies and methods, and provide convincing evidence that they are effective. We interpret the word *teaching* here to signify all professional activity that provides direct support for student learning. That includes not only traditional classroom and laboratory teaching, but also instruction of online courses, and small-group settings, one-to-one teacher-student interactions, student advising, and the scholarship of teaching and communication of its results.

Why should a skeptical professor spend valuable time preparing a portfolio? Because it makes good sense to document teaching activities with the same care and accuracy as he or she uses to document research and scholarship. Portfolios are a step toward a more public, professional view of teaching and reflect teaching as a scholarly activity.

The logic behind portfolios is straightforward. Earlier assessment methods such as student ratings or peer observation were like flashlights: they illuminated only the teaching skills and abilities that fell within their beams and therefore shed light on only a small part of a professor's classroom performance. With portfolios, the flashlight is replaced by a searchlight. Its beam discloses the broad range of teaching skills, abilities, attitudes, philosophies, and methodologies.

PORTFOLIO USES

Faculty members are busy, even harried, individuals. Here are some reasons they should want to take the time and trouble to prepare a teaching portfolio:

- Graduate students are preparing portfolios to bolster their credentials as they enter the job market.
- Professors are preparing portfolios to take on the road as they seek a different teaching position.
- Some institutions are requiring portfolios from finalists for teaching positions.

- Portfolios are being used to determine winners of an institution's teacher of the year award or for merit pay consideration.
- Professors nearing retirement are preparing portfolios in order to leave a written legacy so that faculty members taking over their position will have the benefit of their experience.
- Portfolios are used to provide evidence in applications for grants or release time.
- Institutions are asking faculty to prepare portfolios so they can provide data on their performance to persons and organizations operating off campus, such as government agencies, boards of trustees, alumni, the general public, and advocacy groups.

By far, though, the two most often cited reasons for preparing teaching portfolios are to provide evidence for use in personnel decisions and to improve teaching performance.

PERSONNEL DECISIONS

Providing a rational and equitable basis for promotion and tenure decisions is a central reason for preparing a teaching portfolio. In today's climate of greater accountability, colleges and universities are increasingly looking to portfolios as a rich way to get at the complexity and individuality of teaching. The portfolio provides evaluators with hard-to-ignore information on what individual professors do as teachers, why they do it, how they do it, and the outcome of what they do. And by so doing, it avoids looking at teaching as a derivative of student ratings.

Some argue that professors should be given unrestricted freedom to select the items that best reflect their performance. That approach works well if the portfolio is developed for improvement, but not if it is developed for personnel decisions such as tenure or promotion. Because each portfolio is unique, the lack of standardization makes comparability very difficult for faculty members from different teaching contexts.

One answer is to require that portfolios being used for personnel decisions such as tenure or promotion include certain items, along with those chosen specifically by the professor. Mandated items might include summaries of student evaluations, classroom observation reports, representative course materials, and a reflective statement describing the professor's teaching philosophy and methodologies. The professor would then choose which additional items to include in the portfolio.

If certain items in the portfolio are standardized, comparison of teaching performance (three finalists from different disciplines competing for university teacher of the year, for example) becomes possible.

Because they are based on triangulation of data, portfolios provide evaluators with solid evidence from an array of different sources. This material enables them to better recognize and evaluate the effectiveness of faculty members as teachers inside and outside of the classroom.

The contents page prepared for personnel decisions (that is, evaluations) might include the following entries:

Teaching Portfolio
Name of Faculty Member
Department/College
Date

Table of Contents
1. Teaching Responsibilities
2. Teaching Philosophy
3. Teaching Methodologies
4. Student Evaluations for Multiple Courses (summative questions)
5. Classroom Observations
6. Review of Teaching Materials
7. Representative Course Syllabi
8. New Instructional Initiatives
9. Evidence of Student Learning
10. Statement by the Department Chair Assessing the Professor's Teaching Contribution to the Department
11. Teaching Awards
12. Teaching Goals
13. Appendices

When portfolios are submitted for personnel decisions, the focus should be on evidence that documents the professor's best work as a teacher and demonstrates that significant student learning (cognitive or affective) has taken place. The faculty member's achievements, awards, and successes are the focus. Self-criticism is a key component in a portfolio developed for teaching improvement, but it does not make much sense to include for those who are being considered for promotion or tenure.

It is important to keep in mind that use of the portfolio for personnel decisions is only occasional. Its primary purpose is to improve performance.

IMPROVING PERFORMANCE

There is no better reason to prepare a portfolio than to improve performance. Faculty are hired by institutions in expectation of first-class performance. To help them hone their performance is nothing less than an extension of this expectation. It is in the very process of reflecting on their work and creating their collection of documents and materials that professors are stimulated to reconsider policies and activities, rethink strategies and methodologies, revise priorities, and plan for the future.

A portfolio is a valuable aid in professional development for three important reasons: (1) the level of personal investment in time, energy, and commitment is high (since faculty prepare their own portfolios), and that is a necessary condition for change; (2) preparation of the portfolio stirs many professors to reflect on their teaching in an insightful, refocused way; and (3) it is grounded in discipline-based pedagogy, that is, the focus is on teaching a particular subject to a particular group of students at a particular time in a particular institution.

Do teaching portfolios actually improve faculty performance? For most faculty, teaching portfolios actually improve their performance. Experience suggests that if a professor is motivated to improve, knows how to improve, or knows where to go for help, improvement is quite likely.

When used for improvement purposes, the portfolio contains no mandated items. Instead, it contains only items chosen by the professor working in collaboration with a consultant/mentor.

The contents page in a portfolio for improvement might have the following entries:

Teaching Portfolio
Name of Faculty Member
Department/College
Date

Table of Contents

The improvement portfolio provides a record of performance that details progress and setbacks, successes and disappointments in a framework of honest and thoughtful information analyzed and examined in a timely way. The goal is to establish a baseline of information and then progress through stages of experimentation and development until enhancement of teaching performance becomes evident through assessment.

Sometimes a professor will decide to prepare a teaching portfolio that focuses on a single course rather than an array of courses. The goal is to improve his or her teaching of that particular course by helping the faculty member (1) articulate a teaching philosophy for that particular course; (2) describe, analyze, and evaluate course materials, methods, and outcomes;(4) study student and peer evaluations; and (5) formulate an action plan for improvement.

Whether improvement actually takes place depends on the information included in the portfolio. It will not be successful unless the teaching elements to be strengthened are singled out. If the portfolio is to stimulate improvement in teaching performance, it must have multiple items, and the data must be detailed, thoughtful, and diagnostic.

CHAPTER TWO

CHOOSING ITEMS FOR THE TEACHING PORTFOLIO

The items chosen for the portfolio are based on a combination of availability of supporting materials, the nature of the portfolio, the faculty position, the discipline, and the importance assigned by the faculty member to different items (see the sample portfolios in Part Three). Differences in portfolio content and organization should be encouraged to the extent that they are allowed by the department and the college or university.

Since the teaching portfolio is a highly personalized product, no two are alike. The information revealed in the narrative and documented in the appendix bears a unique stamp that personalizes the portfolio.

Nevertheless, given the nearly universal need in faculty evaluation today that professors document their teaching, the list in this chapter should be helpful. It does not comprise items a professor must include. Rather, it includes many possibilities from which the faculty member can select those that are relevant to his or her purpose and particular academic situation. Also, there may be some items not included in this chapter that are particularly relevant to an individual professor and can be selected for his or her portfolio.

Although this is not an exhaustive list, it illustrates the range of items that might be selected to evidence teaching style and effectiveness. Of course, no single item in the portfolio is capable of providing a comprehensive view of the faculty member's teaching performance. Rather, the reader's impression of that performance comes from a summative review of all of the items in the portfolio.

The portfolio takes a broader view of teaching than the traditional curriculum vitae compiled by faculty to document their achievements because it integrates the values of the faculty member with those of the discipline, the department, and the institution. That is accomplished by work samples and reflective commentary that speak to an integration of values.

A word of caution: all college and university professors have seen poor student work dressed in fancy covers. The point of the teaching portfolio is not a fancy cover. Instead, it is the thoughtful, integrated compilation of documents and materials that make the best case for the professor's effectiveness. The portfolio typically contains a narrative that provides rich details on a professor's teaching activities, initiatives, accomplishments, and goals, as well as thoughtful reflection on his or her performance. The appendices provide evidence that supports the narrative section.

Based on an examination of more than one thousand portfolios prepared by professors in institutions representing all sectors of higher education, we can say with confidence that certain items turn up in portfolios with much more frequency than others. They fall into three broad categories: material from oneself, material from others, and products of teaching and student learning.

MATERIAL FROM ONESELF

Faculty generally find that gathering materials from themselves is easy because they write their own statements of responsibilities, philosophy, methodologies, syllabi, and goals.

STATEMENT OF TEACHING RESPONSIBILITIES

This statement should include course titles, catalogue numbers, average enrollments, and an indication of whether the course is graduate or undergraduate, required or elective. A chart or table is a useful way to present the information.

TEACHING PHILOSOPHY

The focus here is on the philosophy of teaching and learning that drives the professor's classroom performance. Following are some guiding questions to consider as prompts when preparing this section: What do I believe about the role of the teacher? What do I believe about the role of the student? Why do I teach? What does good teaching mean to me? What can my students expect from me?

TEACHING METHODOLOGIES

This section addresses the professor's strategies and methodologies.

Guiding questions as prompts: Why do I choose the teaching strategies and methods that I use? How would I describe my particular teaching style? What do I do in the classroom and outside it? How do I assess student learning? What kind of feedback do I give to students?

DESCRIPTION OF TEACHING MATERIALS

Samples of teaching materials are placed in the appendix, but the highlights are included in the narrative, and the two are cross-referenced. Course and instructional materials could include applications of computer technology, study guides, case studies, handouts, and manuals.

Guiding questions as prompts: How do these materials enhance my teaching? In what ways have they changed in recent years? How do I know these changes are for the better? What kind of student feedback do I have about the effectiveness of these teaching materials?

CURRICULAR REVISIONS

This section concerns new or revised courses, material, and assignments.

Guiding questions as prompts: Have I introduced new applications of technology? Changed course objectives? Used new material? Added (or dropped) guest speakers? Field trips? Laboratory work? Have I developed a new course? Revised a course? Team-taught a course?

INSTRUCTIONAL INNOVATIONS

Highlighted here are the new and different pedagogical innovations the professor uses to enhance teaching and student learning.

Guiding questions as prompts: What new approaches have I introduced in teaching my courses? Which ones worked well? Why were they successful? Which didn't work well? Why didn't they work? How could they be changed so they would be more successful next time?

REPRESENTATIVE COURSE SYLLABI

Samples of syllabi are placed in the appendix, but highlights appear in the narrative, and the two are cross-referenced.

Guiding questions as prompts: What does this syllabus say about my teaching and learning beliefs? What do I want it to say? What does it say about the course and my way of teaching it? Is it a learning-centered syllabus? Does it detail course content and objectives, teaching methodology, readings, and homework assignments in the way I want it to?

DOCUMENTATION OF TEACHING IMPROVEMENT ACTIVITIES

Improvement efforts and professional development activities are highlighted here. Samples of certificates of attendance can be placed in an appendix file, but reference is made to them in the narrative, and the two are cross-referenced.

Guiding questions as prompts: Which faculty development workshops and conferences have I attended? How am I applying what I learned from those programs? What specific steps have I taken to improve my teaching? How have I responded to suggestions for improvement that have come from students?

TEACHING GOALS—SHORT AND LONG TERM

This section of the portfolio asks professors to look ahead and identify some short- and long-term teaching goals. It forces them to crystallize their thinking about possible projects and activities that would continue their development as a teacher.

Guiding questions as prompts: What teaching goals have I been unable to attain in the past that I would like to pursue now? Why are they important to me? How can my department or institution help me achieve those goals? What kind of resource help (people? money? space? time?) do I need to achieve those goals?

MATERIAL FROM OTHERS

Materials from others are trickier to produce than materials from oneself because they comprise student evaluation and classroom observation reports—feedback that varies in availability and utility.

STUDENT COURSE EVALUATIONS

Student course or teaching evaluation data, especially those that produce an overall rating of effectiveness or satisfaction, are placed in the narrative section of the portfolio. As in other sections of the portfolio, all claims must be supported by evidence in the appendix. Student course evaluation data are often presented in a chart or table that shows the course title and catalogue number, number of students, mean score, and, if available, the department or collegewide mean score on each question.

When the portfolio is used for promotion or tenure, it is especially important to provide ratings on each of the questions that the institution's personnel committees consider to be pivotal.

Guiding questions as prompts: Are all claims made in the narrative about student ratings supported by evidence in the appendix? Are there any special circumstances that are affected the ratings? Is the vast majority of the student feedback current or from the recent past (three to five years)? Are student evaluation data included from each class that is regularly taught? Are data from all pivotal questions included?

COLLEAGUE REVIEW OF TEACHING MATERIALS

Excerpts from reports reviewing such pedagogical supports as course syllabi, assignments, reading lists, tests, and PowerPoint slides are placed in the narrative file and cross-referenced to the complete report in the appendix file.

Guiding questions as prompts: Are excerpts included in the narrative that tie in with my teaching philosophy or methodology? What do these teaching aids say about my teaching and learning beliefs? What is significant about each? In specific terms, how do they help students learn?

Classroom Observation by Faculty Colleagues or Administrators

Excerpts from observation reports are placed in the narrative section and are cross-referenced to the complete report, located in the appendix file.

Guiding questions as prompts: Is the observation report dated and signed by the observer? Are any excerpts included in the narrative that tie in with my philosophy of teaching or pedagogical methodology? Did any special circumstances (for example, room too noisy, too large, too small, too cold, too hot) interfere with teaching and learning during the observation?

Documentation of Teaching Improvement Activities

Improvement efforts and professional development activities are highlighted here. Samples of certificates of attendance can be placed in an appendix, with reference made to them in the narrative, and the two are cross-referenced.

Guiding questions as prompts: Which faculty development seminars or workshops have I attended? How am I applying what I learned from those programs in my teaching? What evidence do I have of growth or change in my teaching? How have I responded to students' suggestions for improvement?

Teaching Honors and Other Recognition

This section of the portfolio focuses on teaching honors or other recognition from colleagues, students, administrators, or alumni, such as a distinguished teaching award, student advising award, or teacher of the year designation. Certificates of achievement, award letters, and photographs documenting the teaching recognition should be placed in the appendix.

Guiding questions as prompts: Which teaching honors or other recognition have I won? Who selected me for this achievement: peers, students, or alumni? On what basis was I selected? Have there been setbacks or disappointments that later served as the foundation of any of these honors?

PRODUCTS OF GOOD TEACHING AND STUDENT LEARNING

The most difficult area to address is the products of student learning—an assessment of what and how students have learned. Examinations, written reports, laboratory notebooks, fieldwork reports, and student presentations at conferences can constitute compelling evidence of student learning. But documenting this information in a thoughtful and systematic way can be a difficult task.

A RECORD OF STUDENTS WHO SUCCEED IN ADVANCED STUDY IN THE FIELD

This section of the portfolio is a list of students who have gone on to success in higher-level courses or are now employed in the field.

Guiding questions as prompts: Which of my recent students have gone on to advanced study in my discipline? Which are employed in the field? Do I have evidence of my influence on student career choice or graduate school admission? Have I helped any students secure employment?

STUDENT SCORES ON EXAMINATIONS BEFORE AND AFTER THE COURSE

Highlighted here are the student test scores on examinations. The focus is not on the performance of an individual student but rather the performance of an entire class.

Guiding questions as prompts: Are all claims of student learning in the narrative supported by evidence in the appendix? Are the data showing test score differences in examinations from multiple courses? Are there any circumstances that interfered with student learning? Are there changes that I can make in my teaching that could increase student learning?

SUCCESSIVE DRAFTS OF STUDENT PAPERS

In this section, highlights of successive drafts of student papers showing improvement as a result of the faculty member's comments and guidance are included in the narrative and are cross-referenced to the full work located in the appendix.

Guiding questions as prompts: Have I included my written comments suggesting how samples of student work might be improved, along with the student work itself? Does it reflect graded student work that represents different levels of quality: excellent, good, average, poor? Do the graded student assignments reflect my efforts to direct development of critical thinking skills or written communication skills?

STUDENT PUBLICATIONS OR CONFERENCE PRESENTATIONS PREPARED UNDER THE DIRECTION OF THE FACULTY MEMBER

Especially relevant to faculty who teach on the graduate level, this section is often presented as a list of student publications and conference presentations prepared under the guidance and direction of the professor.

Guiding questions as prompts: What was my role with each student listed: to provide direction or support or to serve as a coauthor or copresenter? Have I included appropriate citations in the narrative and appropriate evidence in the appendix file?

THE APPENDIX

The material in the appendix needs careful attention to be sure that all statements of accomplishment in the narrative are adequately supported. That said, it is best not to engage in overkill.

Just as information in the narrative part of the portfolio should be selective, so too the appendix files should consist of judiciously chosen evidence that adequately supports the narrative section of the portfolio. If the appendix contains nonprint media or items that do not fit within the portfolio three-ring binder—videotapes, photographs, or CDs, for example—the professor may briefly discuss such materials in the narrative and make them available for review in a designated location.

Rather than offer a separate, isolated commentary for each appendix, the vast majority of professors weave references within the narrative portion of their portfolio (for example, "See Appendix A for the original student evaluation summary sheets"). This approach strengthens coherence and ties together the narrative and the appendix files.

Which sorts of evidence might go into the appendices depends on the requirements of the department and the institution, as well as the personal preferences of the professor and the purpose for which he or she is preparing the portfolio. But many of the following items are often included:

- Student ratings of instruction
- Syllabi
- Classroom observation reports
- Samples of graded student work
- Invitations to speak at a conference or another institution on teaching one's discipline
- Copies of course assignments, study guides, exams, and reading lists
- Record of student scores on tests
- Examples of your contribution to curriculum design and course development
- Confirmation of your participation in teaching improvement activities
- Teaching awards and other recognition of your teaching accomplishments

The appendices must be of manageable size if they are to be read. For most professors, six to ten categories of items are sufficient.

A word of caution: sometimes faculty who are preparing teaching portfolios fall into the trap of permitting the appendix files—the supporting documents—to determine the portfolio narrative. In this case, the tail wags the dog. Should that occur, professors may find themselves focusing on a shopping list of possible portfolio items, determining which are easily obtainable, and then creating the reflective section of their portfolios around the evidence they have at hand. The result is that they end up focusing on the what rather than the why. A far better approach is to:

1. Reflect on your underlying teaching philosophy.
2. Describe the strategies and methodologies that flow from that reflection (why you do what you do).
3. Select documents and materials that provide the hard evidence of your teaching activities and accomplishments.

The Mechanics

We have visited several hundred colleges and universities of differing sizes and missions to talk with faculty groups and administrators about the portfolio and its place in the evaluation of teaching. In the course of our discussions, questions about portfolio length and preparation time have come up repeatedly. Our answers to them follow.

Typical Portfolio Length

The typical teaching portfolio is a narrative of approximately eight to twelve double-spaced pages, followed by a series of tabbed appendix files that provide documentation for the claims made in the narrative. Information in both the narrative and the appendices should be carefully selected for relevance and cohesiveness with the other information in the portfolio.

Although disciplines and institutional requirements differ, professors often allocate pages to specific topics as follows:

Material from oneself	Three to five pages
Material from others	Three to four pages
Products of good teaching and student learning	Two to three pages
Total	Eight to twelve pages

Some institutions put a ceiling on the number of pages in order to prevent data overkill in the portfolio. Others distribute a three-ring binder of perhaps two inches and insist that they will read only information housed in that binder for tenure or promotion decisions.

PORTFOLIO PREPARATION TIME

How long does it take to prepare a teaching portfolio? The answer is, it depends. Professors who prepare an annual report probably already have a good deal of the necessary material on hand. For example, they probably have a list of their teaching responsibilities, copies of syllabi, and student rating data. In this case, preparation of the portfolio will probably take between ten and twelve hours spread over a number of days.

But if the professor does not prepare an annual report (or does one but has misplaced it), the needed documents and materials are likely to be scattered and less organized. In that case, it will probably take between fifteen and eighteen hours, spread over a number of days, to put together the portfolio.

CHAPTER THREE

PREPARING THE TEACHING PORTFOLIO

Three crucial cornerstones are the keys to the success of the teaching portfolio: the need to discuss expectations, getting started with portfolios, and gaining acceptance of the concept.

THE NEED TO DISCUSS EXPECTATIONS

The teaching portfolio will have value only when personnel decision makers and faculty members learn to trust the approach. Crucial to the development of trust is the periodic exchange of views between the department chair and professor about teaching responsibilities, ancillary duties, and specific items for the portfolio. This discussion should address expectations and specifics of what and how to report teaching performance. Otherwise there is a danger that the chair may erroneously conclude that the data submitted overlook areas of prime concern and may even cover up areas of suspected weakness. Such possible misunderstanding is largely eliminated by open discussion.

Since there is no guarantee that the current department chair will be in that position when the faculty member is being considered for tenure or promotion, it is a good idea to also talk with recently tenured faculty and to respected, older, straight-shooting professors who can give solid, realistic advice.

The topics of conversation with the chair and with others are the same:

• What do the department and the institution expect of faculty in terms of teaching?

- What evidence of successful performance—both quantity and quality—is considered appropriate?
- How much evidence is enough?
- What are appropriate and effective ways to report the evidence?

Expectations are of great importance even in the case of a portfolio created for improvement and personal growth instead of personnel decisions. Departments and institutions have their own formulas for the evidence of teaching performance they seek in determining teaching effectiveness. They give differing levels of importance to student ratings, syllabi, curricular developments, philosophy, methodology, student learning, and other sources of information that might be included in a portfolio. Those differing levels of importance are why it is essential for professors to know accurately the relative importance given to the items that might be included in their portfolio.

Getting Started with Portfolios

Perhaps the best way to get started is for a group of faculty to develop general standards of good teaching. They should have enough flexibility to accommodate diverse approaches to teaching. The following guidelines should be helpful:

- Obtain public, top-level administrative support for the portfolio concept and an institutional commitment to provide the necessary resources to launch the program successfully.
- Start small.
- Involve the institution's (or department's) most respected faculty members from the start.
- Rely on faculty volunteers; do not force anyone to participate.
- Keep everyone—faculty and academic administrators—informed about what is going on every step of the way.
- Field-test the portfolio process.
- Permit room for individual differences in portfolios. Styles of teaching differ. So do the disciplines.

It is important to allow a year, or even two years, for the process of acceptance and implementation. During this period, draft portfolios should be carefully prepared, freely discussed, and modified as needed. All details of the portfolio program need not be in place before implementation. Start the program incrementally, and be flexible to modification as it develops. But remember that the quest for perfection is endless. Don't stall the portfolio program in an endless search for the perfect approach. The goal is improvement, not perfection.

GAINING ACCEPTANCE OF THE CONCEPT

To say that the teaching portfolio approach is useful is one thing, but to get the approach off the ground is quite another. Some professors automatically resist by evoking various academic traditions. They say that faculty are not comfortable as self-promoters and have neither the time nor the desire to keep a record of their teaching achievements. But in truth, the world of college and university teaching is undergoing considerable change. In an age of accountability and tight budgets, the portfolio is an instrument focused on effective teaching. Professors need to produce better evidence of their teaching effectiveness and must do so in a clear and persuasive way for third-party inspection.

Caution: Not only do some professors decline to embrace the portfolio concept, but some administrators do so as well. At some institutions, administrators are immediately negative at the sight of strangers bearing new ideas, and the portfolio is no exception. People being people, some operate comfortably in well-worn grooves and resist almost any change. Others resist out of an unspoken fear that somehow they are threatened.

If the teaching portfolio approach is ultimately to be embraced, an institutional climate of acceptance must first be created. How can that be done? The following guidelines should be helpful:

- The portfolio concept must be presented in a candid, complete, and clear way to every faculty member and academic administrator.
- Professors must have a significant hand in both the development and the operation of the portfolio program. They must feel, with justification, that they own the program.

- The portfolio approach must not be forced on anyone. It is much better to start with faculty volunteers.
- The primary purpose of the portfolio program should be to improve the quality of teaching, and its approach should be positive rather than punitive.
- The institution's most respected professors should be involved from the onset. That means the best teachers, because their participation attracts other faculty to the program. It also means admired teachers who are also prominent researchers; their participation will signal both the value of portfolios and their willingness to go public with the scholarship of their teaching.
- The portfolio should be field-tested on a handful of respected professors. The fact that faculty leaders are willing to try the approach will not be lost on others.
- If portfolios are to be used for tenure and promotion purposes or to determine teaching awards, all professors must know the performance standards by which their portfolios will be judged. Specifically, they must know what constitutes exemplary, satisfactory, and unsatisfactory performance.
- The portfolio program must recognize the teaching responsibilities of each faculty member and any special circumstances or conditions in effect when he or she was hired.
- Room must be allowed for individual differences in portfolios as long as those differences can be tolerated by the institution. Styles of teaching differ. So do disciplines and career points. The documents and materials in the portfolio of a professor of organic chemistry with twenty-five years of teaching experience will be different from those of a professor of organizational behavior with five years of teaching experience.
- Encourage collaboration. A portfolio mentor (coach) from the same discipline can provide special insights and understandings, as well as departmental practices, in dealing with portfolios. On the other hand, a mentor from a different discipline can often help clarify the institution's viewpoint, that is, the big picture. That can be significant since portfolios submitted for personnel decisions will be read by faculty from other disciplines.

- The portfolio should include only selective information. It is not an exhaustive compilation of all of the documents and materials that bear on individual teaching performance. Instead, it presents selected information on teaching accomplishments and activities. But in the process, it also addresses the why of teaching, not just the what.

CHAPTER FOUR

STEPS TO CREATING A TEACHING PORTFOLIO

Experience suggests that most faculty rely on the following sequence of steps in creating their teaching portfolios.

STEP 1: PLANNING

Before assembling a portfolio, a faculty member needs to think about the purpose for preparing it and the audience that will read it.

PURPOSE

There are many reasons for developing a teaching portfolio—improvement in performance, applying for promotion or tenure (personnel decision), seeking a different (or first) teaching position, in response to a teaching award nomination, or to build a legacy. To a large degree, the purpose drives the content. The professor may intend for the portfolio to serve multiple purposes, but it is important to distinguish between the primary and secondary purposes because the priorities for building a portfolio are likely to influence decisions about its content.

AUDIENCE

Once the purpose for preparing a portfolio is clear, it should be relatively easy to identify the readers: Self? Chairperson? Review committee? Search committee? The list of anticipated readers will inform decisions about how best to structure and draft the portfolio narrative. For example, if the portfolio is prepared for improvement, it is essentially a personal, private document seen only by the faculty member. Therefore, the collection of documents and materials may be in whatever form suits the individual, who can then abbreviate the explanation of teaching responsibilities that would be needed if the portfolio were to be read by someone less familiar with the faculty member's current responsibilities. The goal is self-reflection to enhance teaching performance.

But when the portfolio is prepared for a personnel decision, it educates college or university personnel committees—some of whom will be from outside the professor's discipline who will have little familiarity with the professor's teaching responsibilities—about the teaching philosophy, methodologies, and effectiveness of the professor and how they support the mission of the department and institution. For that reason, it is particularly important that the portfolio be written in clear, concise, easily understood language that avoids jargon and acronyms and embraces clarity and simple language.

Key questions to consider are:

- Who are your primary readers?
- What evidence will they expect to find?
- What types of evidence will be most convincing to those readers?

STEP 2: SUMMARIZE TEACHING RESPONSIBILITIES

Typically this covers such topics as courses currently taught and those taught in the recent past and teaching-related activities such as serving as faculty advisor to student organizations, advising individual graduate or undergraduate students, or serving as a thesis reader or director. It also includes information on whether the courses were required or elective, graduate or undergraduate, and taught online or in a traditional classroom. The focus is on what the faculty member is responsible for as a teacher. Some portfolios describe teaching responsibilities in a two- or three-paragraph statement. Others do so in a chart or table.

STEP 3: DESCRIBE YOUR APPROACH TO TEACHING

Bearing in mind the summary of teaching responsibilities described in step 2, the professor prepares a two- to two-and-one-half-page reflective statement describing his or her teaching philosophy, objectives, and methodologies. The statement addresses the issue of how faculty members carry out their teaching responsibilities from the standpoint of why they do what they do. Some guiding questions to consider are:

- What are your beliefs about teaching?
- How do your actions as a teacher reflect your beliefs about teaching and learning?
- What evidence will demonstrate that your methodologies reflect your beliefs?
- How have your teaching methods changed in response to changes in students, course material, or technology?
- What instructional material have you developed?
- What innovative teaching activities do you use?

STEP 4: SELECT ITEMS FOR THE PORTFOLIO

In addition to the basic portfolio information (summary of teaching responsibilities, teaching philosophy, syllabi), the faculty member will want to select other items that illustrate his or her teaching style and offer evidence of teaching effectiveness. The items that project the style will describe how the professor approaches such activities as classroom teaching, student advising, and curriculum development. The items that indicate the professor's effectiveness will likely include student ratings of instruction, statements from colleagues or administrators who have observed the faculty member in the classroom, and a record of students who have succeeded in advanced study in the field. These items should provide readers with a clear and accurate assessment of the professor's effectiveness in performing their assigned teaching responsibilities.

The selection of items for the portfolio depends on the purpose for which the portfolio is prepared, as well as the audience.

But, importantly, it also depends on the professor's personal preferences, academic discipline, academic career point, and any content requirement of a professor's department or institution.

STEP 5: PREPARE STATEMENTS ON EACH ITEM

The professor prepares statements on activities, initiatives, and accomplishments. The objective is to inform readers of the nature and extent of work performed by the professor in his or her capacity of teacher. If, for example, one teaching responsibility is student advising, the professor may engage in such activities and initiatives as conducting periodic counseling with students in need, starting a mentoring program for majors, or implementing a student portfolio program focused on the skill development of individual students.

Here are some guiding questions to consider when preparing this section:

- Have you provided support documentation for every claim made?
- Have you cross-referenced your narrative with the appendix?
- Have you included names, programs titles, and locations— where appropriate—to document your efforts to improve teaching?

STEP 6: ORDER THE ITEMS

The sequence of statements about accomplishments in each area is determined by their intended purpose. For example, if the faculty member intends to demonstrate teaching effectiveness, student ratings of instruction and classroom observation reports would be stressed. If the faculty member intends to demonstrate curricular revision, current and previous syllabi as well as an explanation of why the curricular revisions were made would be stressed. And if the intention is to demonstrate wide use of a variety of teaching methodologies, a detailed explanation of specifically why each method was used to convey particular information would be stressed.

STEP 7: COMPILE THE SUPPORTING DATA

Evidence supporting all items mentioned in the portfolio should be retained by the professor and made available for review on request. These include, for example, original student evaluations of teaching, samples of student work, invitations to contribute articles or present papers at conferences on teaching one's discipline, classroom observation reports, and letters from the department chair. This evidence is crucial support material and is not included in the narrative. Instead, it is placed in an appendix or, if it is unwieldy or too large, referred to in the appendix and made available on request.

STEP 8: PRESENT THE PORTFOLIO

Experience suggests that the best way to present the entire portfolio is in a unified container, typically a single three-ring binder. A two-and-one-half-inch binder with sleeves on the front and spine is a useful and inexpensive way to secure material and make it easy to add or delete items. Tabs serve to organize and neatly separate the appendix items. We suggest that it is best to label all loose items; three-hole-punch everything; do not use sleeves for materials inside the portfolio (they slip out easily); and use tabbed dividers with computer-generated stick-on labels.

STEP 9: INCORPORATE THE PORTFOLIO INTO THE CURRICULUM VITAE

The portfolio is inserted into the professor's curriculum vitae under the heading of "Teaching." Department guidelines will determine its precise location in the c.v. in relation to the sections on research and service.

CHAPTER FIVE

THE IMPORTANCE OF COLLABORATION

Should portfolios be developed by the professor working alone, or should they be the result of collaborative efforts?

From mounting experience, we know that they are best prepared in consultation with others. The reason is that portfolios prepared by the professor working alone do not include the collegial or supervisory support needed in a program of teaching improvement. And, importantly, there is none of the control or corroboration of evidence that is essential to sustain personnel decisions. Collaboration ensures a fresh, critical perspective that encourages cohesion between the portfolio and supporting appendix material. We examine both working with a mentor and self-mentoring in this chapter.

WORKING WITH A MENTOR

Who might serve as a portfolio mentor? A department chair, a colleague, or a teaching improvement specialist on campus can discuss with the professor important questions:

- Why are you preparing the portfolio?
- What do you hope to learn from it?
- Which areas of the teaching-learning process do you expect to examine?
- What kinds of information do you expect to collect?
- How can the information be presented best?

Although some professors prepare their portfolios in collaboration with their department chairs, experience tells us that most will end up working with another person—typically a faculty colleague at the same institution or at another one in the same geographical area. For example, within the same institution, a professor of organizational behavior might mentor a professor of child and family studies. Or a professor of education might mentor a professor of English. Similar mentoring arrangements might be made between faculty members across institutions.

Some may argue that the portfolio contents will be colored by second-party assistance and therefore be less useful because it represents coached performance. But we believe that portfolio development should involve interaction and mentoring in the same way that a doctoral dissertation reflects both the efforts of the candidate and the advice of the mentor.

To be effective, the portfolio mentor must have wide knowledge of procedures and current instruments to document effective teaching. In this way, he or she can assist the faculty member by providing suggestions and resources. But having such content knowledge alone is no guarantee of effective guidance. The mentor must also have the interpersonal skills and attitudes necessary to develop the relationship needed for effective mentoring. A good mentor, says Devanas (2006), needs to be both a coach and a critic—someone who can motivate the faculty mentor while maintaining an objective perspective.

SELF-MENTORING

Although we recommend that teaching portfolios be developed collaboratively, we are keenly aware that sometimes no willing and able mentors are available. In that case, although the valuable collaborative aspects of portfolio development will be lost, it is still possible to prepare a portfolio. The guiding questions as prompts cited earlier in this volume should help. So should these self-assessment questions:

- What is your purpose in creating the portfolio?
- Who are your primary readers?
- What evidence will they expect to see?

- What types of evidence will be most convincing to those readers?
- What criteria will be used to evaluate your teaching?
- What weight will be given to student ratings?
- What are the valued courses in your department?
- What is the expected balance of portfolio information from yourself, from others, and about student learning?

After the portfolio has been drafted, the following questions can serve as a helpful checklist:

- Does your portfolio clearly identify all of your teaching responsibilities?
- Does the reflective statement adequately and accurately describe your teaching philosophy, strategies, and methodologies?
- Does your portfolio reflect consistency between your reflective statement and your teaching actions?
- Have you included other activities that support or inform teaching and learning—for example, advising, textbook editing, serving on curriculum committees, presenter of teaching workshops, mentoring, or continuing education activities?
- Is every claim made in the narrative supported by evidence in the appendix?
- Is the vast majority of data current or from the recent past?
- Does your portfolio contain performance evaluation data from multiple sources?
- Does it contain evidence of student learning?
- Would including some charts, tables, or graphs contribute to the readability of your portfolio?
- Have you included information on efforts to improve your teaching performance?
- Does the portfolio clearly identify what you teach, how you teach it, and why you teach it as you do?
- Is a complete table of contents included?
- Are appendices included?
- Are numerical student rating results included for several courses over several years?

- Have you included specific information on your short-term and long-term goals with regard to improvement of your teaching?
- Have any department or institutional factors influenced your teaching effectiveness?

CHAPTER SIX

SUGGESTIONS FOR IMPROVING THE TEACHING PORTFOLIO

We have crisscrossed the country explaining the teaching portfolio. We have visited scores of colleges and universities of different sizes, shapes, and missions and discussed with promotion and tenure committees, department chairs, deans, and faculty the place of portfolios in the evaluation of teaching and as a powerful tool for teaching improvement. And we have had the pleasure of working as mentors to hundreds of individual professors (one at a time) as they prepared their personal portfolios. This extensive involvement not just as theorists but also as practitioners has led us to the following suggestions to faculty who prepare their portfolios. Some of these suggestions are minor and may go unnoticed. But in mentoring faculty in different institutions as they developed their teaching portfolios, we have found that these items are frequently overlooked.

HOUSE THE PORTFOLIO IN A BINDER WITH TABS FOR APPENDICES

A three-ring binder that is two and a half or three inches, with sleeves on the front and spine, is a useful and inexpensive way to secure material and make it easy to add or delete items. The tabs serve to organize and neatly separate the appendix items.

Include the Date of the Portfolio

Putting a date on the portfolio enables the professor to establish a baseline from which to measure development in teaching performance. That growth can be gauged by the degree to which the portfolio demonstrates improvement resulting from a reexamination of philosophy and methodologies.

Include a Detailed Table of Contents

A table of contents enables portfolio readers to see the breadth and flow of teaching responsibilities, philosophy, methodologies, and priorities of the faculty member. Built on reflection and evidence, it serves as a road map to the portfolio narrative and appendix.

Include a List of Appendix Items

Positioned on either the table of contents page or on the first page of the appendix itself, this list helps readers find specific evidence for claims made in the narrative.

Cross-Reference the Narrative to the Appendix

Every item in the appendix should be cross-referenced in the narrative section. For example, at the end of a discussion of syllabi, reference would be made to the appendix: "See Appendix A for copies of syllabi." Or at the end of a discussion of a classroom observation by the department chair, reference would be made to evidence in the appendix: "See Appendix B for copies of the chair's observation report."

Number the Pages in the Portfolio

Although this may seem self-evident, our experience as mentors of hundreds of faculty as they prepared their portfolios proved otherwise. Numbering pages in a teaching portfolio is just as important as it is in a student term paper.

BRING THE TEACHING PHILOSOPHY STATEMENT TO LIFE

This should be a reflective, straightforward, well-organized statement of one to two pages that avoids technical terms and favors language and concepts that can be easily understood. A narrative first-person approach is generally appropriate. The goal is to bring the teaching philosophy section of the portfolio to life by creating a vivid portrait of a faculty member who is intentional about teaching practices, objectives, values, and strategies.

DESCRIBE HOW THE PHILOSOPHY IS TRANSLATED INTO ACTION

A crucial section of the portfolio is the description of how a professor's philosophy statement is translated into action. For many readers, this is one of the most revealing parts of the portfolio. Here, professors describe how they conduct classes, develop instructional resources, grade performance, and advise students. They provide details of the teaching methodologies they use, what they want students to experience in the classes they teach, the labs they oversee, and the independent projects they supervise. And they often discuss the climate they try to establish in the settings in which they teach.

EXPLAIN THE EVIDENCE IN THE PORTFOLIO

Unexplained evidence is difficult for readers to understand and interpret. For example, two course syllabi from different years provide evidence of instructional change over time, but the significance of the change and why it took place are not readily apparent. That is why we recommend a commentary explaining why specific changes were made, as well as the reaction of students (for example, e-mailed comments from students that are included in the appendices) as convincing evidence of the professor's efforts to improve instruction.

CONSIDER INCLUDING THE OCCASIONAL DISAPPOINTMENT IN TEACHING OR LEARNING

Teaching improvement depends on risk and experimentation. Not everything new will succeed. But when the portfolio is developed for improvement (as opposed to personnel decision) purposes, a detailed description and assessment of something that did not work can lead to thoughtful revision of the approach so that it is more likely to succeed when tried again. Whether such disappointments in teaching or learning should be described in a portfolio prepared for personnel decisions is an open question. In our experience, most portfolios submitted for this purpose do not include such a section.

INCLUDE SPECIFIC INFORMATION, NOT GENERALITIES

Avoid generalities, and be specific. Identify the dates, names, programs, and titles of courses taught. Instead of, "My student ratings are generally high," it is better to say, "Ninety-four percent of the seventy-six students in my Microeconomics course (fall 2010) stated that they would recommend that their friends take my class," and instead of, "My department chair observed me teaching and had positive things to report," it is better to say that, "My department chair, Hugh Downey, observed my Introduction to Finance course on November 1, 2010, and reported I was 'well prepared, that my students were fully engaged, and that the content was covered in a thorough and interesting way.' (See Appendix A for the chair's complete observation report.)"

FORMAT THE NARRATIVE FOR READER INTEREST

Reading twelve pages of straight narrative can be tedious. Bolster reader interest by the judicious use of boldface type, italics, bullet points, charts, and graphs. Avoid excessive detail. Make your points clear and succinct, and avoid long paragraphs.

ENHANCE THE STUDENT EVALUATION SECTION

Many professors use a graph or chart to present student rating results. Be sure to include the number of students, course titles and catalogue numbers, information on the rating scale (for example, 1–5, with 5 high), and all core questions on the student rating form. (Those are reviewed more closely than others by members of tenure and promotion committees). Sample core questions frequently include: "The professor was well prepared,"

"Overall evaluation of the course," "Overall evaluation of the professor," and "I would recommend this professor to my friends." The portfolio narrative contains a summary of student feedback. Readers should be referred to the appendix for complete student evaluation results.

LIMIT THE NUMBER OF STUDENT OR COLLEAGUE COMMENTS

Some professors assume that the more favorable student or colleague comments they include, the better. But that is a mistaken assumption. Generally just two or three comments each from students and from colleagues are sufficient. Those comments should be specific and tied to the professor's methodology:

- Example from a student: "The discussion method that Professor Abel used was especially effective in engaging us with the material."
- Example from a faculty colleague who observed a class: "Professor Abel's use of directed discussion was effective, engaging, and appropriate for the Introduction to Psychology class that I observed on February 3, 2010."

INCLUDE NAMES AND POSITIONS OF PEOPLE TO WHOM YOU REFER

If reference is made to a peer review of teaching materials or an outstanding student achievement, be sure to include the name and position of that person—for example:

"My department chair, Patricia Streim, reviewed the teaching materials from my Introduction to Creative Arts course on March 1, 2010. Appendix C contains her report. It states (in part) that the materials were 'outstanding, clear, thoughtful, and student-friendly.'"

"Ann Root, a graduate student in my Advanced Statistics course during fall 2010, presented a poster session on Changing Statistical Techniques at the 2010 annual meeting of the American Educational Research Association in Chicago."

SEEK COHERENCE AMONG PORTFOLIO SECTIONS

A well-developed portfolio provides a coherent teaching profile in which all parts support the whole. For example, the philosophy of teaching section outlines a professor's belief in active learning. The methodology section describes how that philosophy is implemented in the classroom. Student rating forms would include several questions asking for the student perspective on the faculty member's effectiveness in using active learning. And peer observers would comment on that effectiveness from their perspective.

MAKE BULKY ITEMS AVAILABLE ON REQUEST

Some items do not lend themselves to being placed in an appendix because they are unwieldy or too large or can be easily lost. Examples are videotapes, large photographs, sculptures, musical scores, and oversize teaching materials. For that reason, if the appendix contains items that do not fit within the portfolio covers, the faculty member may choose to briefly discuss these materials in the narrative and make them available for inspection on request.

UPDATE THE PORTFOLIO EACH YEAR

It is not necessary to completely revise the portfolio each year because certain things are not likely to change. For example, one's teaching philosophy and methodology rarely undergo dramatic changes. But there will be new student rating data, perhaps new courses taught and new syllabi, and possibly new classroom observations.

We recommend an annual updating, perhaps at the end of each academic year. The process should take no more than one day of work. If the professor maintains a file and stores new evidence on teaching assignments, opportunities, and achievements, all of the information needed for the portfolio update will be in one location, and the updating will not be a time-consuming task.

One important reminder is that when new material is added, older, less relevant items are deleted so that the size of the portfolio remains constant.

CHAPTER SEVEN

EVALUATING THE TEACHING PORTFOLIO

Experience suggests that most professors prepare their teaching portfolios for purposes of personnel decisions: tenure, promotion, retention, and hiring. For that reason, this chapter addresses the question, "What should personnel committees look for when they evaluate teaching from a portfolio?"

In truth, the evaluation of teaching performance, from portfolios or any other instruments, is unavoidably an exercise in subjective judgment. Of course, personnel decisions should be based on objective data. But the purpose of objective data is to help shape a subjective decision. This does not suggest, of course, that the judgments cannot be systematized and sanitized. On the contrary, if the evaluation process meets key requirements, the likelihood of making better personnel decisions is greatly enhanced.

KEY REQUIREMENTS

Certain key requirements are especially relevant to the evaluation of teaching performance through portfolios.

PRACTICALITY

Portfolios should be readily understood and easily put to use by personnel committees. They should not demand an inordinate amount of time or energy to read and evaluate. One way to ensure this is to put a page limit on the length of portfolios. Whatever the limit—eight, ten, even twelve pages—the figure should be clearly known by professors and personnel committee members.

Relevance

There must be a clear link between the crucial elements in teaching and learning and the elements selected for evaluation. Put another way, relevance can be determined by answering one question: "What really makes the difference between effective and ineffective teachers in a particular discipline?"

Acceptability

This is perhaps the most important requirement. Unless the portfolio program has won the unqualified support of the evaluators and those being evaluated, it will be on shaky ground. That means that academic administrators and faculty leaders must build support for the program by focusing attention not just on the technical soundness of the portfolio concept but also on its attitudinal and interpersonal aspects. They must engage in frank and open discussions in order to build program acceptability.

The Importance of Mandated Portfolio Items

Because each portfolio is unique, the content and organization will differ from one professor to another. This can possibly create difficulty in using portfolios for personnel decisions. One way around this problem is to require portfolios used for tenure, promotion, and hiring and for teaching excellence awards to include certain mandated items along with the elective ones. By standardizing some items, comparison of teaching performance (for example, of four professors from different teaching contexts who are seeking the university teaching excellence award) becomes possible. Not surprisingly, this approach has been adopted by a great many colleges and universities using portfolios for personnel decisions.

Although the mandated items vary somewhat from one institution to another, they often include a reflective statement on the professor's teaching, summaries of student ratings for the past three years, course syllabi for courses taught in the past three years, innovative course materials, and evidence of efforts to improve one's teaching.

AVOIDING PITFALLS IN THE EVALUATION OF TEACHING PORTFOLIOS

Equipped with hindsight and the benefit of experience, we have identified some common pitfalls in the evaluation of portfolios for personnel decisions. We offer them as two don'ts:

- *Don't assume that everyone must teach in the same way.* It is better to allow individual differences in teaching styles and techniques as long as they can be tolerated by department and institutional goals. In general, it is best to develop criteria within the smallest practical unit: sometimes the entire college or university, but more often a department or a group of similar departments.
- *Don't assume that standards and ratings will be the same across academic disciplines and institutions.* Standards and ratings are mercurial and tend to fluctuate—sometimes widely and even unfairly. Some raters are strict; others are lenient. This may give momentary pause to an institution about to use portfolios for tenure, promotion, and hiring decisions. But, in truth, the same variation in standards and rating exists in all methods used to evaluate teaching. That is why it is no solution to decide not to introduce a portfolio program. Off-the-cuff appraisals of teaching based almost exclusively on student ratings may be currently popular, but they are hardly the answer.

We believe it is better to install a teaching portfolio program that has the advantage of documenting both the complexity and individuality of teaching and then refine the process of portfolio evaluation so that it is accurate, fair, and complete.

GENERAL ITEMS TO CONSIDER
IN EVALUATING PORTFOLIOS

This list of suggested items for evaluating portfolios was developed from detailed discussions with more than 225 members of personnel committees at colleges and universities across Carnegie classifications. They are also based on the work of Miller (2005), Seldin (2002, 2010), and Zubizarreta (2004):

1. If an institution requires core items (for example, student ratings), they must all be included in the portfolio.
2. Evidence must be presented to show that academic institutional goals (for example, the development of critical thinking skills) are met in the classroom.
3. Evidence of accomplishment—not just a reflective statement—must be presented in the portfolio.
4. The vast majority of data must be current or from the recent past—perhaps the past four years.
5. The degree of documentation in the three areas of information (from oneself, from others, and evidence of student learning) must be in general balance, and several sources should be used as documentation in each area.
6. The portfolio must demonstrate teaching consistent with departmental and institutional priorities and missions.
7. The reflective statement of what and why professors teach as they do must be consistent with the syllabus and with student and peer observations of their teaching.
8. The portfolio must meet established length requirements for the narrative and the appendix.
9. Some evidence of peer evaluation of teaching must be presented unless this would be inconsistent with the department and institution's culture.
10. Products or outcomes of student learning must reveal successful teaching.
11. Efforts of improved performance over time—in methods, materials, and evaluations—must be included in the portfolio.
12. The ratings on all common core questions on student rating forms from several courses and several years must be included.

13. The teaching responsibilities section must be consistent with the department chair's statement of the professor's responsibilities.
14. The portfolio must profile individual style, priorities, and teaching achievements.
15. The portfolio must reflect consistency between a professor's reflective statement of teaching philosophy and his or her teaching actions in the classroom, the lab, or the studio.
16. All claims made in the portfolio narrative must be supported by evidence in the appendix.
17. The reflective statement of what and why professors teach as they do must be consistent with the syllabus and with student and peer evaluations of their teaching.
18. Evaluators must focus attention on the evidence supporting teaching effectiveness and ignore an elegant cover or attractive font.
19. Review committee members must allow individual differences in teaching styles, techniques, and priorities and not assume that every faculty member must teach in the same way.
20. Evaluators must avoid relying too heavily on any one source of evidence, for example, student evaluations. No personnel decision—for promotion, tenure, hiring, or even merit pay—should be made on the basis of a single source of evidence. The focus should be not on a single stone but rather on the mosaic formed by all of the stones.

SPECIFIC QUESTIONS TO CONSIDER IN EVALUATING PORTFOLIOS

Much of the time when a college or university decides to evaluate teaching through portfolios, a committee is named to develop criteria and suggested focus for examining portfolio materials. Then faculty and administrative feedback is obtained, and the criteria and suggested focus are redrafted and eventually tested for reliability and validity. If this time-consuming approach increases acceptability, the lengthy developmental process may well be justified. But instead of creating an original list, most institutions can benefit from the experience of others.

Obviously the criteria and suggested focus for examining portfolio materials must be congenial with the institutional and departmental objectives and goals of a particular institution. In general, therefore, it is better to adapt—not adopt—already developed criteria and suggested focus of others and reshape them to meet local conditions.

The following criteria and suggested focus for evaluating portfolios should be considered not as the definitive word but as a starting point for campus discussion intended to mold and reshape the model for a better fit with institutional or department needs.

Suggested Portfolio Evaluation Form

COURSE DESIGN

Suggested Portfolio Materials

- Instructor's statement of teaching responsibilities

- Statement of teaching goals and objectives

- Syllabi

- Course goals and objectives

- Student ratings summary

- Teaching materials (tests, homework, reading lists, handouts, assignments)

- Graded term papers, projects, assignments

Suggested Focus in Examining Course Materials

- Are materials and course content appropriate for the course level?

- Do they represent the best work in the field?

- Are they appropriately challenging?

- What level of performance do the students achieve?

- Do course requirements appropriately address critical thinking development? Writing skill development?

- Are the teaching materials consistent with the course's expected contribution to the department curriculum?

Rating (circle one):   1   2   3   4   5
Ratings based on a scale of 1 = poor, 2 = fair, 3 = good, 4 = very good,
5 = excellent.

Teaching Methodologies

Suggested Portfolio Materials

- Summary of student ratings

- Videotape of the professor teaching an entire class

- Information about special circumstances that may have affected teaching

- Chair or faculty peer classroom observation

- Statement from department chair assessing teaching performance

- Description of steps taken to evaluate or improve one's teaching

- Honors or other recognition of teaching excellence

Suggested Focus in Examining Portfolio Materials

- How do this faculty member's student ratings compare with others teaching similar courses?

- What trends are apparent across courses?

- What are this faculty member's teaching strengths? Weaknesses?

- Is there evidence of teaching improvement over time?

- Is there evidence of meaningful curricular development?

- Does the faculty member engage in team teaching? Interdisciplinary teaching?

Rating: (circle one)   1   2   3   4   5

Content Knowledge

Suggested Portfolio Materials

- Evidence in teaching materials

- Record of attendance at disciplinary-based conferences resulting in presentations to faculty or application to classroom

- Record of public lectures or performances, reviews of scholarly or creative work

- Record of student research directed
- Evidence of consultations and invitations related to teaching
- Participation in faculty colloquia

Suggested Focus in Examining Portfolio Materials

- Are the teaching materials current?
- Is the best work in the field represented?
- Is the faculty member sought out as a resource in the discipline area by peers or students, or both?
- Does he or she seek opportunities to learn more about the subject?
- Is there evidence that the professor uses expertise in settings outside the classroom?
- Does the faculty member actively involve students in scholarship?

Rating: (circle one)   1   2   3   4   5

STUDENT LEARNING

Suggested Portfolio Materials

- Statement of evaluation criteria for student grades
- Grade distribution
- Copies of graded exams and student papers
- Successful drafts of student work, along with the professor's suggestions as to how each draft might be improved
- Pre- and posttest performance by the class
- Videotape of student presentations at the beginning and the end of a course
- Student learning portfolios
- Statements by alumni on their learning

Suggested Focus in Examining Portfolio Materials

- Is the grading philosophy appropriate for the courses taught?
- How suitable is the professor's grade distribution?

- Is there evidence of real cognitive or affective student learning?

- Are the professor's comments on student work appropriate? Thorough? Motivating?

- Is there evidence of assistance provided by the professor to students who are preparing publications or conference presentations?

- Do student essays, creative work, or fieldwork reports indicate deep, reflective thinking and earning?

Rating: (circle one)   1   2   3   4   5

ASSUMING DEPARTMENTAL TEACHING RESPONSIBILITY

Suggested Portfolio Materials

- Record of service on teaching-related committees (curriculum, grading policies, faculty development)

- Evidence of design of new courses and programs

- Evidence of involvement in student advising or career development

- Record of teaching improvement activities

- Record of teaching load, class size, grade distribution

Suggested Focus in Examining Portfolio Materials

- Is this faculty member a "good citizen" with regard to teaching responsibilities

- Are classes met on time? Missed classes made up?

- Does the professor instruct an appropriate number of students?

- Does he or she take an active role in the improvement of instruction in the department?

- Does the faculty member seek feedback about teaching performance, explore alternative teaching methods, make changes to increase student learning?

- Does he or she make an appropriate contribution as a student advisor?

Rating (circle one):   1   2   3   4   5

PART ONE: COMPOSITE RATING

Write your rating here for each of the above five components:

Component	**Rating**
Course Design	_____
Teaching Methodology	_____
Content Knowledge	_____
Student Learning	_____
Assuming Departmental Responsibility	_____
TOTAL SCORE:	_____

PART TWO

After reviewing your ratings in the five components above, please comment here on your overall rating of this professor as a teacher.

CHAPTER EIGHT

ANSWERS TO COMMON QUESTIONS

Over the past fifteen years, we have visited hundreds of colleges and universities to talk with faculty members and administrators about the teaching portfolio and its place in the evaluation and improvement of teaching. And we have served as individual mentors to nearly nine hundred professors across disciplines as they prepared their portfolios. In the course of this activity, professors and administrators have asked certain questions with much greater frequency than others. This chapter is devoted to answering those questions.

IS THE TEACHING PORTFOLIO CONCEPT IN ACTUAL USE TODAY?

In truth, it has gone well beyond the point of theoretical possibility. More and more colleges and universities—public and private, large and small—are nurturing and rewarding teaching performance through portfolios. Some institutions use them to improve performance. Others use them in tenure and promotion decisions. Still others use portfolios for both improving performance and personnel decisions.

IS THE PORTFOLIO RESTRICTED TO TRADITIONAL CLASSROOM TEACHING?

Absolutely not. We define *teaching* as all professional activity that provides direct support for student learning. That includes not only traditional classroom and laboratory teaching but also online instruction, as well as instruction in computer laboratories and small-group settings, one-to-one teacher-student interactions, student advising, and the scholarship of teaching and communication of its results.

HOW DOES THE TEACHING PORTFOLIO DIFFER FROM THE USUAL FACULTY REPORT TO ADMINISTRATORS AT THE END OF EACH ACADEMIC YEAR?

First, the portfolio empowers faculty to include the documents and materials that they feel best reflect their performance in teaching. It is not limited to items mandated by administrators. Second, the portfolio is based on collaboration and mentoring rather than being prepared by the faculty in isolation. Third, in preparing the portfolio, professors engage in structured reflection about why they do what they do, and for many faculty—almost as a by-product—it produces an improvement in performance. Fourth, professors describe the nature and significance of their work as teachers in clear, simple language, and that is of enormous help to members of tenure and promotion committees, especially those not in the professor's discipline.

IF PROFESSORS DESIGN THEIR OWN PORTFOLIOS, HOW CAN THEY BE SURE THEY ARE PRODUCING WHAT ADMINISTRATORS ARE REALLY LOOKING FOR?

From mounting experience, we know that portfolios are best prepared in conjunction with others. The reason is that portfolios prepared by professors working alone lack the control or corroboration of evidence essential to sustain personnel decisions. A related point is that since most faculty prepare portfolios with someone other than their department chair, it is of special importance to have a periodic, written exchange of views between chair and professor about such items as teaching responsibilities, the general content and structure of the portfolio, and how teaching performance is to be reported.

Can an Impressive-Looking Portfolio Gloss Over Weak Teaching?

No. In truth, that is a contradiction in terms because weak teachers lack evidence of effective teaching performance. The evidence is just not there. Supporting materials must be provided for every claim made. For example, a professor who claims that her student ratings were outstanding must provide rating forms that bear out this statement. An elegant cover and attractive graphics cannot disguise weak performance for a professor any more than it can for a student.

Why Are Portfolio Models And Mentors So Important to Professors Who Are Preparing Their Own Portfolios?

The models enable them to see how others in different disciplines have combined documents and materials into a cohesive whole. Some institutions make available portfolio models of exemplary, satisfactory, and unsatisfactory quality. In a similar way, most faculty come to the portfolio process with no prior experience with the concept. That is why the resources of a mentor are so important. The mentor, much like a dissertation advisor, makes suggestions, provides resources, and offers steady support during portfolio development.

How Are Mentors Recruited?

Once faculty have been taught about the portfolio and coached by an experienced, trained mentor (usually from outside the institution), a core group of faculty emerges as experienced campus leaders who can help others develop their portfolios. They can sponsor in-house workshops, help faculty connect with mentors, and set up a library of relevant reading materials and sample portfolios, for example.

Must the Mentor Be from the Same Discipline as the Professor Who Is Preparing the Portfolio?

The process of collaboration is not discipline specific. True, a mentor from the same discipline can provide special insights and understandings as well as departmental expectations and practices.

But a mentor from a different discipline can often provide the big picture, that is, the institution's viewpoint. That can be a significant help since portfolios submitted for tenure and promotion are read by faculty and administrators from other disciplines.

WHO OWNS THE PORTFOLIO?

Without question, the professor who prepared the portfolio owns it. Decisions about what goes into it are generally cooperative ones between the mentor and the professor. But the final decision on what to include, its ultimate use, and retention of the final document all rest with the professor.

DON'T ALL PORTFOLIOS LOOK ALIKE?

Not at all. In truth the portfolio is a highly individualized product, and no two are exactly alike. Both the content and organization vary widely from one portfolio to another. (See the sample portfolios in Part Three in this book.) Different disciplines cater to different types of documentation. For example, an introductory economics course is a world apart from a genetics honors seminar, and a graduate course in American history since 1900 is far removed from a freshman studio arts course.

DO CERTAIN ITEMS SEEM TO APPEAR CONSISTENTLY IN MOST PORTFOLIOS?

A review of hundreds of portfolios suggests that the following items are most often selected for inclusion: (1) a reflective statement by the faculty member discussing his or her teaching objectives, strategies, and methodologies; (2) syllabi for all courses; (3) student evaluation data; (4) a statement of the professor's current teaching responsibilities; and (5) participation in faculty development seminars and workshops designed to improve teaching.

HOW TIME-CONSUMING IS PREPARATION OF A PORTFOLIO?

Although it may appear that putting together a portfolio would take an inordinate amount of time, this has not proved to be the case. In fact, most professors can complete their portfolios in just a few days. They already have much of the material on hand, such as end-of-the-year annual reports, student ratings, and letters of invitation or thanks. Updating the material demands no more than keeping files of everything relating to teaching, in the same way that professors keep files of everything relating to their research and publication. When those sections of a curriculum vitae are updated, so too is the teaching section.

How Much Time Does It Take to Prepare a Portfolio?

Most faculty members construct the portfolio in twelve to fifteen hours spread over several days. Much of that time is spent thinking, planning, and gathering the documentation for the portfolio.

How Long Is the Typical Portfolio?

The typical portfolio has a narrative of seven to ten pages, followed by a series of appendices that document the claims made in the narrative. For most faculty, a three-ring binder holds the portfolio, and tabs identify the different items in the appendix. Just as information in the narrative should be selective, so should the appendix consist of judiciously chosen evidence. If the portfolio contains nonprint materials or items that do not fit within the portfolio cover—such as books, videotapes, or CDs—the professor may briefly discuss these materials and make them available for inspection on request.

Should Administrators Develop the Teaching Portfolio Program and Then Tell Faculty to Prepare Them?

Absolutely not. Imposing a portfolio program on faculty is almost certain to lead to strenuous faculty resistance. Far better is to involve faculty in both developing and running the program. The program for portfolios, for both improvement and promotion and tenure, should be faculty driven.

CAN GRADUATE TEACHING ASSISTANTS DEVELOP WORTHWHILE PORTFOLIOS?

Yes. Although they lack extensive teaching experience from which to draw materials and evaluations, graduate teaching assistants can write detailed portfolios that include substantive information on their teaching goals and objectives for achieving those goals. At Harvard University, for example, the portfolio programs are in fact designed to assist graduate students in documenting what they taught, why they taught it that way, and how well they taught it to give them a leg up when entering the job market.

THE PORTFOLIO CONCEPT SEEMS USEFUL FOR JUNIOR FACULTY, BUT WHY WOULD SENIOR FACULTY WANT TO PREPARE ONE?

All professors stand to benefit from writing a portfolio. At institutions where post-tenure review is required, the portfolio can play a major role in describing and documenting a professor's ongoing commitment to teaching excellence. Portfolios can also be instrumental in determining salary increases, merit pay, fellowships, awards, grants, and teaching release time. Moreover, because improvement in performance is the primary motive for engaging in the reflection and documentation that comprise a teaching portfolio, senior faculty member can prepare portfolios to sharpen their performance or set the stage for innovation and creativity in the classroom.

SHOULD AN INSTITUTION SEEK OFFICIAL FACULTY ENDORSEMENT OF THE PORTFOLIO?

Our recommendation is not to do this, at least in the early stages. The process of preparing a portfolio carries its own endorsement, and voluntary participation works best. A pilot group of early participants serves as a catalyst for encouraging others to take part in future portfolio programs.

Should All Evidence in the Portfolio be Explained?

Yes, because unexplained evidence is difficult for readers to understand and interpret. For example, including copies of current syllabi and those from five years earlier provides evidence of change over time. But the significance of change and why it took place may not be not readily apparent. That is why the addition of a commentary explaining why specific changes were made provides more convincing evidence about the professor's efforts to improve performance.

How Would You Suggest Encouraging Resistant Faculty to Prepare Portfolios?

Some faculty automatically resist portfolio development. They say they are not comfortable as self-promoters and have neither the time nor the desire to keep a record of their achievements. But their arguments can be disposed of by pointing out that this is an age of accountability, and faculty need positive documentation to support their accomplishments. They also need to convey those accomplishments clearly and persuasively to others for inspection and review.

How Often Should the Portfolio be Updated?

Most professors do so every year. Updating demands no more than keeping records of everything related to teaching performance, in the same way that records are kept of everything relating to a professor's research or publication.

Is the Syllabus Actually Inserted into the Portfolio? Are Students' Ratings? Peer Observations? Letters of Invitation?

Typically these appear as appendices, but specific references to them are made in the body of the portfolio—for example, "Appendix A includes copies of my current syllabi for all courses currently taught. Each syllabus contains course goals and objectives, a daily breakdown of course content, the dates for major papers and tests, and information on grading, attendance, and general classroom management." For student ratings, peer observations, and letters of invitation, a slightly different approach is recommended: place the actual material in the appendix, but include highlights of that material in the body of the portfolio. This is especially important if the material is being prepared for purposes of tenure or promotion. Here is one example:

Student Ratings Example

My student ratings are consistently higher than the Department of Classics average. For the fall 2010 semester, the thirty-one students in my Introduction to Classics (Classics 290) rated my teaching as follows:

Question	Department Average	My Score
Interesting assignments	4.10	4.23
Motivates students	3.95	4.12
Explains clearly	3.98	4.26
Overall course quality	4.18	4.31
Overall instructor quality	4.09	4.42

Scale: 1 is low, and 5 is high.

Why include highlights of selected sources of information in the body of the portfolio? Because promotion and tenure committees are often overworked, frequently tired, and usually pressed for time. In truth, they may tend to skim the appendices. Highlights, like peaks of mountains, cannot be overlooked.

HOW DO TEACHING PORTFOLIOS IMPROVE TEACHING?

Implicit in the process of assembling the portfolio is a learning experience for the professor. That process offers the opportunity to step back and reflect on one's teaching. Following are some guiding questions to help structure that reflection:

- What kinds of activities take place in my classroom? Why?
- Which courses do I teach most effectively? Why?
- How has my teaching changed in the past five years, and are these changes for the better?
- Would it help to offer more contemporary or real-world material in the course?
- How heavy a workload can I reasonably impose on my students?
- Should I encourage collaborative work in class? On homework assignments?
- Am I easy for students to talk to and easy to make a mistake in front of?
- What does learning look like when it happens?
- How do I want students to be changed by my teaching?
- How do I choose specific assignments and experiences for my students?
- How do I assess student learning?
- What kind of feedback do I give students on their work?
- What kind of course materials do I prepare? Why?
- How sensitive am I to differences (ability, culture, gender, learning style, race) that may have an impact on learning in my classes?
- If I overheard my students talking about my teaching, what would I want them to say?

How Important Is Strong Administrative Backing?

This backing is crucial. Unflinching administrative support is key in persuading faculty to invest time and energy in preparing high-quality portfolios. Administrators must vigorously and publicly commit themselves to the portfolio concept and provide the needed financial support. And the concept must be presented candidly and clearly to faculty and department chairs before it is implemented. Importantly, it must also be made crystal clear that the portfolio is viewed as an additional—not replacement—source of information on teaching.

WHAT SEEMS TO SURPRISE FACULTY AS THEY PUT TOGETHER THEIR PORTFOLIOS?

Following are some comments from a group of professors who developed their portfolios at a state university during a recent intensive five-day summer workshop:

"I knew that I was a good teacher. Now I have the proof."
"I wish I had saved the evidence that I threw away in the last few years."
"The process took much less time than I expected it would."
"Now I'm ready to apply for promotion."
"Before this program, I never really thought about why I do what I do as a teacher."
"I wish I had done my portfolio ten years ago!"
"Fabulous process. Wonderful product."
"Working with my portfolio mentor was a real joy."
"My portfolio helped me explain to my mother what I do!"

WHO SHOULD INTRODUCE THE PORTFOLIO AT A COLLEGE OR UNIVERSITY?

Faculty development specialists are especially well qualified to introduce the concept and to serve as mentors. Why? Because they are trained in multiple approaches and techniques to demonstrate teaching effectiveness and are experienced in working with faculty to improve teaching performance. Assuming they have the training, department chairs and members of teaching enhancement committees can fill the same role.

ARE THE TIME AND ENERGY REQUIRED TO PREPARE A PORTFOLIO WORTH THE BENEFITS?

In our view, and in the view of virtually every one of the nine hundred faculty members we have personally mentored as they prepared their portfolios, the answer is a resounding yes. It usually takes no more than a few days to prepare, and the benefits are considerable. The teaching portfolio allows professors to describe their teaching strengths and accomplishments for the record, a clear advantage when evaluation committees examine that record in making promotion and tenure decisions. But the portfolio does more than that. Many professors report that the very process of reflection and collecting and sorting documents and materials that reflect their teaching performance serves as a springboard for self-improvement. And, importantly, many colleges and universities find that portfolios help to underscore teaching as an institutional priority.

The key to developing successful teaching portfolio programs is to proceed slowly, carefully, and openly. Success does not come automatically, but it comes. The proof is in the many successful programs operating around the country.

CHAPTER NINE

E-PORTFOLIOS FOR TEACHING IMPROVEMENT

Monica A. Devanas

Increasingly our academic lives have moved into the digital world: we e-mail and text students, post syllabi online, use course management programs to provide resources to our classes, interact with groups of students in chatrooms, and collect student work electronically. It is not surprising, then, that creating and reviewing a teaching portfolio might also be done within this digital world.

Teaching portfolios—those collections of descriptions of courses we teach, reflections on our purpose and principles, and the evidence we offer to prove our effectiveness as professors—have their beginnings for most of us in the digital environment. We design our courses, learning goals, activities, and assignments at our computers; collect references using indexes and databases in digital libraries; and send messages to students over the Web. We generate our publications for scholarship, teaching, and service elements in an electronic format, and even publish electronically.

Initially the first electronic portfolios (e-portfolios) were displays of student materials. These were an extension of the traditional student learning portfolios, now offered as a collection of digital materials demonstrating what the student learned. Much of the history and applications of e-portfolios has been the scholarship of Helen Barrett, who has been researching strategies and technologies for e-portfolios since 1991 and publishing a Web site, "Technology and Alternative Assessment," since 1995 (Barrett, 2000).

But e-portfolios did not become widely used in higher education for documenting teaching for almost a decade. Batson (2002) suggests this move to digital documentation of teaching is the result of three areas of impact: students' work products are increasingly in electronic format, Web-based databases allow dynamic Web environments, and our own habits of working in digital formats contribute to the ease with which we can organize, search, collect, and assess entire curricula, programs, personal teaching records, student work, and the learning process and learning progress.

THE E-PORTFOLIO

The e-portfolio holds promise as a tool for the improvement of teaching. But before it can become useful, one must think about how it is different from the typical paper-driven teaching portfolio. Using digital technologies effectively requires more than simply scanning documents into a pdf file.

An electronic version of a teaching portfolio, like the traditional paper-based portfolio, is still a documented narrative statement of a faculty member's teaching responsibilities, philosophy, goals, and accomplishments as a teacher. As with the paper-based portfolio, one of the biggest challenges is choosing materials to include (Piernik-Yoder, 2009)—a challenge that Barrett (2005) describes as one of finding and gathering all of the materials and artifacts from different storage spaces, which makes a strong argument for having an online digital archive.

To illustrate the challenge in choosing materials to include in the e-portfolio, three variations are presented in Figures 9.1, 9.2, and 9.3. They are included here to illustrate a sample of different approaches and materials that might be considered when deciding what to include. Note that a commonality of each version is that links are provided to specific sections of the e-portfolio.

A significant effect and frequent purpose of creating a teaching portfolio is to focus on improvement of teaching. This can mean the improvement of an individual who reflects on his or her teaching and its effectiveness or the improvement of a collection of faculty members as they consider implementing new teaching strategies department-wide or as part of an ongoing

FIGURE 9.1   AN E-PORTFOLIO INCLUDING A PERSONAL PHOTOGRAPH

▶ Rutgers University   ▶ CTAAR   ▶ Contact

Monica A. Devanas

During my twenty-five years at Rutgers, my perspectives on teaching and higher education have been greatly influenced by my experiences in teaching microbiology, mentoring research students, designing new courses, science education reform, faculty development and assessment programs.

▶ Vita and Biosketch
▶ CTAAR
▶ Workshops
▶ SENCER
▶ CASTL
▶ Teaching Portfolio
▶ Biomedical Issues of HIV/AIDS Course site

As the Director of the Center for Teaching Advancement and Assessment Research, I have seen many new trends in pedagogy, curricula and instructional technologies. My work at the Center has given me the opportunity to observe and understand issues of teaching from a worldwide perspective and apply these ideas in higher education in my classes, at Rutgers, and at other institutions here and abroad.

As a microbiologist, I have been able to bring new practices into traditionally established fields, generate research opportunities for undergraduates, link science content with civic issues and demonstrate that these connections create deeper learning. My work with the National Science Foundation funded "Science for New Civic Engagements and Responsibilities," (SENCER.net) has been a forum for blending both of my worlds, that of faculty development and science education.

With more than two decades of work and collected experiences, this is a good time to synthesize the outcomes of my efforts in this space and detail them in a *Teaching Portfolio.*

Site created by Chris Moore, 2010

---

interest in improving student learning. In both cases the individual needs to engage in the three basic steps: describe his or her teaching, reflect on the purposes of teaching in a philosophy statement or discussion of strategies and methods, and then present documents and data to demonstrate the claims of teaching effectiveness (Seldin, 1991, 1997; Seldin & Associates, 1993; University of Texas at El Paso, n.d.).

The first two steps of the description of teaching responsibilities and self-reflection happen regardless of the format for the teaching portfolio—whether paper or digital. However, the transition from old ways of developing a portfolio structure to new ways of e-portfolios requires more than just substituting one format for another. It requires rethinking the whole process under transition. "Folio thinking," as it is described in student learning

FIGURE 9.2 A TEXT-ONLY APPROACH TO AN E-PORTFOLIO

▶ Rutgers University ▶ CTAAR ▶ Contact

Teaching Portfolio

"Chance favors the prepared mind" is a statement that has guided me for much of my life. The quote is attributed to Louis Pasteur, a father of microbiology, during his address at the inauguration of the Faculty of Science, University of Lille, Lille France, December 7, 1854. I saw it first on the cover of microbiology journals in graduate school. Since then it has become a mantra for much of my professional life. I do like the Idea that to "Be Prepared" has positive, if not undetermined, outcomes, perhaps even rewards.

▶ Vita and Biosketch
▶ CTAAR
▶ Workshops
▶ SENCER
▶ CASTL
▶ Teaching Portfolio
▶ Biomedical Issues of HIV/AIDS Course site

Teaching Portfolio
Courses
Teaching Philosophy
Teaching Strategies
HIV/AIDS Course
Student Projects
Assessment of Teaching

Prodded by such a motto, I never shrank from the chance to learn something new and microbiology offered many opportunities. Graduate school and post-docs, new theories, new places, new people, new experiences. In graduate school I had the opportunity to be chief scientist on a research cruise, only to have the crew mutiny. My first post-doc was a chance to link environmental microbiology elements to molecular biology practice, as well as fly a single engine plane and plow a field. During my second post-doc I had the chance to bring molecular practice back to another environment and found invitations to present in Wales and Communist Yugoslavia. Back teaching at Rutgers, I found lots of projects, such as working on grants for women in science and hosting mobs of undergraduate research students.

The most rewarding opportunity for all my preparedness was the chance to create a new course on the Biomedical Issues or HIV/AIDS in 1991 when there were few such courses in the country. Abandoning the inadequate offering of textbooks, I generated my own study guide blending content areas of infection disease with epidemiology, immunology and virology, pharmaceutics and politics. Students read primary reserach papers for background on populations with HIV issues, and designed solutions. Lots of deep and complicated content became attractive to the students since they saw the relationship between the real world problems and the information that biomedical sciences offered to understand the phenomenon and dare to attempt solutions. The basic premise of teaching science through the lens of complex public issues was a marked difference in approach to learning for the students. They grappled with cell-to-cell interactions and chemical signals of the immune system and novel genetic pathways of retroviruses, determined to understand the puzzle of AIDS and thoroughly approved of the process. This concept of science linked to real issues with extensive student engagement became a pilot for the core in a new reform in science education, i.e. Science Education for New Civic Engagements and Responsibilities, or SENCER (see SENCER.net).

Site created by Chris Moore, 2010

applications of e-portfolios, is a reflective practice to guide students in the meta-analysis of their learning process and the development of their learning portfolios (Greenberg, 2004). The same sort of approach to teaching needs to be developed by faculty as they consider developing an e-portfolio for improving their teaching. For example, it is a simple step to take a syllabus, make it a pdf file, and post it on a Web site for students to retrieve. This level of transition makes life more convenient for students and instructor and has low costs of transition for anyone who types up a syllabus in the first place.

Even if the faculty member is manually collecting the materials and scanning them or uploading digital files to a Web site or into a predesigned e-portfolio template program, the process still requires considering the material to include. The purpose in selecting each item, as well as the audience accessing the e-portfolio, also needs to be considered. As with the paper-based portfolio constructions, faculty members need to take the time to reflect and evaluate, alone or with others.

FIGURE 9.3 AN AUTOBIOGRAPHICAL APPROACH TO AN E-PORTFOLIO

Monica A. Devanas
Rutgers University
Center for Teaching Advancement and Assessment Research
Director, Faculty Development and Assessment Programs
Teaching Portfolio
Spring 2010

Teaching Philosophy

Teaching Responsibilities

Strategies and Methods

Biomedical Issues: HIV/AIDS

Student Projections

Assessment of Teaching

    Student Comments

    Ratings

    Peer Reviews

Teaching Awards

Efforts to Improve Teaching

During my twenty-five years at Rutgers, my perspectives on teaching and higher education have been greatly influenced by my experiences in teaching microbiology, mentoring research students, designing new courses, science education reform, faculty development and assessment programs. As the Director of the Center for Teaching Advancement and Assessment Research, I have seen many new trends in pedagogy, curricula and instructional technologies. My work at the Center has given me the opportunity to observe and understand issues of teaching from a worldwide perspective and apply these ideas in higher education in my classes, at Rutgers, and at other institutions here and abroad. As a microbiologist, I have been able to bring new practices into traditionally established fields, generate research opportunities for undergraduates, link science content with civic issues and demonstrate that these connections create deeper learning. My work with the National Science Foundation funded "Science for New Civic Engagements and Responsibilities," (SENCER.net) has been a forum for blending both of my worlds, that of faculty development and science education. With more than two decades of work and collected experiences, this is a good time to synthesize the outcomes of my efforts in this space and detail them in a Teaching Portfolio

---

The step of collecting and storing documents and data in an organized structure so that it is easily retrievable is usually not a standard practice of most faculty. Most busy faculty focus their time and energy on their core functions of scholarship, teaching, and service. The discipline to save and be able to retrieve portfolio materials is usually a secondary concern to most faculty members until there is a need, such as for reappointment, tenure, or promotion. This part of the process—the collection, organization, and retrieval of data and documents—can be significantly supported by using a digital approach to document handling.

In using the simplest format of an e-portfolio, the faculty member's narrative statement is frequently linked to materials of interest or adding material to a program. Either way, materials are available and accessible with little or no effort. The challenge in creating or reviewing a teaching portfolio regardless of format is the time it takes to select the materials for review, and with a digital collection system, the risk is that everything that is collected will be included. This could present a problem because now faculty members need to devote time to the decision of where to start, what to use, and what to compare. So much is available that they can become overwhelmed with what is relevant since all of it is potentially available.

Creating an electronic portfolio from a paper-based one is a difficult transition. The reason is simple: uploading a raft of digital documents to a Web site or storage space does not necessarily create much value or convenience for the user because those documents have to be read and reviewed to make them useful. This is always the stumbling block in electronic student learning assessment portfolios; the first question faculty members ask about them is, "Just who is going to read and review them?

CREATING AN E-PORTFOLIO

Considerable thought and effort must go into the design of an e-portfolio if it is to be useful for faculty development. It requires considerable time organizing, planning, and designing the portfolio itself. What helps greatly is to use the power of technology to make the review of all related documents focused, meaningful, and rapid so that we can incorporate change more quickly into our teaching.

Just how to do that will come out of learning by doing, with changes made as we proceed with the development of the portfolio. But some obvious steps make good sense.

STEP 1: GOALS

It is useful to make a list of the components or items that are important to your teaching, such as learning goals, level of content, variety or effectiveness of presentation skills, or engagement of students. To do this using the portfolio approach, it is probably best to list several goals and design a rubric for each component. Examples for rubrics for e-portfolio evaluation are found at these Web sites:

Penn State University: www.schreyerinstitute.psu.edu/pdf/e_
    portfolio_rubric.pdf

ePortfolio Portal: www.danwilton.com/eportfolios/rubric.php

University of Wisconsin–Stout: www.uwstout.edu/soe/profdev/
    eportfoliorubric.html

STEP 2: STANDARDS

This involves simple statements of what a professor expects of himself or herself and what one thinks a good syllabus design, or a good level of student engagement, should be. Essentially it is asking questions such as those asked in scholarship of teaching (Piernik-Yoder, 2009).

The simplest format for an e-portfolio is to collect these items as independent documents with links between the main narrative document and the digital documents. This is not a very different process from simply collecting hard-copy documents. The power of using a digital environment is in being able to use a database structure for all the components and items that will allow the categories of elements to be accessible, collectable, reviewable, and comparable.

STEP 3: DATABASE CONSTRUCTION

To be useful, data must be entered into the e-portfolio in folders that can be searched independent of the documents themselves. In many ways, this is the most challenging aspect of the e-portfolio, since it requires an immediate investment in preparation and organization. For example, suppose a professor would like to compare the effectiveness of her office hours over time. That is going to require keeping records on office hours on such issues as whether students attended and, if so, how often. This information should be put into the e-portfolio separately so it can be searched and compared. In other words, an effective e-portfolio should be more like a database than like a list of documents.

The design and creation of such a database-like program is the basis of most commercially available e-portfolio programs, such as Epsilen (www.epsilen.com), elgg (http://elgg.org/), Rcampus (www.rcampus.com/), Foliospaces (www.foliospaces.com/), and many other free online tools to create interactive eportfolios (Barrett, n.d.).

To take advantage of the power of databases for e-portfolios requires entering into an electronic diary all items, thoughts, materials, and engagements with students (see the Electronic Portfolio Consortium Web site: www.eportconsortium.org/). Not all aspects are anticipated at the time of database creation, so from time to time (perhaps every five years), the process needs to be redone to include new elements and restructure or reprioritize those less meaningful.

The need for confidentiality and permission to use student work also needs to be addressed. This becomes an increasingly important need when e-portfolio software articulates with learning management systems where students have been placing their work (LaGuardia Community College, 2007; Reese & Levy, 2009). Lorenzo and Ittelson (2005) note that teaching e-portfolios are not to be a collection of teaching materials from an entire career; rather, they need to be selective to avoid information overload. Although graphics, audio, and video can showcase innovative teaching strategies, not many faculty members are familiar with multimedia technology. Also, there may be copyright and privacy issues when authentic examples of student work are included in a faculty member's e-portfolio.

Technical challenges and barriers abound also with questions about format, sustainability, hosting, server space, and accessibility. As e-portfolio structures improve their articulation with campus learning software programs, the numbers of questions explode. Groups discussing and debating these issues can be found at the Electronic Portfolio Consortium (www.eportconsortium .org), Helen Barrett's blog (http://electronicportfolios.com/ blog/), and Academic Commons (www.academiccommons.org/ commons/essay/future-eportfolio-roundtable).

There are many more questions, issues, and challenges before e-portfolios are integrated into day-to-day academic routines and are seamlessly connected to learning systems where students are uploading course projects and institutional systems with data on courses, faculty, and students. Digital natives will have no hesitation in engaging in these tools and habits. Digital immigrants will find the process of transition from a paper-based format to digital as a challenge in time and in the process of adapting folio thinking to make the most of integrated systems.

STEP 4: ASSESSMENT

Once the e-portfolio is created, there remains the process of self-reflection and self-assessment, which is essential for using any materials for improvement. Digital environments and word processing tools can help organize, collect, and compare, but some of the review process needs to include collaboration with colleagues who can assist with objective perspectives, advice, and support.

CONCLUSION

The digital systems in which e-portfolios are created have many additional tools designed for communication and collaboration. Every day new networking systems are introduced through which faculty can share their materials with colleagues for feedback and constructive criticism and suggestions. The newest tools for these communications are integrated into digital natives' lives, such as social networking and the ability to exchange and share teaching materials, reflections, assessments, and real-time collaboration tools where all materials are instantly available. Among the most recent ideas on e-portfolios is the idea of using mobile devices to maintain mobile portfolios (m-portfolios) such as on Internet-enabled mobile phones (Rate, 2009).

The future for e-portfolios as a teaching improvement tool is unlimited. Technology innovation on campus is dramatically altering the way we teach and the way students learn.

CHAPTER TEN

CLINICAL EDUCATION PORTFOLIOS

Annalise Sorrentino

I am a teacher, but I do not have a specific class load; do not give midterms and finals that are graded, plotted on a graph, and compared to previous years; and do not teach Pediatrics 101 or Pediatrics 210 with an optional lab. But I am an effective teacher, and I know that from the evidence contained in my clinical educator teaching portfolio—both the narrative and the appendix.

SOME BACKGROUND

When I finished my fellowship in pediatric emergency medicine and prepared to join the faculty at the University of Alabama-Birmingham (UAB), I tried explaining to my parents what I would be doing. Although it seemed perfectly clear to me, it proved to be somewhat confusing to them. My title would be assistant professor, and despite the fact that most of my work would be done at the bedside, I was considered a teacher. Academic faculty, as we are often referred to, are asked to instruct at the bedside but also lecture in the classroom. We are expected to be able to modify our methods and our emphasis based on who we are teaching and what level of instruction they need.

Our audience ranges from junior students to senior medical fellows, from people who have dedicated their careers to following in our footsteps to those who cannot wait to leave. There is usually a curriculum in place (most of the time put there by someone else) that we try to follow to meet current guidelines and requirements, all the while knowing that medicine is constantly changing, aware that what we are saying now may be considered out of date relatively quickly.

We are not teachers in the traditional sense, but many of the templates for portfolios are structured to complement the more conventional fashion. So much of what we do as clinician educators or academicians seems intangible and difficult to quantify. However, our contributions are significant, and it is to our benefit to illustrate what we do and how well we do it.

Every teaching portfolio is first and foremost a personal document. It is not a meticulous outline of everything we have done for, say, the past five years, but rather a presentation of the three or four aspects of our careers that are most rewarding. There is no right or wrong, and for many of us in medical-related fields, that concept is very frustrating. For years, we have been taught to memorize and follow algorithms. We are detail oriented and at times may even have had attempts at creativity and individuality stifled. Now, the outline to follow is the one we are creating. This is our chance to show division directors and department chairs that our methods are innovative, appropriate, and successful.

GETTING STARTED

As with most of the rest of medicine or other clinical specialties, there are different approaches to reach a goal. I present my approach as one example, in anticipation that it will guide you on your task, knowing that it should differ in many ways from mine.

The idea of getting started on a portfolio can be quite intimidating, so to make it more approachable, I suggest that you divide it into two main categories: the narrative and the evidence. I also like to refer to it as the story and the proof. And here is where the fun part comes in: you get to write your own story and decide what to include. Now is the time to be proud of your accomplishments and pat yourself on the back.

THE NARRATIVE

One of the best pieces of general advice I can give about how to write your narrative is to assume the reader has no idea what you do. Write it so your mother would understand your responsibilities. So instead of writing, "I teach medical students," write, "I give a one-hour lecture to third-year medical students on their pediatric rotation six times a year. The topic of the lecture is catastrophic illnesses in children presenting with common complaints. There are typically ten to twelve students in attendance."

The narrative can be divided several different ways but should include several key sections, which I elaborate on next. There is some overlap in the topics, and it allows flexibility and creative license as the portfolio is built. Since this is a personal document, add the areas you deem necessary. As you are contemplating what to include, review what your individual institution's requirements are for promotion and tenure. This record will serve as an excellent template to use while preparing documents and materials.

TEACHING PHILOSOPHY

This section should describe how you teach as a clinical educator, why you teach that way, and how your teaching methods have changed over time. This will help readers understand your current style and can offer insight into who you are and the principles that guide you as a teacher. This section might include examples of your previous efforts and your own personal educational goals. Some questions can help you get started:

- How do I teach most effectively?
- How does the fact that I am teaching adult learners affect my methods?
- How has my approach to teaching changed over time?
- What are my strengths as an educator? What areas would I like to improve?
- How would I like my educational efforts to be remembered?

Example: In the constantly changing world of medicine, the concept of lifelong learning is crucial. What I learned in medical school may or may not be applicable to current medical strategies. So as I strive to teach trainees, I am also learning myself. I change my teaching style to meet the needs of my students. Since most of my teaching occurs on an individual basis, my goal is to identify the way each person learns the best and then use a suitable teaching method. I find that many adult learners do not like to be challenged, especially with something they may not know. But they tend to learn and remember things better when faced with such a situation.

I am an innovative educator who is passionate and enthusiastic about teaching. I want to be known not just as a "good" teacher of clinical medicine, but as a medical educator who has developed methods, curricula, and improved understanding of educational processes that make a difference in the development of the next generation of physicians.

TEACHING RESPONSIBILITIES

Depending on the job description, there are a number of ways to arrange this section. One way is to separate the topics into the different groups that you teach (for example, students, residents, fellows, community; or nurses, therapists, physicians), or into the different types of teaching you do (for example, bedside, didactic, simulation).

Example: My teaching responsibilities include education at all levels. Working in the pediatric emergency department affords me the opportunity for bedside teaching on a regular basis. In this capacity, I instruct pediatric emergency medicine fellows, pediatric residents, internal medicine/pediatrics residents, emergency medicine residents, family practice residents, senior medical students, and nurse practitioner students. My role with each of them is distinctly different and is described in detail in my personal teaching portfolio.

EVIDENCE OF SUCCESSFUL INNOVATIONS

Much of what clinical educators do is set by a medical or nursing school curriculum or hospital or other training guidelines. But often there are programs or courses that a medical educator creates. Have you arranged any new rotations or experiences for your students? Is there something for which your department looks to you as the expert? Have you taken part in professional development workshops or seminars? In what ways have you applied what you learned?

Example: The opportunity to attend the Association of American Medical Colleges Early Career Faculty Development Seminar for Women was very beneficial. There were successful women from all over the country who were there for the sole purpose of helping us plan our careers. I was so energized by that experience that I wanted to share it with other people, both men and women. A colleague and I have put together a workshop on strategic career planning for clinical educators that addresses such issues as these:

- Basics of career planning
  - Identifying your passions
  - Strategizing to achieve your goal
  - Self-reflection
- Mentoring
  - How to be a successful mentee
  - How to be your own best mentor
  - Mentoring as a team approach
- Career advancement options
  - Local resources
  - National opportunities

ACCOMPLISHMENTS AND AWARDS

This is the time to boast about the recognition others have given to you. These can range from formal awards, to acknowledgment of service, to serving on local committees. Attaining membership status in professional organizations takes time, effort, and dedication so should be viewed as an achievement. This is not the time to be modest; this is the time to shine.

Example: As I reflect on my career, there are a few accomplishments of which I am particularly proud. The first is *The Polhill Report*, a quarterly newsletter that I edit and publish. It honors the memory of a pediatric emergency medicine physician who died unexpectedly in 2002. Rud Polhill was a mentor of mine during my training and introduced me to the concept of lifelong learning. As editor, I enjoy writing about issues that affect all of us in a day-to-day practice of pediatric medicine.

Another accomplishment I have been able to achieve is my "fellow" status in both the American Academy of Pediatrics and the American College of Emergency Physicians. The latter required three years of active service to local and national efforts of the college.

PROFESSIONAL GOALS

The previous sections have been about the past. It is just as important to plan the future. This can also serve as a checklist to monitor your professional progress. Keep in mind, though, that objectives change. This should be a fluid section—one that you review and adjust on a regular basis. This is an opportunity for self-reflection and can help put the smaller pieces together into the big picture.

Example: My overall purpose continues to be to deliver quality health care to the children of Alabama and to teach others to do the same. In order to do that, I will continue to provide pediatric medical care at the local level, but I also want to become more involved in pediatric emergency medicine at the national level, specifically through the American College of Emergency Physicians. Another goal I have is to help others promote themselves. I hope to do this through continuing to host workshops on career development and by introducing others to the art of developing their own academic or professional portfolio. I feel fortunate that I became aware of these opportunities early in my career, and I hope to help other junior-level faculty do the same.

THE EVIDENCE

Displaying the evidence of accomplishments makes up the remainder (and the majority) of the portfolio. The activities referred to in the narrative are cross-referenced with the proof of these activities in the appendices. Just as there are several ways to organize the narrative, there are also various ways to organize the evidence so that it mirrors the narrative. The sections in which teaching responsibilities are divided provide a good start.

When referring to a particular responsibility or activity, there must be proof of that action. This may be a summary of a lecture, an outline of a program or curriculum, or a class roster. Evaluations are key in the appendices, as they illustrate how well teaching has been performed. For large groups or programs offering continuing education credits, this is done as part of the program, so do not forget to ask for that feedback. Not only is it important for the portfolio, but it is also important for your overall development. For smaller groups, there may not be a prearranged evaluation. One solution is to give one to the participants at the time of the event. It can be very simple and quick to fill out, but can give valuable feedback on the topic, the presentation, and the methods.

Medical school classes have class numbers (just like English 101), and these are very easy to list. Get to know the people in the student services department of the school and discipline involved; although these evaluations are usually just an e-mail away, they are often distributed only if requested.

Copies of any publications that relate to teaching one's discipline should be included, whether they are original research, peer-reviewed, review articles, or abstracts. If there are other teaching-related publications to which you contribute (newsletters, bulletins, updates), they should be included as well.

For many of us, giving lectures is a mainstay of our existence. A lot of work goes into each one of those, and they should be listed in some fashion. I suggest including the title slide with a brief explanation of the purpose of the lecture (evidence-based medicine, case conference, review topic) and the intended audience.

For those involved in direct patient care, cards and letters from patients or families are a valuable addition to a portfolio. In the era of 360-degree evaluations, they may even be a requirement for certain board certifications. This is perhaps the most important evidence of all. It is evidence of directly affecting a patient's life; no matter how minor it may have seemed at the time, it was significant to someone.

CONCLUSION

The clinical education portfolio has a specific niche that can help academic faculty display their accomplishments and goals. It assists not only in outside evaluation but also in self-reflection, which is vital to successful faculty development and advancement. My portfolio sits on the right-hand corner of my desk and has become my most frequently used reference book. As the process begins, persevere and work through it. The final product will be well worth your effort.

PART TWO

HOW PORTFOLIOS ARE USED

The chapters in Part Two describe in detail how four institutions and one administrator have implemented portfolios on their campuses. The institutions—large and small, public and private—represent by design diverse settings and practices reflecting the broad differences in history, context, purpose, and academic culture among colleges and universities where teaching portfolios have had an impact.

The portfolios described in the following chapters have varying purposes and practices. They are used for teaching improvement, tenure and promotion, and preparing new professors to teach. These representative institutions—Loyola University of Maryland, University of Massachusetts Amherst, Elgin Community College (Illinois), and Florida Gulf Coast University—illustrate the diverse needs of their faculty, the history and evolution of their programs, and lessons learned as teaching portfolio programs have been developed on their campuses.

From Loyola University, we learn how portfolios have been evaluated. From the University of Massachusetts Amherst, we see how portfolios can be used to enhance graduate education and how e-portfolios have been evaluated. From Elgin Community College, we see how a program is established and how collaboration with institutional stakeholders develops. From Florida Gulf Coast, we view the development and impact of teaching portfolio institutes. And in the final chapter in this part, we hear the reflections of the chief academic officer at Florida Gulf Coast University on faculty preparation for tenure and promotion.

A cautionary note: The full range of teaching portfolio use can best be understood and appreciated by reading all of the institutional reports.

CHAPTER ELEVEN

TEACHING PORTFOLIOS AT LOYOLA UNIVERSITY MARYLAND

Peter Rennert-Ariev

Loyola University is a Jesuit university located in Baltimore, Maryland. Founded in 1852, Loyola has experienced transformation from a small, male-only, local college to a diverse, dynamic, coeducational university providing undergraduate and graduate education to a diverse population of more than six thousand students. The Jesuit tradition at Loyola has prompted the development of student-centered education with undergraduate and graduate programs rooted in the liberal arts tradition. At the undergraduate level, all students complete a core curriculum, representing the traditions of the liberal arts and designed to equip students with skills of cogent thinking, careful analysis, and clear communication. Graduate programs prepare students as leaders in their professional fields in teaching, scholarship, and community service. Loyola's programs are distinguished by a focus on meaningful professional service and leadership and an emphasis on academic achievement, excellence in teaching, and engaged, meaningful scholarship.

In pursuit of these goals Loyola has established the Center for Teaching Excellence, designed to enrich opportunities for faculty to develop teaching skills and habits of discernment and reflection toward student learning. The center sponsors a variety of faculty development opportunities focused on strengthening the quality of teaching, including Ignatian pedagogy and service-learning teaching seminars, teaching workshops (such as an annual teaching enhancement workshop) that provide opportunities for faculty to share best teaching practices, and the annual Teaching Portfolio Workshop. The Teaching Portfolio Workshop, in particular, has been central to deepening Loyola's institutional commitment to teaching and fostering faculty development in teaching. The workshop has occurred annually since 2003, and each year, it has included a diverse group of faculty participants representing a range of academic departments, both graduate and undergraduate education, and levels of faculty experience and rank. The number of participants has ranged from ten to twenty-five each year, and approximately one hundred faculty members have now completed the workshop.

The portfolio workshops, lasting four to five days, have helped participants construct their own teaching portfolios as they work individually and meet for three or four individual consultation sessions with their portfolio mentor. The program also provides several opportunities for whole group discussions involving all participants to clarify the content of, and processes associated with, teaching portfolios and to share strategies to broaden institution-wide faculty involvement in teaching portfolios and mentoring programs in general. The program culminates in a session in which participants share their final portfolios, and the mentors publicly comment on attributes of each participant's work.

The portfolios are designed to serve as a collection of materials that document teaching performance. In promoting the portfolio workshops, Loyola administration has encouraged faculty to use portfolios to serve one or both of the following goals: as a tool for organizing evidence to be used for tenure and promotion decisions and as a vehicle for self-reflection and teaching improvement. Mentors typically discuss these goals with their mentees to help them think about suitable evidence. The portfolios themselves generally provide eight to twelve double-spaced pages of written narrative, followed by appendices that contain products of good teaching, examples of student work, assessment, and information provided by others (statements from colleagues who have observed the professor's teaching or student evaluation data, for example).

This chapter focuses on analyzing the experiences of faculty from Loyola who have been engaged in constructing teaching portfolios. The first year of the workshop, I produced my own teaching portfolio and have subsequently served as a member of the mentoring team each year. My experience in this process and the deep levels of reflection about teaching that it promoted have led to my interest in pursuing scholarship on the processes and outcomes involved in creating teaching portfolios.

METHOD

The analysis in this chapter is based on a sample of twenty-five faculty participants who participated in the portfolio workshop in 2006. This sample included representation from all three academic divisions at Loyola: social science, the humanities, and business and management. I analyzed each of their completed teaching portfolios and, following the workshop, conducted an interview with each of the twenty-five faculty members. In addition, I have included participant observation data of my own work as a mentor with four participants from this group of twenty-five. I recorded and transcribed all of my mentoring meetings with these participants for twelve total meetings. Using a semistructured approach, I interviewed participants to reflect on three central questions:

- Why did they elect to participate in the workshop?
- What was the process of constructing their teaching portfolio like?
- How, if at all, did constructing their portfolio and participating in the workshop provoke reflection on their teaching and assessment practices?

FINDINGS

Virtually all participants sought to participate in the workshop because they perceived that the experience would help them prepare their materials for annual faculty evaluation, midterm tenure review, or tenure review, or some combination of these. All participants were untenured faculty, and two-thirds had completed their second or third year as full-time faculty.

While the primary goal of participants was to achieve a positive evaluation, participants reported that the portfolio process helped them to reflect more meaningfully on their teaching and to learn to consider—and assemble—appropriate evidence. Half of the participants, for example, reported that the process helped them see the links between their philosophy and teaching methods in more profound ways than they had previously considered. Most reported having previously submitted a philosophy statement (it is required all faculty applicants), but they reported that the teaching portfolio provoked a deeper level of analysis of their teaching philosophy. Also, three-quarters of the participants said that the process helped them to consider evidence of their teaching effectiveness they would not have otherwise considered. They had made deliberate choices, based on careful selection of materials, to obtain a representative sample of their teaching rather than a compilation of everything they had accomplished. In this way, participants learned to employ a sampling methodology to select appropriate evidence.

It should be noted that individual departments coordinated the annual and midterm tenure review process. In most cases, departments required untenured faculty to submit some reflective commentary on their contributions toward teaching, research, and service, as well as evidence of teaching effectiveness, usually including end-of-course student evaluations. The midpoint tenure review and tenure review materials generally consisted of a more extensive compilation of accomplishments in teaching, research, and service. Most faculty considered how to edit their portfolio in ways that could be submitted as part of their tenure review documents as, for example, submitting the teaching portfolio for the section on "teaching" in their tenure dossier.

Faculty also noted how their student assessment practices were represented in the teaching portfolios. A common theme discussed by faculty was that their students have prior knowledge that can be useful for instruction. References to the importance of accessing students' knowledge and enabling opportunities for students to construct and share knowledge in the classroom were prevalent within the philosophy statements and descriptions of teaching strategies.

For most participants, the essential function of the portfolio was to represent their accomplishments in the most favorable way. Most participants felt it would be counterproductive to show aspects of their teaching in which they had struggled. That is, they felt that the portfolio was not a vehicle to "show the bombs" or aspects of their teaching that had proven particularly challenging or difficult to resolve. In this sense, the portfolio's potential as a formative tool to help faculty identify aspects of their teaching in need of improvement may have been diminished by the overall effect of the portfolio as a means of representing exemplary practice. When faculty participants were primarily concerned with using the portfolio for purposes of their own evaluation, the usefulness of the portfolio as a tool for formative assessment and the improvement of teaching may have been somewhat diminished.

The use of teaching portfolios at Loyola University has contributed to the institution in several important ways. Most academic departments now recommend that all untenured faculty complete the teaching portfolio and include it as part of their annual evaluation. In addition, the requirements for tenure now recommend that faculty complete a teaching portfolio and include the reflective analysis of teaching and a sample of documentary evidence commonly seen in teaching portfolios in their dossier. Some departments are revising their faculty evaluation criteria to reflect less heavy emphasis on only a few traditional measures of teaching effectiveness, such as aggregate values derived from student course evaluations. Instead many departments now recommend a broader sample of the many types of evidence available to demonstrate effective teaching and a thoughtful, reflective stance toward teaching.

Although Loyola is not exempt from the silo effect, where faculty tend to work only within their academic disciplines, the teaching portfolio has brought awareness of central themes and connections to the university mission that might have otherwise been missed. For instance, *curapersonalis*—a central theme in Jesuit education, meaning care for the individual—was also central to several teaching philosophy statements in one year's workshop. Recognizing this common ground led to deeper understanding across disciplines and ultimately resulted in collaborative work among the faculty, culminating in a faculty-led teaching workshop the next year.

IMPLICATIONS

Loyola's experience with teaching portfolios demonstrates some lessons for other institutions. There are strong indications that teaching portfolios can be used effectively as a tool for development of teaching capacity and reflection on teaching in ways that simultaneously inform the individual and the institution. The criteria that are used to evaluate and mentor faculty in the area of teaching can be deepened by the use of portfolios. Portfolios also can help reveal areas in which faculty show incomplete understanding of tools for student assessment and thus suggest possible content for faculty development experiences.

The friction between the portfolio as a tool for development and a tool for evaluation makes clear that its use should be understood in the context of the institutional climate around faculty evaluation. The literature of faculty evaluation stresses that faculty and administrators should support a balanced evaluation process that includes greater emphasis on development (Mills & Hyle, 1999). If portfolios are to be used a tool for development, faculty should be encouraged to reveal aspects of their teaching they would like to improve. In that regard, the institution may need to negotiate better strategies for faculty to disclose less positive information about their teaching and how they might improve, even though doing so may be perceived as professionally risky within existing evaluative processes. If, however, the teaching portfolio is constructed strictly as a dossier that reflects exemplary practice and makes the strongest possible case for a positive review, then it may make sense to reformulate, and make flexible, the structure of the portfolio to reflect exactly that format to which faculty are held accountable. To this end it appears that Seldin and Miller's (2009) *The Academic Portfolio: A Practical Guide to Documenting Teaching, Research, and Service* provides a useful model for faculty.

Our experiences with teaching portfolios at Loyola have had a positive impact on the institution. Faculty who have participated have gained both a deeper understanding of their teaching prompted by the portfolio process and by increased opportunities to collaborate with colleagues across disciplines. The institution has increasingly recognized the value of portfolios, and they are now used to inform annual and tenure review processes. In addition, institutional tools for assessment of student learning have been favorably influenced by faculty development of teaching portfolios. Further research on the impact of the teaching portfolio at Loyola University no doubt will show a positive influence on students, faculty, and the university itself.

CHAPTER TWELVE

EXPLORING THE FUTURE OF TEACHING PORTFOLIOS WITH GRADUATE STUDENTS AT THE UNIVERSITY OF MASSACHUSETTS AMHERST

Mathew L. Ouellett

For the past twenty years, the Center for Teaching (CFT) at the University of Massachusetts Amherst has served a central goal of helping the university to achieve excellence in teaching and learning through many programs. These programs support teachers from junior, early-career, and senior faculty to graduate students—the future faculty. Since the 1980s, researchers and practitioners have concluded that the teaching portfolio is a useful method to promote better teaching, document teaching development efforts, and evaluate teaching effectiveness (Seldin, 2004). As the demands of accountability for higher education have increased, many graduate schools and faculty development programs sponsor teaching portfolio development for current and future faculty.

At the University of Massachusetts Amherst, the CFT began working with teaching portfolios in the early 1990s as a method for supporting faculty members (especially junior pretenure instructors) interested in documenting their efforts for the promotion and tenure processes (Sorcinelli, 1993). In conjunction with these efforts, the CFT offered workshops on teaching portfolios for faculty members. The goals of these workshops were multiple: fostering collegial discussion on teaching, promoting individual refection and improvement, and placing the responsibility for evaluating teaching in the hands of faculty. In addition, we distributed a free print resource, *Teaching Portfolio*, which outlined the rationale for portfolios and offered models for teaching statements (Sorcinelli, 1993).

UMass recognizes that graduate students provide essential contributions to the excellence of undergraduate education at the university. These contributions include teaching, instructing labs, acting as discussion leaders and graders, and tutoring. In addition, many graduate students have found that these teaching-related experiences contribute significantly to their development of discipline-based expertise and content presentation skills.

In many graduate programs, students receive comprehensive feedback on their research interests through the ongoing supervision and mentorship provided by faculty members. Therefore, doctoral-level students often leave graduate school with a clear understanding of their research, writing interests, and strengths. However, rarely are graduate students mentored in the development and documentation of teaching skills. In many cases, even if students have had the opportunity to teach during their time in graduate school, teaching is often a secondary commitment (Ouellett, 2007).

Like many other peer institutions, graduate students at the University of Massachusetts Amherst are paying increasingly close attention to the importance of teaching effectiveness for their long-term career success. They are seeking ways to reflect on and to document their strengths as teachers. However, the polish of the faculty examples included in *Teaching Portfolio* initially overwhelmed some graduate students and kept them from attempting to create their own (Mues & Sorcinelli, 2000).

TEACHING DOCUMENTATION PROGRAM

In response, the CFT launched the Teaching Documentation Program (TDP) in 1998, a modularized self-paced program, in an effort to recognize and support the substantial commitment graduate students make to their teaching (Sorcinelli & Ouellett, 1998). The TDP strengthens graduate student education by formalizing university graduates' teaching development efforts and providing them with a competitive advantage in their future career goals. Specifically, the TDP documentation contributes to graduate student development in three ways: as an increasingly necessary part of the academic job application, as a useful tool for interviews, and as an opportunity for graduate students to think about and reflect on their teaching in a substantial way (Ouellett, 2007). An important issue, for example, is raised by Armstrong, Stanton, and Mannheimer (2005) in "How Would You Teach This Class?" They stressed the importance for graduate students to think about their teaching "in a sustained way" before academic job interviews. They further suggested that before entering the job market, graduate students should begin considering how they would answer questions about promoting student learning in their classes. The TDP gives them the opportunity to do so.

Now in its tenth year, nearly one hundred senior graduate students have taken advantage of some or all aspects of the TDP. By far, the most popular service is support in developing a philosophy of teaching statement, with about a quarter of participants completing a full teaching portfolio. Word-of-mouth recommendation from one graduate student to another sustains the popularity of the TDP.

The TDP addresses efforts in three key areas: introduction to theory and research of teaching excellence, evidence of self-reflection and some experience with teaching assessment, and teaching improvement. In addition, it encourages participants to document evidence of teaching development activities that may be useful in the future (for example, developing a philosophy of teaching statement, a syllabus, or an exercise or lab assignment). Each component of the program emphasizes learning by active participation, developmental feedback, and critical self-reflection (Sorcinelli & Ouellett, 2002).

At the conclusion of the TDP, participants receive a formal letter of documentation from the CFT that inventories and describes their teaching development efforts. Such evidence that participants have collected throughout the PDP can be useful when seeking a position with teaching responsibilities, preparing a formal teaching portfolio, or articulating future teaching development goals (Sorcinelli & Ouellett, 2002).

E-PORTFOLIOS

The conventional hard copy portfolio usually contains a statement of teaching philosophy, teaching experience and responsibilities, reflection and refinements—objective and subjective evaluations of teaching skills, lesson plans, and prepared and prospective syllabi. As technology has evolved, the teaching portfolio has also started to evolve from paper binders to laptops, CDs, and Web-based applications.

Kilbane and Milman (2003) described the e-portfolio as "a goal driven collection of a teacher's work produced and displayed in digital format that demonstrates their goal in knowledge and skills over time" (p. 4). The UMass program determined that there might be several advantages of an e-portfolio for graduate students seeking to prepare a teaching portfolio.

The e-portfolio supports the traditional portfolio material format but can be represented with a format that is much easier to update. It also can showcase multimedia samples of the graduate student's work. For example, a short video segment from a lecture, lab, or discussion session led by the student could be included. An e-portfolio could also visually display the prominent pedagogies the student has successfully adopted. E-portfolios allow readers to navigate within the portfolio with hyperlinks; one can easily click from a lesson plan to a grading rubric or from a methodology to an example assignment.

E-portfolios can be packaged into CD-ROMs or uploaded to a server to give graduate students an opportunity to share their materials with peers, parents, or potential future employers. E-portfolios can be used for job applications and interviews, easily and inexpensively sent by the Web or on portable media. By the very process of creating their own portfolios, graduate students become more skilled in new technologies and have greater awareness of the technology resources available (Reynolds, Labissiere, & Haack, 2004).

Thus, it seemed that e-portfolios would be the ideal tool for graduate students to host multiple types of materials (evidence) and to serve various purposes: formative—an ongoing process to support new professional development; summative—contained within a formal evaluation; and marketing—used to seek employment (Barrett, 2009).

THE E-PORTFOLIO PILOT EFFORT

The uses of portfolios nationally by tenure system faculty have shown promising results (Seldin, 2004). We were interested in seeing if we could expand the TDP to include an e-portfolio component. Based on interest expressed by graduate students participating in Introduction to College Teaching in the spring 2004 semester, we reviewed the research and current practices related to electronic teaching portfolios and sought support for a pilot initiative. Introduction to College Teaching is a three-credit, interdisciplinary graduate-level seminar that provides an introduction to the principles and performance of college teaching through an examination of current research and best practices related to teaching and learning in higher education settings.

Underwritten by a grant from the graduate school, we launched a pilot e-portfolio program in spring 2005 that supported fellowships for six graduate students from various disciplines. The fellowship included an orientation meeting, regular seminar meetings, individual teaching development meetings with consultants from the CFT, and technical support as needed from the Office of Instructional Technology/Academic Computing. The fellows met in a seminar setting about once a month for two semesters. In these sessions, they received instruction in creating a teaching portfolio, participated in hands-on technology training sessions, and, most important, exchanged resources and processes with one another for developing an effective e-portfolio. Participants also received a copy of Dreamweaver software to develop their e-portfolios and a modest stipend to support participation (approximately five hundred dollars per person).

ASSESSMENT

During the fellowship, we regularly sought out the feedback of participants on seminar materials, exercises, discussions, and the usefulness of technical assistance. Assessment also included a follow-up survey conducted in spring 2009. All six fellows completed the pilot e-portfolio program, and all successfully secured teaching positions in universities and colleges. The feedback was vital in reviewing what had been helpful to them.

The aggregated results of these surveys indicated that the pilot e-portfolio program was effective in helping the graduate fellows document their achievements in teaching and prepare them for future teaching careers. In particular, they found value in engaging each other in discussion, organizing their thinking about teaching before entering the job market, and learning how best to present their teaching to future colleagues. Participants were enthusiastic about the benefits of learning new technologies, about engaging in structured discussions with peers on teaching, and about the support they received from teaching consultants in organizing and reflecting on their teaching development.

On the negative side, graduate fellows ultimately found the time required by the technological components of creating an e-portfolio outweighed the benefits. The largest negative factor was the great deal of time it took these students to develop the technical proficiency required to move their materials from paper to Web. Even given a basic template, time became the enemy as participants balanced their efforts to collect and reflect on their materials with time spent putting them on the Web. Participants underscored the importance of the opportunity to draft ideas and get feedback from a variety of perspectives. They felt that their results were much more polished than they would have been otherwise due to access to technical training and support. However, based on their feedback, we discontinued the e-portfolio project after the pilot program.

In the final analysis, the perception of a lack of utility of e-portfolios in job search processes by both graduate students and their faculty advisors became insurmountable. In fact, some faculty advisors openly questioned the benefit of the teaching portfolios at all, given the large amount of time they took to develop and polish. In addition, none of the graduate fellows were required to provide a teaching portfolio in their quest for a junior faculty position, although they were all glad to be able to offer one to search committees. It also became clear that search committee members had limited interest in receiving or reviewing e-portfolios. Finally, none of the respondents to the survey reported continued use of their e-portfolio beyond the job search process. Based on this feedback and our own reflection, we concluded that the utility of e-portfolios did not sufficiently justify the time commitment required of graduate students to compose them.

LESSONS LEARNED

We learned a number of important lessons from our experiences with the pilot e-portfolio program. It confirmed for us that the portfolio process is fundamentally beneficial for the growth and development of preparing future faculty members. Our experiences reinforced the importance of individualized support for the development of teaching documentation materials and the enduring benefits of "good talk about good teaching." The following lessons learned may be of help to other colleges and universities as they explore the potential benefits a teaching portfolio program may have for the professional development of their graduate students:

- *Help graduate students become more comfortable with writing from a first-person point of view.* The style of writing for a portfolio is unlike the writing style often demanded of graduate students. A well-written portfolio does not generally read like a research paper. Portfolios at their best are individual expressions of goals, values, and accomplishments; therefore, no two are alike. Although this stylistic departure can feel risky to some graduate students, the results have the potential to be genuine and engaging.
- *Encourage graduate students to think of their teaching portfolio as nested within a set of job search documents, each serving a specific and unique purpose.* This broad set of materials is composed of up-to-date curriculum vitae, a well-crafted cover letter, a statement of research activity and evidence of accomplishments, and a teaching portfolio. Regrettably, portfolios can never convey everything there is to say about a teacher. Each element contributes something unique and answers particular questions in providing persuasive evidence of preparation for, and the promise of success in, a faculty position.

- *Portfolios change constantly.* They can easily be adapted as one creates new materials, fresh data emerge, and values and priorities have evolved by simply adding and removing materials. And portfolios are generally most effective when they demonstrate patterns over time while addressing specific goals at hand. Materials that provide evidence gathered over the context of several semesters or years are more persuasive (Ouellett, 2007).
- *It is essential to be concise, to direct and align materials included in a portfolio to highlight top priorities, and to help readers see the evidence of the student's teaching development efforts.* The reason is that portfolios are often read under less-than-ideal conditions such as during a search committee or other personnel-related processes.

Our campuswide e-portfolio project was generally ahead of its time. However, it may be worth experimenting with e-portfolios within certain disciplinary contexts where digitized media and electronic information is welcome, such as computer science or digital art.

CONCLUSION

We look forward to reanimating the e-portfolio program when the use of digital information in higher education job searches is more common. Until such time, branching out to explore the contributions possible by e-portfolios highlighted values and practices that continue to frame all of our teaching portfolio consultations with graduate students. These enduring attributes include providing theoretical as well as practical models for teaching development; making explicit how portfolios fit within the context of a job search in academia; normalizing the ever-changing nature of portfolios; and the importance of an authentic voice in holding readers' attention.

CHAPTER THIRTEEN

DEVELOPING TEACHING PORTFOLIOS AT ELGIN COMMUNITY COLLEGE

The Early Years

Kimberly Tarver

Elgin Community College's mission is to improve people's lives through learning. The college, which was established in 1949, serves a five-county area in northern Illinois. More than 125 full-time faculty and 350 part-time faculty provide instruction for a diverse population of more than eighteen thousand students enrolled in credit programs.

Formal and informal learning experiences and professional development activities are encouraged and supported at departmental, divisional, and institutional levels. The college offers internal development activities through the department of human resources and the Center for Enhancement of Teaching and Learning (CETL), in addition to financial support for external professional activities. Participation is further reinforced by offering credit for professional development, which translates to an increase in faculty salary.

Commitment to effective teaching is demonstrated in hiring and evaluation processes and support for ongoing professional development of faculty, all established through contract negotiations. Faculty attain tenure and conduct annual self-assessments through self-evaluation, content assessment, and reviews of student evaluations.

The Teaching Portfolio Initiative at Elgin Community College began with a few hallway conversations regarding the annual self-assessment process. Discussion revolved around exploring a more meaningful process of self-reflection and creation of opportunities to have more conversations about teaching and learning. One member of the group said, "It's exciting to talk about different teaching strategies and learn from each other." After multiple hallway meetings, this small group decided to research what other institutions were doing to promote reflection and sharing. Several of the articles found referred to publications on the teaching portfolio.

This small group of "hallway trailblazers" committed to learn more about teaching portfolios and planned to develop a workshop to be offered to fellow faculty. We sought support from our division's academic dean and were encouraged by his direction to maintain faculty ownership. The outcome of that initial communication resulted in Elgin Community College's hosting a one-day introductory workshop on the teaching portfolio in October 2007. The workshop provided participants with an overview of the purpose and process of developing a teaching portfolio. Faculty from other community colleges in the region were also invited as word of the event spread.

In June 2008, ten faculty members, both full time and part time, participated in a three-and-one-half-day workshop with outside facilitators to develop teaching portfolios. The group met initially as a whole and then came together daily for lunch and scheduled breaks. Individual daily meetings were scheduled between each participant and his or her assigned mentor. All participants opted to house their teaching portfolios in a notebook, and one instructor of performance arts provided digital video of student work as evidence of learning.

Faculty appraisal on the impact on teaching was immediate and positive. One professor said, "It got me reenergized about my teaching. . . . [The teaching portfolio] helped me see what I do that is fun and exciting and helped me think of new ideas. Once you're tenured, it can be hard to find time to look back and reassess your teaching. . . . It's good to see the development of your work over time." Another professor said, "It forced me to stop, think, and reflect [on] where I need to focus my professional development time and prioritize the changes I need to make in the classroom. . . . It has made me a better teacher."

Throughout the course of the workshop, we were visited by our college president, vice president, and several academic deans. Our teaching portfolio showcase and graduation event was attended by many key administrators and fellow faculty members. Overall it was a great success.

Funding and support for these initial steps came through the office of the vice president of teaching, learning, and student development. Following successful completion by our first ten participants, these faculty members presented at a meeting of the college deans and requested further support and funding for future workshops and mentor training. One year later, another workshop was held, during which two Elgin Community College faculty members participated in the first step to becoming teaching portfolio mentors. Training in-house mentors will serve to create an ongoing, affordable, and sustainable program. Similar comments were heard from participants the second year— for example, "This process gave me more confidence as an instructor. . . . I realized what areas I am skilled in and what areas I should be focusing on more as a teacher."

The mentors-in-training spent time reviewing a mock case, role playing, providing support, and acting as consultants to workshop participants. One mentor in training said, "The training allowed me the chance to reflect on my mentoring style. The role-play activities provided me the chance to practice and process what I liked and didn't like about my style. Although intense, the training prepared me for the next step to become a teaching portfolio mentor." The other mentor-in-training felt the training equipped her to be more effective in other contexts, including serving on tenure committees and mentoring new faculty.

Another workshop was scheduled in 2010 for ten more faculty members and the two mentors-in-training, who successfully completed the process and are now prepared to offer future teaching portfolio workshops for the college faculty. After reviewing other institutions' experiences with alternate models of delivery and the negative impact on satisfaction and successful completion, Elgin Community College will continue to follow the three-and-a-half-day model. The 2010 session was offered in January with the idea that future sessions will alternate annually between January and June. The June session has been offered twice and has consistently been in conflict with other conferences and summer courses. We anticipate that scheduling will continue to be a challenge.

The teaching portfolio process and product provided us with opportunities to focus on teaching and what we do well in the classroom. We are now able to document and demonstrate teaching effectiveness with evidence. We also created opportunities for interdisciplinary collaboration and sharing of ideas. The most valuable aspects of the teaching portfolio initiative at Elgin Community College have been maintaining faculty ownership as a faculty-driven process, administrative support, financial resources, individual purpose and ownership of the teaching portfolio, interdisciplinary peer interaction, and benefit of the mentor relationship and feedback.

One faculty summed it up in this way: "I appreciate the opportunity to share, discuss, and review other methods and manners of teaching and encouraging student learning. The teaching portfolio provides a format in which to monitor my self-development and manage the information and evidence." She also valued the institutional impact on the improvement of teaching and learning and the potential impact on perceptions of the community and potential employers of this college's graduates.

Teaching portfolio participants have presented at local and state conferences as a panel during which they discussed their personal experiences and the purpose and value of the teaching portfolio. Regional and statewide exposure creates opportunities for collaboration with other institutions participating in similar initiatives. It also serves as a tool to attract similarly dedicated professionals to seek a teaching position at Elgin Community College, as excellence attracts excellence.

Although the required annual self-assessment and the teaching portfolio overlap in several areas, they do not serve the same purpose. The teaching portfolio is flexible enough to meet the self-assessment criteria, but it has not been encouraged as a substitute because of the nature of the faculty contract and challenges in developing consistent use across divisions. However, elements of the teaching portfolio may easily be inserted into the self-assessment format. The teaching portfolio is voluntary and will remain a faculty-driven and faculty-owned initiative. Because we do not think the teaching portfolio should be mandated, we would not recommend that it now become part of the formal evaluation process. That might lead to a climate of distrust and detract from the value of the process and the product.

Teaching portfolio participants at Elgin Community College value their experiences of developing and sharing their portfolios. One participant was a full-time administrator and part-time instructor at Elgin Community College. Following the workshop, she applied for, and subsequently was offered and accepted, a full-time teaching position. She viewed "creating a teaching portfolio [as] an excellent opportunity to reflect on my teaching philosophy, goals, and methodology. . . . I truly believe the teaching portfolio was instrumental in clarifying and solidifying my career goals! I actually utilized my teaching portfolio during the interview process!"

Personally, the teaching portfolio has been the single most important professional development activity in which I have participated, and it has had a significant impact on my teaching. It has been an invaluable resource and time saver for course-level and program-level assessment. It has helped me evaluate the effectiveness of my instructional strategies and provided me with a mechanism to directly assess my goals and the effects of my participation in professional development activities. Moreover, I can now more clearly articulate how my activities, such as efforts at infusion of multicultural perspectives, can be seen in my teaching.

As a result of these past two years, which include a one-day introductory workshop and three teaching portfolio workshops following the three-and-a-half-day model, we have more than twenty successful portfolio completers and two mentors-in-training. We have managed to generate considerable interest among the faculty and enjoy the support and encouragement of the administration.

Teaching portfolio development is in its infancy at Elgin Community College. Future steps for the teaching portfolio initiative at the college include creating a sustainable process of offering annual or semiannual workshops with in-house mentors, developing a process to support ongoing portfolio updates and revisions, and creating opportunities to showcase or share portfolios across disciplines. It will remain a faculty-driven process, and we can expect ongoing institutional support as long as we continue to demonstrate a positive contribution to improvement of the teaching and learning process and support for achievement of the college's mission to improve lives through learning.

CHAPTER FOURTEEN

IMPLEMENTING THE TEACHING PORTFOLIO AT FLORIDA GULF COAST UNIVERSITY

Donna Price Henry

Florida Gulf Coast University (FGCU) in Fort Myers opened its doors to its first students in fall 1997. A new university in the State University System of Florida, FGCU was approved by the Florida legislature to support burgeoning population growth and meet the needs of the southwest Florida region for access to university academic degree programs. Student enrollment grew from twenty-six hundred in fall 1997 to over eleven thousand in fall 2009. In that same period, the full-time faculty have grown from 162 to just over 400. Over the past five years, the College of Arts and Sciences has welcomed on average 22 new faculty each fall semester. Historically, about half of the faculty recruited to FGCU have just completed graduate school or postdoctoral fellowships. With this growth in new faculty, it is important to offer supportive professional development programs as faculty begin their academic careers.

At FGCU, faculty are hired on multiyear continuing contracts (rolling contracts). They prepare professional development plans for the academic year, which are reviewed annually by department chairs for performance assessment. Satisfactory performance on annual reviews ensures recurring three-year contracts. Promotion tracks exist for both ranked faculty with terminal degrees in their disciplines and for instructors at FGCU. The promotion process includes college-level peer review and independent assessments from the department chair, dean, and provost. For annual and promotion reviews, faculty submit a portfolio documenting teaching, service, and scholarship. In the College of Arts and Sciences, criteria for promotion are broadly defined and build on the work of Boyer (1990) and Glassick, Huber, and Maeroff (1997). The integrated use of portfolios for faculty evaluation and promotion provides a unique opportunity to implement professional development through the use of the teaching portfolio.

PROFESSIONAL DEVELOPMENT PLAN

One of FGCU's greatest challenges is to provide an enriching and supportive environment for new faculty as the university's student body and academic programs rapidly expand. To meet this need, the deans from the Colleges of Arts and Sciences and Professional Studies, with support of the provost and vice president for academic affairs, offered a faculty professional development opportunity through a teaching portfolio institute in late spring 2007. Fifteen faculty accepted the open invitation to participate in this four-day teaching portfolio institute. Over the summer, faculty participants were sent materials to prepare for the August institute, which included the third edition of *The Teaching Portfolio* (Seldin, 2004) and a worksheet that outlined materials needed as evidence for their portfolios. Most faculty who volunteered to participate were planning to apply for promotion and viewed the portfolio development as a means to begin developing their promotion portfolios. One faculty member offered this description of the effect of the institute: "I brought the draft of my promotion portfolio self-reflection on teaching to the institute. I thought a few tweaks would be all I needed to wrap things up. In four days, I prepared five additional drafts, and left with a document that made me excited about my fall classes!"

After the institute, feedback from faculty indicated that the workshop was more than a means to seek promotion. Faculty indicated a clear impact on their teaching—for example, "The

Teaching Portfolio Institute allowed me to take quality time to reflect on my teaching. I hadn't thought about my teaching philosophy since I applied for my current position. I was in the middle of finalizing my syllabi for the fall semester, and through the discussions with my mentor, I made modifications that better reflected my teaching style."

THE TEACHING PORTFOLIO INSTITUTE

The Teaching Portfolio Institute has a specific, prescribed agenda. A central meeting room is assigned, and each day starts with coffee, tea, and pastries, with snacks and beverages kept in the central meeting room all day. Each mentor is assigned a specific location to meet individually with his or her mentees. Over the four days, faculty have discussion time with their colleagues, one-on-one time with their assigned mentors, and individual time to draft and redraft their portfolios with generous feedback from their mentors. Participants are informed to expect fifteen to twenty-five hours of individual work time over the four-day period to complete the teaching portfolio to the third draft stage. Here is an overview of the process:

Teaching Portfolio Institute Agenda
Day 1
- Overview of the teaching portfolio
- One-on-one meetings with mentors to begin process
- Homework developing the teaching portfolio
Day 2
- Continuing individual development of the teaching portfolio
- One-on-one meetings with mentors to review drafts
- Homework developing the teaching portfolio
Day 3
- One-on-one meetings with mentors to review drafts
- Luncheon to share progress on teaching portfolios with faculty colleagues
- Homework developing the teaching portfolio

Day 4
- Graduation ceremony and teaching portfolio sharing
- Certificates of completion awarded

Teaching Portfolio Institutes are built around one-on-one interaction between individual faculty and their assigned faculty mentors. Assignment of mentor is made without regard to discipline as long as the two are not from the same disciplinary area. Should that random occurrence take place, a new assignment is made. This underscores the point to faculty that the audience that will be reading their portfolio will come from an array of academic disciplines, not just their own. In addition, time is intentionally devoted to support faculty while they are so intensely focused on drafting their portfolio. In the middle of the institute, a teaching portfolio luncheon is held for faculty to talk about their portfolios and share ideas on how best to present materials in their portfolios. The luncheon provides an opportunity for faculty to share and compare teaching strategies with other faculty, as this faculty member noted: "I enjoyed talking to colleagues from other disciplines about my teaching. It forced me to be extra thoughtful about disciplinary jargon as I described what I do. I never would have thought to incorporate a writing workshop used in freshman composition to help my students to be better writers in senior-level science classes."

At the conclusion of the Teaching Portfolio Institute, a graduation ceremony is held, and college deans and the provost are encouraged to attend. The first part of the morning is used for faculty to display their portfolios for review by everyone attending. For the formal part of the ceremony, each mentor introduces his or her mentees. Mentors present details that illustrate the strong teaching qualities of the individual faculty. One faculty member had this to say about the experience: "The workshop was intense! I dedicated my time 24/7 over the entire four days. On the final day, it was great to see my dean review my portfolio. She commented on the great organization—as well as the stylish cover! I will definitely recommend this workshop to my colleagues."

After the introduction, each participant is awarded a certificate of achievement signed by his or her college dean and the provost.

LESSONS LEARNED, FEEDBACK, AND NEXT STEPS

Fall college meetings followed quickly after the first Teaching Portfolio Institute, and College of Arts and Sciences and Professional Studies faculty were asked to present information and feedback from the institute to their colleagues. Much interest was generated, and we began planning the second Teaching Portfolio Institute for August 2008. Offering a second institute afforded us the opportunity to train internal faculty to be teaching portfolio mentors. With internal faculty mentors, we would be able to expand the professional development for faculty in our colleges beyond the institutes offered once a year. We selected three teaching portfolio faculty who expressed an interest in mentoring. For their work in the institute, they were provided a modest honorarium.

The August 2008 Teaching Portfolio Institute included eighteen additional faculty from the two colleges. One lesson learned was to have faculty on a waiting list for the institutes because with each program, two or three faculty withdrew from the institute a week or so before it started. With a waiting list, other faculty stepped in. The new internal mentors benefited from working with other faculty and looked forward to working with colleagues in their departments. One mentor noted learning "a great deal from working with colleagues through the portfolio development process. It would be great to involve peer review teams in the portfolio development process. It would definitely have a positive impact on the promotion process at the university."

Again, faculty response about the workshop indicated that a lot of work was covered in just a week, but the final product offered them a new outlook on their teaching. Many faculty participating in the workshops began to share their enthusiasm with colleagues in the departments. Chairs began coming forward asking when the next Teaching Portfolio Institutes would be offered.

A new provost and vice president for academic affairs joined FGCU just before the second workshop. After participating in the graduation ceremony, he embraced the concept of professional development around faculty portfolios. Time was allocated at dean's council to discuss the benefits of portfolio development for faculty across all colleges. The deans had questions about the process, content, and faculty interest in the Teaching Portfolio Institutes.

For the benefit of deans whose faculty had not participated in prior portfolio development, the provost sponsored a luncheon for all former Teaching Portfolio Workshop faculty. All academic deans and the provost attended, and faculty were asked to share the information and feedback regarding the institutes. Faculty agreed that the portfolios provided a framework for faculty to thoughtfully reflect on their academic work and present their accomplishments in an evidence-based way. In general, the strengths reported included the reflection time and quality portfolio that faculty had as a finished product at the end of the institutes. Faculty concurred that developing the portfolio improved their teaching and that they were excited about maintaining and updating their personal portfolio. One faculty member suggested that department chairs be encouraged to attend the Teaching Portfolio Institute. The only weakness reported was that faculty had not totally cleared their calendars in anticipation of the upcoming workshops. They recommended that future institute participants be made aware of the workload in advance of the Teaching Portfolio Institute so that they could benefit more fully during the intensive sessions.

Through further discussions at dean's council meetings, the provost centralized portfolio professional development for all faculty at FGCU and considered training for the academic portfolio as well as the teaching portfolio. The academic portfolio is an innovative and highly promising way to get at the individuality and complexity of faculty work in teaching, research, and service (Seldin & Miller, 2009).

With the support of the six college and library deans and the provost, FGCU implemented its first Academic Portfolio Institute in June 2009 with rave reviews and waiting lists double the size of space available. A second institute was planned for August 2009 to include training for a new cohort of internal academic portfolio mentors. With two sets of internal mentors, we are now planning ongoing professional development for our faculty. The two types of portfolios, teaching and academic, serve different purposes and are appropriate for different faculty. Newer faculty and instructors benefit from the teaching portfolio to support their growth and development in teaching. This focus on strong teaching is essential for FGCU with our development as a quality comprehensive university. More experienced faculty who have been on campus and are nearing time for promotion find the academic portfolio process quite beneficial. We look forward to continuing the momentum with faculty portfolio development at FGCU. The strong support from the provost and other deans provides faculty with clear expectations for assessment as they develop their careers at FGCU.

CHAPTER FIFTEEN

REVIEWING THE TEACHING PORTFOLIO

Considerations from a Provost/ Vice President of Academic Affairs

Ronald B. Toll

Little else on a university campus approaches the level of emotional fervor as discussions of faculty performance review. A common perception regarding the process is that the further the tenure and promotion portfolio review moves through the institutional hierarchy, the more inherently mysterious that process becomes and the less the process is linked to the real work of teaching and learning. At most institutions, the final authoritative consideration of the portfolio is the purview of the chief academic officer (CAO), variously referred to at different institutions as the vice president for academic affairs (VPAA), dean of the faculty, or provost. Faculty are typically not in a position to ask the CAO what he or she is looking for in a portfolio in terms of content or format. Even if an opportunity to engage in meaningful discussion on this topic with the CAO does arise, faculty can feel inhibited about asking meaningful and probing questions beyond those related to simple formatting issues, fearing that the line of questioning may reveal shortcomings, lack of confidence, or simply be politically incorrect.

This chapter is meant to serve as surrogate for that conversational opportunity. It contains the reflections of one of those CAOs: I am a former regular faculty member and now an administrator whose responsibilities include rendering decisions on faculty performance. My views have been shaped by my own experience as a faculty member, department chair, dean, and provost/vice president of academic affairs, and heavily influenced by my review of about five hundred portfolios associated with tenure, promotion, and post-tenure performance at several institutions, both public and private. All of these schools have a mission emphasis on teaching and learning, and, by extension, the area of teaching serves as a primary criterion for faculty success, along with expectations for creditable scholarly and creative productivity and service to the campus and surrounding community.

Demystifying the process of tenure and promotion review, especially at the senior academic levels, is essential to promoting a campuswide atmosphere of transparency, equity, and efficacy. In this way, the anxiety of the tenure decision and, to a lesser extent, the promotion decision can be reduced. As academicians, we must accept that some degree of apprehension will remain an inextricable part of the review process, no matter how clear and explicit the protocols and the criteria.

In 2009, at Florida Gulf Coast University, we conducted about fifty faculty searches. In aggregate, over the course of the full academic careers of these faculty, presumably about thirty-five years, my institution was committing about a third of a billion dollars to the continued vitality, growth, diversity, and success of our faculty and, by extension, our students. With such an enormous investment, it is incumbent on us to evaluate faculty carefully, thoughtfully, comprehensively, and fairly. From the faculty perspective, it is essential that their teaching portfolio be prepared in a manner commensurate with its importance.

Certainly standards, policies, practices, guidelines, and interpretations vary from institution to institution. But there is more commonality among institutions of higher learning with regard to expectations placed on faculty concerning their teaching performance than might otherwise be assumed. That said, all institutions should address modalities related to demonstration of superlative teaching efficacy and learning outcomes in clear and transparent ways.

With that in mind, what follows are suggestions for faculty as they prepare their teaching portfolios for tenure, promotion, or post-tenure review. They are provided from the perspective of an end user, that is, a provost who personally reviews and renders decisions on these critical career stages based on faculty portfolios.

THE STATEMENT ON TEACHING PHILOSOPHY

The portfolio section covering teaching philosophy often includes an introductory overview that establishes the candidate's overarching educational construct. Because of its location near the beginning of the portfolio, it can and should serve to set the stage. However, it is imperative that this preliminary view be followed by and rooted in substantial evidence supplied in the methodology section of the portfolio. Regrettably, too often, it has been my experience that the opening statement is bereft of follow-up supporting information. As a stand-alone, these reflections of intentionality often look something like the following hypothetical contribution:

> I want my students to learn how to read and understand the material that I present in my classes. Therefore, I go to great lengths to organize course material and to assign regular, required readings that my students must complete prior to coming to class each day. In this way I know that they have the information they will need to be successful in my class and beyond.

> Ultimately, I want my students to be reflective decision makers whose lives have been enriched by an understanding of [discipline] and how it relates to the greater world around them. I want to help my students develop a love of lifelong learning as strong as my own. By my modeling this behavior for them, they will come to understand that learning is the greatest gift that they can give to themselves.

This opening statement could potentially be a solid start to a well-developed section on philosophy, expanded on in the teaching methodology section. But too often, this is where the entire section ends: no evidence to support these desired goals is provided. These goals are certainly meritorious, but stating goals as rhetorical aspirations without providing evidence that there has been actual achievement in attaining those goals is a vacant exercise. There is no reason to suggest that these superlative outcomes have been achieved.

American higher education has witnessed a paradigm shift from faculty acting as sage on the stage to guide on the side. Along with this change, teaching, programmatic, and institutional success and effectiveness are increasingly being viewed in terms of a series of demonstrable and measurable outcomes as compared to simple inputs. What follows is another brief hypothetical statement, with a very different emphasis, that might appear in the methodology section of a teaching portfolio:

> Students in my classes are required to turn in six one-page discussion response essays at regular intervals throughout the semester. Their papers are graded using the rubric presented in Appendix H. Graded exemplars of student essays showing trends in overall improvement during the semester in the area of stating a position and defending it are also included.

This type of presentation, based on demonstrable outcomes evidence, serves to make the faculty member's case.

OUTCOMES-BASED SUPPORT

One of the primary means to demonstrate the efficacy of your teaching is to explicitly identify, with various forms of evidence, the degree to which learning has taken place. Certainly the true demonstration of learning outcomes varies from discipline to discipline. Some of the expected outcomes placed on a performing arts major are different from a nursing major and those of a physicist, for example. But there are many commonalities regarding essential skills such as critical thinking, effective communication, and multidisciplinary problem solving. Do not let the differences be an impediment to documenting your case on your teaching. To the contrary, exploit the differences to demonstrate your mastery of the discipline and any specific methods that support exemplary outcomes.

It is essential to begin gathering evidence about your teaching early in your career. Collecting evidence regularly during the period under review will be of tremendous value in annual reviews, in assessing your own efforts along the way, and for demonstrating a dedicated long-term strategy for continuous improvement.

Some aspects of the true long-term learning by your students may not present themselves until they have left your class to pursue additional course work at your institution or have graduated to put those practices into effect. I remember vividly the biology student who was an outspoken critic of my teaching during his time in college. When he came back to visit our department near the end of medical school education, he told me that he understood why I "made him do" the work that he was required to undertake in my class. He then remarked that he came to find that he was one of the best-prepared students in a particularly difficult class in medical school because of it. There really is no better outcomes evidence.

Because of the unavoidable lag time, these jewels of comprehension can come too late for tenure review but perhaps not too late for a future promotion. Also, while the full impact of your teaching on your students may not surface for years, many of your instructional efforts are demonstrable almost immediately. These are the items for inclusion in your portfolio.

PORTFOLIO REVIEWERS

The further your portfolio moves along the review process, the less direct knowledge that the individual reviewers will have of you and your accomplishments outside of what is contained within your portfolio. Therefore, I cannot overemphasize the importance of having your portfolio speak for you, strongly and explicitly, in the absence of other means of knowing what efforts, however exemplary, and what outcomes, however significant they may be, you have identified. The language that you use must be free of disciplinary jargon, or such terms need to be clearly defined. Core educational outcome goals encompassing such skills as the ability to reason, the capacity to draw inference, and the ability to communicate effectively generally transcend disciplines and specific program or course objectives. Often these are expressed as undergraduate student learning outcomes and are mapped to the curriculum. Collectively they constitute a common language set that all in academe can speak and understand.

WHAT TO PUT IN AND WHAT TO LEAVE OUT

Including materials in your portfolio without explanation is not only a shortcoming; it may demonstrate a lack of understanding of, or appreciation for, the task at hand. Consider that the CAO may be reviewing dozens of portfolios and be required by guidelines found in the various policy manuals to render decisions within a relatively short time frame. Careful organization and explanation of the contents of the portfolio is critical.

For example, simply inserting course syllabi from the past twelve semesters of teaching demonstrates little. The CAO cannot be expected to survey all of them in direct comparison to each other and find the changes made to these documents over time. Moreover, if the reviewer identifies the changes, he or she will have no idea as to what motivated the changes and whether the changes resulted in increased, decreased, or no net change in teaching efficacy.

Including materials that contain evidence without delineating that evidence, and drawing inference and conclusions, is substantially lacking in value to any review.

WHEN FAILURE CAN BE A GOOD THING

I tend to visualize improvement in instructional skills, and presumably concomitant improvement in learning outcomes, as a rising curve that never quite reaches its maximum terminus point, an asymptotic increase, always with a bit of additional room for continued growth. To suggest that as academicians we all start lower on the curve and then improve our instructional skills through time seems almost naively simple, and it is. But what seems to be particularly difficult for some of us is to allow ourselves to provide examples where experiments in pedagogy were less than enormous successes.

Most of us have no problem reflecting back to our personal lives and recognizing that some of the most valuable lessons that we learned were directly attributable to mistakes that we had committed. We should not be afraid to apply that same logic to our development as professors. In this context, the advice of some well-meaning colleagues, "Don't put anything in your portfolio that can be used against you," is counter to the enterprise of the natural and healthy methods of professional growth: learning from mistakes made and following a course of iterative steps that contribute to the process of constant improvement.

Therefore, presenting examples of pedagogical experiments that apparently did not work can be beneficial as part of your portfolio as opposed to detracting from it. In fact, I believe that a full-blown pedagogical failure is a highly unlikely event. The time and care that you have placed into trying some new approach, begun as an offshoot to something that you have already done in your classes or as an extension of a new idea that you picked up from a colleague, at a professional meeting, or from a scholarly publication on instructional methods, has more than likely resulted in at least a partial success. You may have fallen short of achieving the complete goal you intended by the change. But it is the desire and the effort to try new modalities that is key to advancing the educational enterprise. These less-than-fully-successful attempts to improve on what you already do can provide some of the most meaningful and informative perspectives into your teaching, for your own self-reflection as well as the purpose of your portfolio review.

Being able to state that you added selected reading assignments to your syllabus in order to encompass a greater range of genres and to demonstrate, with evidence, that this change was beneficial can be a valuable contribution to your performance review. In comparison, a multistep sequence of innovative refinements based on partial goal accomplishment can be exceptionally illuminating.

I have often told faculty that I want them to take risks in the classroom. After all, we ask our students to take intellectual risks, so we must be willing to demonstrate this behavior to them. Risk, by its very nature, can lead to frustration and potential failure. How we respond to suboptimal outcomes when taking risks is, to me, a better indicator of teaching innovation than minor incremental changes that break no new ground. But to encourage risk also means that the institution and the various constituents of the review process must demonstrate that risk, as a behavior, and the positive outcomes that can result from engaging in it, is truly valued and rewarded. At any particular institution, the development of a culture of pedagogical risk taking can take several years to develop and will become systematized only if the risk takers are rewarded with successful emergence from the end of the review pipeline.

NOT A TIME TO BE MODEST

The time of your candidacy for tenure or promotion is not the time for professional humility. I have been surprised by the number of times while speaking to a candidate during a review conference that I have learned of additional information that helped to demonstrate involvement in pedagogical novelty and superlative teaching outcomes but was missing in the portfolio. Substantial endeavors should be included and briefly explained in every portfolio. This is especially true at institutions where direct candidate consultation with the CAO is not part of the review process.

Your case can perhaps be more easily interpreted by colleagues close to you—those in your department or in disciplines related in some manner—if for no other reason than the interactions that you have had with these people. But typically the CAO will require and expect that you have provided within your portfolio a well-documented case based on various forms of evidence, both direct and indirect.

SOME FINAL THOUGHTS

My experience indicates that the overwhelming majority of CAOs are enormously dedicated academicians who take great pride in the achievements of their faculty and the reputation of their institutions. In fact, many aspire to return to the faculty because they entered higher education with the mind-set of an instructor and want to get back to the considerable rewards of being in the classroom.

You must put your best foot forward in developing and submitting the strongest, most complete, evidence-driven, well-organized, and compelling argument for why you should be tenured or promoted. That will not happen if the portfolio contains grammatically poor teaching philosophies, documents with numerous typos, and references to appendices that were not provided or lead to the wrong document or supporting material. Worse are unsubstantiated statements—for example, "This change to my pedagogy was highly effective." How did you know? How is the CAO to know if you do not spell it out and support it with evidence? The portfolio should demonstrate a level of deep introspection and circumspection that warrants the awarding of tenure or promotion. Your portfolio, the reflection of a sum total of years of effort, should be a compendium of documents that not only exhibit care and precision but, more important, demonstrate achievement.

CONCLUSION

It has been my privilege to review many portfolios that reflected well the work of exceptionally talented and dedicated academicians. I remember these documents as having been thoughtful, reflective, and intentional. Through these experiences I have come to appreciate the portfolio as the best available mechanism for faculty to find and present their own voice in the critically important process of faculty performance evaluation. Take this marvelous opportunity to find your voice. At the end of the process, I believe that you will come to appreciate that this personal and professional journey of discovery with regard to your teaching and your students' learning was enormously valuable and rewarding, and served to lead you to even greater levels of instructional accomplishment. Certainly at the end of the day, that is exactly what teaching is all about.

SAMPLE PORTFOLIOS FROM ACROSS DISCIPLINES

Part Three contains twenty-one sample teaching portfolios that are arranged in alphabetical order by discipline. Each sample portfolio refers to appendix material that is part of the actual portfolio but is excluded from this book because of its length and unwieldy nature. Importantly, because each portfolio reflects the unique scope and quality of a professor's teaching, different professors assign varying importance to different items. While some discuss an item at length, others dismiss it with just a sentence or two, or even omit it. *Important: As you read through these portfolios, consider how other disciplines often provide helpful information and insights applicable to your own discipline.*

CHAPTER SIXTEEN

BIOLOGICAL SCIENCES

Martha S. Rosenthal

Department of Biological Sciences
Florida Gulf Coast University
Spring 2010

CONTENTS

TEACHING RESPONSIBILITIES

As a faculty member in the department of biological sciences as well as in the Collegium of Integrated Learning, I currently teach a number of undergraduate courses. Recent courses are shown in the next table. For a complete list of courses taught, please see Appendix A.

Course	Catalogue Number	Type of Course	Credits	Typical Enrollment
Human Physiology	PCB 3703C	Elective for upper-division biology majors	4	30–33
Neuroscience	ZOO 4743C	Elective for upper-division biology majors	4	30–33
Biology of Human Sexuality	BSC 2026	General education course for nonscience majors	3	60
Issues in Science and Technology	IDS 3303	Interdisciplinary course in the Collegium of Integrated Learning	3	35–40

TEACHING PHILOSOPHY

I love the wonder and magic of the human body. Every day in the classroom is a new opportunity for me to help one more person discover the magic for themselves. I want them to learn because, yes, they will need the knowledge and skills to pursue a career. But I also want them to appreciate the awesome capacity of the body, and to instill in them the desire to continue to question and learn throughout their lives.

I feel that my job is not just to present information—there is a surplus of information available to all—perhaps even too much information (a recent Internet search for the term *kidney* produced more than 49 million entries). My job as a teacher is to sort through all this information, to determine what's important, to organize it into a coherent, cohesive package, and to teach the students how to **evaluate** the vast amount of information. Whenever there is an enormous supply of anything, even information, it loses its value. Students must learn how to assess the value of the information. Of course, it is important to teach the foundation of knowledge that the students need to succeed. But my job goes beyond that; it is also important to teach them **how to think critically**. Helping students to develop critical thinking skills is my most significant long-ranging challenge as a teacher. I have therefore made critical thinking a focus not only in my classes, but have also made it the foundation of my sexuality textbook.

The world is an **interdisciplinary** place. One of the foundations of my teaching style has always been to focus on the relationship among different fields. I find it beneficial to put things in terms of **"real life."** For instance, instead of having students simply memorize the cranial nerves, I demonstrate what is involved in a clinical neurological exam.

> I feel that this class was very beneficial for life in general, and that the way it was conducted helped me to gain knowledge of the things that I would never have known before but are very important in society. (Interdisciplinary Studies, 2007)

> She makes the class very interesting by relating the concepts that we learn in the textbook to real life cases. (Physiology, 2007)

> I enjoyed speaking about not only the biological aspects of human sexuality, but critical social issues pertaining to the subjects that were addressed. Learning about social issues in conjunction with the biological aspects of human sexuality greatly added to my understanding of the course. (Sexuality, 2007)

Enthusiasm is key. I truly *love* the courses I teach, and with every lecture, I am amazed anew at the magic and mystery of the subject I am teaching. I teach students about their brains and bodies, sex, love, gender, and drugs—aspects of vital importance to us all. So I want them to learn, love, and care about the material, not just for a semester, but for a lifetime. As I am sincerely excited by the subject, it is easy to pass this enthusiasm on to the students. **Humor** can also increase learning. I am fairly laid back and informal in the classroom, and have found that this increases the comfort level of the students and makes it easier for them to contribute, especially in emotionally laden courses such as human sexuality. I also try to be as **accessible** to students as possible. In addition to office hours, students are encouraged to contact me at any time for help.

> Dr. Rosenthal is a great professor who has a lot of respect for her students. It was very easy to talk with her in and out of class not only about class material but also asking her advice on life (graduate school, etc.). (Physiology, 2006)

> Excellent class, mainly because of Dr. Rosenthal. Excellent instructor, would definitely take her again. Tests are hard, but she shows respect and concern for students. (Sexuality, 2006)

> Dr. Rosenthal is an exceptional teacher. She has a passion for teaching that is evident in each of her classes. She is also always there to help the students in class or out of class in regards to anything. (Sexuality, 2007)

> Amazing teacher! Great at answering questions and very respectful towards students and made the class fun and interesting. I would recommend her to everyone! (Sexuality, 2008)

In summary, my goal as a teacher is to teach material in a way that the students are going to enjoy and remember; to teach them how to learn, so they can go out on their own and evaluate the constantly changing data to which they are exposed; and to cherish the intellectual journey so that they will become lifelong lovers of learning.

TEACHING METHODS AND STRATEGIES

I have taught classes of freshmen and classes of graduate students, classes where the average age of the students was eighteen, and classes where the average age was twenty-eight. I have taught classes with 9 students and classes with 175, classes of scientists and classes of humanities majors. Different classes require different styles of teaching. In content-laden courses such as physiology and neuroscience, my role may be that of a guide and interpreter to help the students understand the material. In these courses, of course, I also coordinate activities that give the students the tools necessary for them to continue the learning process throughout their lives. In interdisciplinary courses that focus more on discussion and development of ideas, I see my role as more of a facilitator. In addition to providing the foundation of knowledge the students need, I lead discussions and help the students to discover ideas and to learn to properly express and defend their ideas. Teaching human sexuality requires the skills of both—it is a content-laden course with emotional baggage. When I teach this course, I must be respectful of the wildly varying views of students, be sensitive in the way the material is presented, encourage students to think critically about the issues, and encourage respect for differing points of view. *In all courses, the goals remain the same: to learn the material; to learn to think, question, judge, and assess; and to appreciate the scope and wonder of the subject.*

I feel it is imperative that material is well **organized**. Learning is enhanced by beginning with a "big picture" overview of the subject and then adding details. Difficult material is broken into simpler units, on which I build to clarify the more challenging concepts. Providing an outline to follow makes it easier to present small, digestible, retainable sections of material.

She is very organized and methodical and is always willing to go the extra mile to assist the student with any questions. The test is a true representation of what she teaches in class and never misleading. Overall I think she is a great asset to the university staff. (Physiology, 2007)

She is one of the best professors I have had. She is very good at communicating difficult ideas and breaking it down so everyone can understand it. (Physiology, 2007)

The use of technology in the classroom can also be a very effective tool, *when used appropriately.* I use PowerPoint presentations for many lectures, but there is some material that is best covered by using whiteboards, videos, discussions, or labs. Interactive physiology CDs may be an excellent tool for illustrating the concept of the reflexes, but having the students test each other's pupillary and muscle reflexes gets the point across better than any CD ever could. The skill is to consider the best tool for each lesson you want to teach.

As Ellen Langer describes in *The Power of Mindful Learning*, while "work" is associated with compulsion, pressure, deadlines, fear of failure, lack of choice, and delayed gratification, "play" is associated with freedom, choice, creativity, and instant gratification. Although learning should be the most joyous experience of a lifetime, too often students feel that the experience, which should be their greatest pleasure, is instead work and drudgery. To combat this phenomenon, I employ various activities in the classroom. These activities include the use of games, clinical demonstrations, laboratories, and discussions. Examples and a more thorough description of these activities are available in Appendix B.

> Various teaching styles were assessed—labs, group work, games, homework, quizzes, tests, and PowerPoints, making the class very interesting and not boring. I would recommend her to anyone. Fabulous teacher! (Physiology, 2006)

> The projects and assignments are always fun, interactive, thought provoking, and require just the right amount of work. (Interdisciplinary Studies, 2008)

COURSE MATERIAL AND STUDENT ASSESSMENT TOOLS

A lot of time and thought have gone into making my syllabi conform to my teaching philosophies and goals. My syllabi are clear, organized, and complete, and give the students detailed course objectives, expectations, and goals. The grading scale and assignments are clearly laid out, as are the various teaching and assessment methods used.

There are a number of activities in these classes that differentiate these classes from those of other professors. One example for each class is given below; the complete syllabi for these courses can be found in Appendix C.

- *Issues in Science and Technology:* Students are encouraged to develop their critical thinking skills, to evaluate the wide array of information about drugs and pharmaceuticals to which we are all exposed. To this end, we spend time learning the basics of critical thinking, and then critically evaluate a number of articles, presentations, and films so students will be able to question information that impacts their lives and health.
- *Human Sexuality:* Students come into this class with a wide variety of values and opinions. In this class, they prepare two short video presentations, one on each side of a "hot topic issue." In this way, they are encouraged to consider both sides of an issue and learn to present the pertinent facts in a coherent and compelling manner.
- *Human Physiology:* In this class, students receive a number of case studies of patients, each of whom is suffering from a different disorder. Students must apply their theoretical knowledge to these "real-world" examples, and understand the etiology, symptoms, and treatment for these patients.
- *Neuroscience:* Students can create a game on different topics of neuroscience. Creating games allows them to think creatively about the topic, to consider its organization, and to essentially "teach" the topic to others in a fun way.

For many classes, I provide **lecture notes** to help the students follow the lecture and to enhance their full understanding of the concepts. This way, the students can focus and understand and ask questions, rather than simply acting as note-taking machines. I also include **study guides** for each test. These guides include a basic guide for how to study and how to take tests. The study guides include learning objectives for each lecture, as well as sample test questions, important points to review, and a review of some of the more difficult concepts. I also include graphs and charts to complete, and suggest different ways for the students to organize their notes to maximize their learning and understanding. A sample lecture and study guide may be found in Appendix C.

Students learn in different ways. Because of this, I use a number of **assessment tools**. In addition to tests (mixed format), students are evaluated by means of case studies, video presentations, papers, and "brief thoughts." Examples of these student assessment tools are available in Appendix D.

As you can see from the scope of my teaching responsibilities, I continually teach new courses. As a lifelong learner, I embrace the opportunity to grow as a scholar by teaching new subject matter and by presenting familiar subjects in new ways. Volunteering to teach a new course—human sexuality—a number of years ago has led me down a new career path. I recently began team-teaching a new course on gender for the Interdisciplinary Studies Minor. I also revise existing courses. I constantly reassess my teaching and classroom activities. While we may not consistently upgrade from Lung 3.1 to Lung 4.1, every year (every day!), *I reevaluate my courses and think what I can do to make them clearer, more fun, and more memorable*—to try to truly educate the students. I review each day's lecture after class to consider what worked, what didn't work, and how it might best be changed to make it as clear as it possibly can be.

ASSESSMENT AND EVALUATION OF TEACHING

I try to give students the tools and desire to learn. My standards and workload are high, but I find that students rise to meet the challenge. Being open, respectful, and accessible encourages students to achieve. I believe my teaching evaluation scores illustrate my success in classroom. Over the last ten years, my average score is 4.71 out of 5.0, with an average class size of 43.7. Although I've been teaching at FGCU for almost 12 years, I'm not getting complacent; in fact, **over the last three years, my teaching evaluation score is 4.81 out of 5** (see the next table). The score is taken from the "overall assessment of the professor" from the student evaluation forms. The scores for all classes, as well as sample written comments, are available in Appendix E. Letters of support, notes, and e-mails from students are also available in Appendix E.

Semester	Course	Enrollment	Score
Summer 2005	Issues in Science and Technology	28	4.9
Fall 2005	Human Systems	175	4.4
	Physiological Psychology	34	4.9
Fall 2006	Human Sexuality	60	4.7
	Human Physiology	31	5.0
Spring 2007	Human Sexuality	62	4.5
	Issues in Science and Technology	38	4.7
	Neuroscience	33	4.9
Fall 2007	Human Sexuality	60	4.9
	Human Physiology	31	5.0
Spring 2008	Human Sexuality	60	4.8
	Issues in Science and Technology	35	5.0
	Neuroscience	26	4.9
Fall 2008	Human Sexuality	60	4.8
	Human Physiology	34	4.8
Average		**51.1**	**4.81**

I encourage *student feedback* about both the course and my teaching style. At least once during each semester, I hand out index cards on which I ask the students to write what is working for them in the course and what improvements they would like to see. I carefully examine these evaluations and implement their suggestions when they will improve the learning experience for the student.

As a senior faculty member here at FGCU, I like to *mentor colleagues* with fewer years of teaching experience. I served on the Mentoring Task Force, designed to help the development and retention of junior faculty, and participated in the College of Arts and Sciences teaching seminar, where senior faculty shared their expertise with junior faculty. I also observe other professors'

classes and have them observe mine. I have had numerous conversations about teaching, students, and courses with other faculty. I relish this opportunity as I always learn something about
teaching from observing another professor or from having
conversations regarding common classroom situations. Some
excerpts from the peer evaluations of teaching are below (the
complete letters are available in Appendix E):

> Dr. Rosenthal encouraged active involvement. . . . [Her] presenta-
> tion was organized, interesting, and challenging, while remaining
> attainable by the students. (Dr. Laura Sullivan, Psychology, College
> of Arts and Sciences)

> When students did not understand, she welcomed their questions
> and created a safe environment for inquiry and discussion. She
> communicated very complicated course material in a way that
> made sense to the students. (Dr. Maggie Calvin, Communications,
> College of Arts and Sciences)

> You held your students captive with your delivery. Your excitement
> for knowing stuff and teaching in a way that learning takes place
> easily was evident. . . . Your students are excited by the content
> because you make the content relevant to their lives. . . . The schol-
> arly depth of your knowledge was obvious from your presentation.
> (Dr. Margaret Bogan, College of Education)

> She has the rare capacity to combine intellectual rigor with a per-
> former's instinct for how to hold an audience's attention. There is an
> outline and a body of facts that one must learn from her lectures (the
> tests are not easy), but she also goes out of her way to provide mne-
> monic aids, to tie the material to everyday experiences and to bring
> in humorous but relevant anecdotes to keep the students' interest.
> (Dr. Glenn Whitehouse, Philosophy, College of Arts and Sciences)

TEACHING AWARDS AND RECOGNITION

I was honored to receive *FGCU's senior faculty teaching excellence
award* in 2002. I was also honored to be named the teacher of
the year at the University of Florida in 1997. I was nominated to

receive FGCU's "student's choice award," and have been named an honorary member of Phi Eta Sigma and The Golden Key International Honour Society. I have also been recognized by "Who's Who Among America's Teachers," and I was chosen as a speaker in the Honors Program Last Lecture Series, where students vote on the professor they would most like to hear if they could only go to one more lecture. Evidence of these recognitions is available in Appendix F.

EVIDENCE OF STUDENT LEARNING

A person's skill as a teacher cannot be measured just by awards or evaluation scores. Student success must be taken into consideration. Students have completed some exemplary work in my classes, including the creation of games, presentations, and papers. Students have also had the opportunity to present their work at the Southern Regional Honors Council and the Florida Collegiate Honors Council. Through these opportunities, students not only learn, but are able to pass their experiences on to others. Examples of student work and conference presentations are available in Appendix G.

Over the years, many of my students have gone on to professional graduate programs. Marc Pepin is a pharmacist for cardiothoracic and orthopedic surgery teams; Shae Sammons is now a dentist; Charity Hamilton is a physician; Joy Caangay is in medical school; and many other students are now enjoying success in their chosen fields. I have been honored to receive letters and notes from these students and others thanking me for my role in their success. Some of these notes are available in Appendix G.

TEACHING OUTREACH

I joined the faculty of Florida Gulf Coast University in 1997 because I was committed to FGCU's mission of student-centered learning. Not only my teaching, but my service and scholarship are largely student focused. Creating innovations in pedagogy and sharing those innovations with our peers is a cornerstone of the academic process. I have presented at a number of conferences on the use of games in the classroom, and I am currently finishing a **textbook on human sexuality, which will be published by Houghton Mifflin/Cengage Learning**. It is broad and interdisciplinary in scope and addresses issues of sexuality from a critical thinking perspective. A list of scholarly and service activities related to teaching or pedagogy can be found in Appendix H.

FUTURE TEACHING GOALS

I recognize that I can always improve as a teacher, and I *strive to improve* myself and my class every day. I take student feedback seriously and constantly work to address issues of concern. I attend conferences and workshops to improve my teaching skills. I work to stay current in my fields. Writing the textbook has helped me greatly, not just in the field of sexuality, but by improving my skills in critical evaluation and presentation of material.

There are a number of things that I would like to improve about my teaching. I think I lecture on more material in class than I should. I should rely on the students' reading the material outside of class more than I do. I am working to change this by cutting some lecture material and giving students more responsibility for reading. This has cleared up more time for activities, which the students enjoy. Another area for improvement is that I am more comfortable with planned lectures, activities, and laboratories than I am with discussion. You never know what will happen in a class discussion, especially in my courses on sex and drugs—two very emotionally laden subjects! I have worked on this by observing the class discussions led by colleagues who are particularly skilled in this aspect. I have also learned to "loosen the reins" a bit and let the discussion go. This has led the class in some very interesting directions, and I am getting more comfortable with this over time. I try to play devil's advocate, no matter what position is being presented, and that keeps the students considering different viewpoints.

Regardless of the degree of success of different strategies, there is always something to learn. I've learned a number of things in the years I've been teaching:

- I've learned that the information is not as important as teaching the students the *value* of the information and critical thinking skills.
- I've learned that each class is different, and I must always make adjustments in my teaching for each course.

- I've learned that I don't teach the students—I need to help the students teach themselves.
- I've learned that if students feel that you are on their side, they will try harder, and that if you have high standards, the students will rise to meet them.
- I've learned that even if I'm thrilled and excited about the spleen, not everyone will share my glee. The students need a break, and it's best to break the class into twenty-minute blocks. I've also gotten very good at reading the students. I can tell when they are getting it, when they're not getting it, and when they've had enough.
- Perhaps the most important lesson I've learned is that I will never be finished trying to improve as a teacher.

APPENDICES

Appendix A: Teaching Responsibilities
Appendix B: Teaching Methods and Strategies
Appendix C: Course Materials
Appendix D: Student Assessment Tools
Appendix E: Evaluation of Teaching
Appendix F: Awards and Recognitions
Appendix G: Evidence of Student Learning
Appendix H: Teaching Outreach

CHAPTER SEVENTEEN

CHEMISTRY AND BIOCHEMISTRY

David E. Smith

Department of Chemistry and Biochemistry
New Mexico State University
Spring 2010

CONTENTS

TEACHING RESPONSIBILITIES

My teaching responsibilities in NMSU's Department of Chemistry and Biochemistry are distributed between general chemistry and physical chemistry. My teaching load is generally two courses per semester, distributed as shown in Table 1. Representative syllabi for each of these courses are given in Appendix A.

TABLE 1. COURSES TAUGHT

Course # (credits)	Avg. size	Title	Fall 2006	Spring 2007	Fall 2007	Spring 2008	Fall 2008	Spring 2009
111 (4)	120	General Chemistry I					x	
112 (4)	120	General Chemistry II			x	xx		
115 (4)	50	Gen. Chem. I (Majors)	x					
116 (4)	40	Gen. Chem. II (Majors)		x				
152 (3)	7	The Molecular World						x
217 (3)	30	Gen. Chem. III (Majors)	x		x		x	
536 (3)	6	Chem. Thermodynamics		x				x

Brief descriptions of the courses are as follows:

- CHEM 111–112 is a two-semester general chemistry course sequence for science and engineering majors. It is a multisection course with enrollments ranging typically from 100 to 140 students per section.
- CHEM 115–116 is a two-semester general chemistry course sequence designed for chemical sciences (chemistry, biochemistry, and chemical engineering) majors. Enrollments are usually 40 to 60 students in CHEM 115 and slightly smaller in CHEM 116.
- CHEM 217 is a third-semester general chemistry course designed to supplement the CHEM 111–112 course sequence and required for majors who do not take CHEM 115–116.
- CHEM 152 is a hybrid mathematics/chemistry distance education course with a target audience of dual-enrollment high school students located throughout New Mexico.
- CHEM 536 is a graduate course in chemical thermodynamics. It is designed to provide a rigorous introduction to the physical chemistry topic of chemical thermodynamics with applications drawn from diverse fields of chemistry and biochemistry.

TEACHING PHILOSOPHY

A few years ago, my daughter discovered odd numbers. She called them "numbers with a middle." When you hold up three fingers, there is a middle finger, but when you hold up two or four, there isn't. She started listing them, "3, 5, 7, 9, 11 . . ." I asked her, "Does the number 1 have a middle?" She eventually decided it does.

Teaching is an odd endeavor. It has a middle, too, a beautiful and mysterious middle. How does a person take sensory input—all of the information they receive from me as a teacher, for example—and then develop a new understanding, all their own? I must admit I don't have much of a clue about how this happens. I understand one end quite well: how to provide input for my students with different types of input for different learning objectives. I think I know something of the other side also—the assessment end where I figure out what they've learned—though that seems to be a more challenging task. *But what happens in the middle?*

This is what I do know. From family and educational background to a good night's sleep, a wide range of factors influences how each student functions. What happens in the middle, then, is highly individual. Identical inputs for 100 students yield 100 different outcomes. This is an enormous challenge for a teacher! To address it, I focus on two principles. The first is that *each student has intrinsic value.* This ideally self-evident truth is frequently ignored or discarded by instructors, and students themselves often fail to believe it. The second is that *all students can learn, though what seems effortless for one may be an arduous chore for another.* Thus assured of the significance of my task and the hope of my success, I set out to "meet them in the middle." And when they learn, I have the honor of participating in something beautiful. What could be more inspiring?

The specific elements of my philosophy of education grow out of these two principles of intrinsic student value and the hope of success. These elements may be expressed in terms of the following responsibilities I have toward my students:

- Provide an inspiring learning environment in which students feel secure, significant, and connected with both the instructor and other students. Students often lack either the confidence or the focus to learn effectively, and without addressing these issues, instruction is seldom successful. I believe they are best addressed through a well-designed learning environment.
- Provide organized, accurate instructional materials to guide students through the learning process and aid in their self-organization. Learning often fails to happen because the "sensory input" a student receives is so scrambled it becomes unrecognizable. This can be the fault of either the instructor or the student. Organizational strategies I employ in my teaching and suggest for my students are designed to optimize the input process.
- Present course materials in a way that is sensitive to the range of student backgrounds and learning styles. I believe that frequently varying delivery methods for course material and keeping students actively involved in the instructional process give every student the best opportunity to learn.

TEACHING OBJECTIVES, STRATEGIES, AND METHODOLOGIES

My teaching makes use of a wide range of methods spanning traditional lecture to informal group work and active classroom participation. It is characterized by a high level of organization, enthusiasm of presentation, and encouragement of student achievement. Strategies and implementation details associated with the elements of my instruction are summarized as follows, with specific examples highlighted in the following section and the appendices:

- PowerPoint presentations are used extensively in all of my courses. They are designed to:
  - Welcome students into the classroom, provide a visual road map for the day's activities, and aid students in organizing essential information.
  - Provide a mechanism for graphical presentation of quantitative information.
  - Deliver questions related to the course material, including review questions at the start of each class period, and subsequently to collect answers using remote response devices.
  - Establish real-world context for course material.
  - Provide a review structure for students via handouts posted each day after class.
- Remote response devices ("clickers") are an integral part of my general chemistry instructional methodology. They provide immediate, valuable feedback on student comprehension that is otherwise inaccessible to me. In addition, clickers keep students actively involved in class, stimulate their interest and enthusiasm in the learning process, and help them to evaluate their own learning nearly instantaneously.
- Chalkboard lectures form a small, significant part of my classes. They are used mostly for worked examples and are delivered in an alternating fashion with projected materials.
- Handouts and worksheets, given daily in all classes, serve multiple purposes, including:
  - Providing administrative information and content summaries

- Focusing students' attention on the most important concepts and computational skills in that day's material while keeping them attuned to the flow of the presentation
- Encouraging active student participation (either individually or informally in groups) through activities ranging from "fill in the blank" to critical thinking exercises
- Providing a valuable study tool
- WebCT, a course-specific virtual learning environment, is used to provide significant organizational assistance to students in all of my classes.
- Enthusiasm and humor are used liberally to establish a learning environment that is both stimulating and enjoyable. Enthusiasm is contagious, and appropriately directed it significantly enhances student engagement in the learning process. Someone recently called my sense of humor "corny," and I decided there was a kernel of truth in that statement. Humor not only makes class more enjoyable, but also makes various learning experiences more memorable and builds a valuable connection between the student and instructor.

DESCRIPTION OF TEACHING MATERIALS

This section begins with a description of general instructional materials that are used in most or all of my courses, followed by a brief discussion of additional materials that target specific courses. Supporting materials for this section are included in Appendix B (general materials) and Appendix C (distance education materials).

Daily Handouts and Worksheets

"[Dr. Smith's] worksheets provide excellent in-class learning for each individual concept and lesson." The first materials students encounter each day when entering my classroom are a handout and a worksheet. The handout is an organizational document with current administrative information that also includes important definitions or content summaries. The worksheet includes one or more review questions, as well as questions related to that day's new material. Worksheets are either collected at the end of class, or answers are submitted using clickers. In a survey conducted in

the middle of the spring 2008 semester, students were asked to rate various aspects of the course with regard to being *beneficial to their learning*. Results, summarized in Table 2, show that over 90 percent of these students considered handouts and worksheets to be either "helpful" or "extremely helpful."

Content Delivery

"The way Dr. Smith utilizes the clickers is effective because we get immediate feedback. It's much better to attempt problems and calculations and figure out what you're doing wrong than wait to find out on a test." Content delivery during class is done in a back-and-forth fashion between PowerPoint content slides, clicker questions and answers, chalkboard lectures, and student work. Keeping the delivery varied helps maintain student attention and caters to different learning styles. Elements of my teaching style related to content delivery include the following:

- Questions are posed regularly to students even in content-rich delivery segments, with answers often submitted using clickers. Student questions are also encouraged at all times.
- Student work is done either individually or with others according to the student's preference.

TABLE 2.   CHEM 112 SURVEY SUMMARY (150 PARTICIPANTS)

Category	Percentage of Responses			
	Not Helpful at All	A Little Helpful	Helpful	Extremely Helpful
Handouts and worksheets	0.6%	7.2%	32.3%	59.9%
In-class use of clickers	3.0%	18.0%	53.3%	25.7%
WebCT posting of notes, handouts, keys, etc.	1.2%	20.0%	28.5%	49.7%
OWL*	12.0%	38.6%	38.6%	10.8%

*OWL: Online Web-based Learning system (owl.cengage.com).

- Humor is often used in conjunction with content delivery to reinforce a concept.
- References to real-world applications and everyday experiences are interspersed liberally.
- Enthusiasm is my norm, and I'm never bashful about my own love of science. The world is a fascinating place, and getting that point across to students may be more important than any specific topic I teach.

Of all the content delivery methods I use, clickers have a singular value in *directing me.* They put me "behind the wheel," while lectures without clickers now seem like driving by remote control. Student response to clickers has been enthusiastic, with almost 80 percent of students rating them as either helpful or extremely helpful (Table 2).

Study Tools

"The daily handouts and worksheets are by far the most helpful tools for studying I've used in any of my classes." I use a variety of study tools with my students. Handouts, worksheets, and worksheet keys are all posted on WebCT shortly after class, as are handouts of PowerPoint slides that contain all clicker questions with answers. After each midterm, I post blank copies of the exam along with exam keys. Students have a very favorable response to WebCT resources, as evidenced by their almost 80 percent "helpful" or "extremely helpful" rating (Table 2) and numerous comments I receive each semester.

Other Instructional Materials

The instructional materials discussed above are used in the majority of my courses. Additional materials that I use in targeted classes include:

- Commercial study tools, currently used in CHEM 111–112. I use an online study system primarily for assigning homework as it provides real-time feedback to students as they answer questions. Student perceptions of the system are mixed (Table 2, OWL category).

- Virtual laboratories, currently used only in my distance education course, CHEM 152. Each laboratory involves a molecular-scale simulation that allows students to visualize behavior that is otherwise inaccessible to direct observation. Each simulation is accompanied by a written laboratory procedure, a post-laboratory self-test lecture (delivered online), and a post-laboratory assignment used to assess student learning. Examples are given in Appendix C.
- Interactive lecture videos, currently used only in CHEM 152. These lecture videos contain self-test questions embedded within PowerPoint-style lecture slides. Branching of the lecture for review of important concepts may be done based on student responses.
- Writing assignments are used occasionally in majors courses (CHEM 217, 115, and 116) and as a significant component in CHEM 536 to provide students an opportunity to communicate scientific thoughts and explore real-world implications of material related to the course.

Efforts to Improve Teaching

It has long been my goal to make regular and significant efforts toward improving my teaching. I pursue this goal primarily through events sponsored by NMSU's Teaching Academy. For example, between the fall of 2007 and spring of 2009, I participated in the following programs:

- "Assessing Students' Learning and Development Along the Chronology of Their Education" (09/13/2007; 3 hours)
- "Peer Coaching! for Classroom and Distance Educators" (02/14/2008; 13.5 hours)
- "Engaging Students with 'Clicker' Technology" (2/26/08; 1.5 hours)
- "Scaffolding for a Successful Inquiry-Based Learning Experience" (12/04/2008, 2 hours)
- "Developing a Teaching Portfolio" (01/30/2009–02/02/2009, 15 hours)
- "Teaching Portfolios: Document Your Greatest Teaching Accomplishments" (05/26/2009–05/29/2009; 15 hours, served as a mentor)

In addition, in the summer of 2008 I participated in ITAL (Institute for Technology Assisted Learning), an intensive three-week training session exposing instructors to technology related to distance education course offerings.

TEACHING-RELATED GRANT WRITING AND SERVICE

I've been involved in the following teaching-related grant writing:

- "Analysis of Performance Factors and an Intervention Strategy for CHEM 111, a Physical Sciences Gateway Course." David E. Smith and Deanna Dunlavy. (Funded, NMSU College of Arts and Sciences, $8,000, 2006).
- "MESH: Mathematics, Engineering, Science Hybrids." David Finston, Kitty Berver, Carolyne Sweezy, David E. Smith, and several others. (Funded, U.S. Department of Education, $540,000 2006–2009). Renewal submitted, 2009.
- "Inquiry-Based Learning Implementation for General Chemistry Laboratories and Beyond." William Quintana, Antonio Lara, David Smith, and several others. (Not funded, National Science Foundation CCLI Phase II).

I also engage in a wide variety of teaching-related service activities, including acting as a mentor or instructor in Teaching Academy events and serving on committees related to curriculum or faculty development.

TEACHING EVALUATIONS AND AWARDS

Student Evaluations

A form for student evaluations used in my department is reproduced in Appendix D. Instructors are rated in seventeen different categories on a scale from A (excellent) to E (very poor). Summaries of student responses are reported as a "grade point average" of the student responses, with a maximum value of 4.0 corresponding to all A responses.

A semester-by-semester summary of numerical student evaluations in my large general chemistry courses (CHEM 111 and CHEM 112) is given in Table 3. Numerical student evaluation scores for other courses, averaged across semesters, are displayed in Table 4. The categories included are those most closely related to material emphasized in this portfolio. Complete evaluation results are included in Appendix D. *I'm very pleased that scores from these evaluations are uniformly high, with only slight variation between sections and courses.*

Student comments often emphasize how they appreciate my organizational structure: *"I think clickers and especially the handouts and in-class worksheets helped a lot."* Some focus on their overall experience: *"The instructor is amazing, he does a great job teaching!"* Others even note my use of humor: *"Jokes are lame but keep 'em coming."* Additional student comments are collected in Appendix D.

Peer Evaluations

My teaching was evaluated by three peers from outside of my department through the Peer Coaching program in the spring of 2008. All three of these peers viewed an informal "teaching slice" of my instructional methods prior to visiting an actual classroom session. Two of the peers in addition collected survey information from different sections of my CHEM 112 students. A summary of peer evaluations and student surveys is collected in Appendix E. *Peer evaluations were enthusiastically positive, particularly about my use of worksheets and clickers and my general dynamic with students.*

Student comments collected by my Peer Coaching colleagues were in response to the question, "What most helps you learn in this class?" Highlights from these comments include:

- *"The in-class handouts and examples help me better understand the topics being taught. This helps me engage my mind and by having to answer clicker questions it keeps my mind focused on what is being taught in the course."*
- *"What helps me most is doing worksheets and working together as a class. It's better having to talk to people around you because we can all help each other."*

TABLE 3. SUMMARY OF STUDENT EVALUATIONS FOR CHEM 111 AND CHEM 112

Survey Question	Fall 2007 (112) N = 63	Spring 2008 (112 Sec. 1) N = 96	Spring 2008 (112 Sec. 2) N = 58	Fall 2008 (111) N = 76	Average
Organization	3.86	3.83	3.86	3.79	3.84
Enthusiasm	3.90	3.80	3.84	3.86	3.85
Attitude toward students	3.94	3.83	3.90	3.86	3.88
Willingness to acknowledge and answer questions	3.94	3.89	3.93	3.95	3.93
Encouraging students	3.78	3.65	3.79	3.82	3.76
Visual aids, handouts, demonstrations	3.82	3.80	3.81	3.82	3.81
Overall rating compared to others at NMSU	3.89	3.61	3.84	3.83	3.79

TABLE 4.   SUMMARY OF STUDENT EVALUATIONS FOR VARIOUS COURSES

Survey Question	CHEM 115/116 Avg. N = 41	CHEM 217 Avg. N = 25	CHEM 536 N = 6
Organization	3.87	3.54	3.83
Enthusiasm	3.96	3.88	4.00
Attitude toward students	3.98	3.90	4.00
Willingness to acknowledge and answer questions	3.94	3.96	4.00
Encouraging students	3.93	3.80	4.00
Visual aids, handouts, demonstrations	3.86	3.57	3.83
Overall rating compared to others at NMSU	3.89	3.57	4.00

- *"Worksheets and clickers really keep me involved and engaged in the class material. Clickers give instant feedback, which really helps. Also, Dr. Smith is awesome. I don't know how he makes chemistry fun!"*

Teaching Awards and Nominations

I was nominated by my students for the *National Society of Collegiate Scholars (NSCS) National Teacher of the Year* award in 2006. Although I did not receive this award, it was a great honor that my students would think me worthy of a national award nomination. In 2009, I received the **NMSU Teaching Academy Innovation Award** for "Innovative Use of Remote Response Devices in the Classroom." The single recipient of this annual award is selected from a university-wide competition.

EVIDENCE OF STUDENT LEARNING

Evidence of student learning in my classes currently takes two forms. The first involves surveys of student perceptions drawn from both midsemester and end-of-semester evaluations. Examples have already been highlighted above in Table 2 and in the section on peer evaluations. Students are generally enthusiastic about how my teaching approach helps them learn.

The second form of evidence I have gathered involves specific examples of student learning demonstrated via clickers. These generally take the form of pre- and post-presentation quiz questions in which students show marked improvement on concept questions following instruction. Several examples of student learning demonstrated via clickers are included in Appendix F.

TEACHING GOALS

My short-term and long-term teaching goals are related to both improvement of instruction and development of skills in the scholarship of teaching.

Short-Term Goals (Next Six Months)
- Read two books related to the scholarship of teaching and begin reading regularly from the *Journal of Chemical Education*.
- Design methods for gathering information from future general chemistry classes that will supply additional evidence of student learning.
- Work with the PRIMOS (education grant) faculty development committee to identify methodologies for assessing student learning in science and math disciplines across NMSU.

Long-Term Goals (Next Three Years)
- Engage in a regular reading program related to the scholarship of teaching and chemistry education.
- Collect publishable data on student learning in at least one general chemistry course, and submit one paper for publication using those data.
- Implement regular instructional activities which provide feedback on student learning.

APPENDICES

Appendix A: Representative Course Syllabi
Appendix B: Teaching Materials: CHEM 112
Appendix C: Teaching Materials: CHEM 152
Appendix D: Student Evaluation Materials
Appendix E: Peer Coaching Summary and Comments
Appendix F: Clicker-Based Evidence of Student Learning

CHAPTER EIGHTEEN

CHEMISTRY AND MATHEMATICS

Richard Schnackenberg

Department of Chemistry and Mathematics
Florida Gulf Coast University
Spring 2010

CONTENTS

TEACHING RESPONSIBILITIES

At Florida Gulf Coast University, I have taught courses ranging from general education and the calculus sequence to senior and graduate courses. The next table is a representative sample:

Term/Year	Course Name	Course Number	Students (mean)	Type of Course
Sp05	Linear Operators and Diff. Eq.	MAS 2121	13	Required for math major
Su05, Fa06, Sp07	Calculus I	MAC 2311	26	Required for math major
Su06, Su07, Su08, Fa08, Sp09	Calculus II	MAC 2312	24	Required for math major
Fa04	Calculus III	MAC 2313	14	Required for math major
Fa05	Elementary Calculus	MAC 2233	110	Required for business major
Fa04, Fa05, Sp06, Fa07, Sp08, Fa08	Foundations of Mathematics	MHF 2191	16	Required for math major
Sp05, Sp06	Discrete Math	MAD 3107	18	Required for computer science major
Fa04, Fa05	Abstract Algebra I	MAS 4301	7	Required for math major
Sp06	Abstract Algebra II	MAS 4312	4	Offered as an elective
Sp05	Matrix Analysis	MAS 4106	4	Offered as an elective
Sp06	Topics in Abstract Algebra II	MAT 5932	6	Graduate course taught in conjunction with MAS 4302
Fa05, Sp06, Fa07	General Math	MGF 1107	35	Gen ed course
Su08	College Algebra	MAC 1105	127	Gen ed course

TEACHING PHILOSOPHY, METHODOLOGY, AND OBJECTIVES

Philosophy of Teaching

As I begin my forty-fourth year in the classroom, I have two constants in my philosophy of teaching.

- Pass along knowledge.
- Inspire students.

That does not mean that I have remained stagnant in the means of passing along the knowledge and inspiring my students, as the following paragraphs will illustrate.

I believe one of the primary responsibilities of a teacher is to pass along the knowledge of the ages, including the current age. What took Newton and Leibniz years to create, we now teach in our calculus sequence. Every year new texts appear that include new material. The Math for Liberal Arts sequence book now contains chapters on voting theory and graph theory, much of which was not available fifty years ago, even twenty years ago.

Objectives and Methodology

My manner of **passing along information** ranges from straight lecture to group work, online work, quizzes, exams, projects, and presentations. I try to cover only the important concepts and techniques in the lecture, relegating omitted material to the worksheets done in class. Students confront this material in a **group** and work it out together.

I feel my primary focus in the classroom is to inspire students to perform at their best level. Math is a difficult subject for most students—**math anxiety** is a very real presence in class. I try to make it as painless as possible for a student to "fail" in his or her attempt at a problem. No mathematician has ever done every problem correctly on the first attempt. I therefore instill in students that I value highly their **effort** at solving a problem. When I first ask students to demonstrate work on the board, I tell them the best thing they can do is mess up the problem because that is how we learn. And when they inevitably make a mistake, I sound very excited and thank them profusely, and then have them seek advice from the "peanut gallery." This instills a "we-are-in-this-together" mentality, and the class as a whole rejoices when a proper solution is discovered.

In other classes I collect the homework, but do not grade the problems for correctness. Instead, if I see a **good attempt** at solving most of the assigned problems, I award the student 100 percent for that homework assignment. If I do not see such an effort, I award 0 percent. I want to see erasures, scribbling, restarts—all the things that indicate thinking has occurred.

For many of my exams, I allow one sheet of handwritten notes. The purpose of this is twofold: one, it encourages the student to review important concepts and formulas, and two, it places **critical thinking** above memorization. I think true understanding of the material is knowing which formula(s) or methods to use, identifying variables and constants, and then correctly applying this information to the problem. This method also relates to the relief of **math anxiety**; it removes the excuse of not remembering a formula.

For many exams, I permit students to make test corrections and earn back points they lost on their first attempt. This also reinforces the idea that it is **all right to fail**, but if given a chance, to work very hard to reach the correct solution and be rewarded for that effort.

When I use online quizzes/homework such as those in CourseCompass or MyMathLab (an online delivery system powered by Blackboard), I allow students to do the quizzes as many times as they want, up until the final exam. Since the quizzes are algorithmically generated, they never see the same question twice, but will see similar questions with different numbers each time. There is an old Russian saying, which I *shout* in Russian, "*ПОВМОРЄИИЄ МАМЪ УЧЄИИЄ!*" (*repetition is the mother of learning*).

I foster excitement in the class by my own excitement at good insights into problems or correct answers to difficult problems by awarding "Gold Stars" in a loud, enthusiastic voice. These are absolutely meaningless in terms of grades, but students often ask if they get a Gold Star for an answer or observation. I often **encourage** students to applaud a student's efforts on the board. After one or two times, it occurs naturally throughout the remainder of the semester. I think this peer recognition is especially valuable. Usually by the end of the semester, most of my students feel comfortable doing their work on the board in front of the class.

SYLLABI

As an illustration of the changes in emphasis from lecture to group problem solving, I present in the next table a portion of the syllabus for my MAC 2312 Calculus II, Summer 2006 class and my MAC 2311 Calculus I, Fall 2006 class. In the former syllabus, the first three days were devoted to lecture and only two days to problem solving. In the latter syllabus, the emphasis is placed on class participation. (See Appendix A.)

MAC 2312 Calculus II, Summer 2006	MAC 2311 Calculus I, Fall 2006
5/8 Chapter 6.1—Sigma Notation Chapter 6.2—Area 5/10 Chapter 6.3—The Definite Integral Chapter 6.4—The Fundamental Theorem of Calculus 5/12 Chapter 6.5—The Substitution Rule Chapter 6.6—The Logarithm Defined as an Integral 5/15 Review 5/17 Review 5/19 Test 1 (Chapter 6)	**Class Participation** Students will demonstrate their solutions to problems in the class. Your grade for this section will be based on how well prepared you are and how many problems you do. Note: You do not have to get the problem correct in order to receive full credit.

A similar change in emphasis on *group work* is apparent in the change in my syllabi in MAC 2312 Calculus II from Summer 2007 to Fall 2008 (see the next table).

Summer 2007 Grading Criteria		Fall 2008 Grading Criteria	
Chapter Exams (4 @ 100 pts)	400	In-Class Worksheets/Quizzes	100
Final Exam	200	Homework Notebooks	100
	600	Chapter Exams (2@ 100 pts)	200
		Final Exam—cumulative	100
			500

STUDENT LEARNING

With my encouragement, several of my former students are now working as instructors or lab coordinators at FGCU. Anecdotally, I have found when teaching a class made up of my former students and others, my former students are distinctly different in their attitude toward attempting problems, not fearing failure, and more poised before the class.

An older, returning student professed her absolute fear of math: "I can't do math," etc. She was very bright and just needed the encouragement to succeed. A few years after graduating, I met her in a department store and was thrilled to learn she was nearing completion of her Ph.D. in statistics. She thanked me for getting over her *math-phobia* hurdle.

EVALUATION OF TEACHING

My student assessment scores in the next table range from 3.0 to 5.0, while most of the more recent assessment scores are in the mid- to upper 4's. With the exception of the fall 2008 assessment scores in Calculus II, the mean scores showed a significant increase from the summer 2006 and spring 2007 levels to the summer 2007 to summer 2008 levels. I attribute the change to group work as the reason behind this increase. (See Appendix B.)

Term/Year	Course Name	Course Number	No. of Students Responding	Overall Assessment of Instructor (mean) 5 = Excellent; 1 = Poor
Sp05	Linear Operators and Diff. Eq.	MAS 2121	10	4.8
Fa06, Sp07	Calculus I	MAC 2311	Sp05 (21); Fa06 (22); Sp07 (18); Sp07 (13)	Fa06 (4.2); Sp07 (4.3); Sp07 (5.0)

Su06; Su07; Su08; Fa08; Sp09	Calculus II	MAC 2312	Su06 (12); Sp07 (18); Su07 (25); Su08 (6); Fa08 (13); Sp09 (30)	Su06 (3.2/3.5); Sp07 (4.3/4.0); Su07 (4.6/5.0); Su08 (4.8/5.0); Fa08 (3.7/3.0)
Fa05	Elementary Calculus	MAC 2233	Large Lecture—45	Fa05 (3.0)
Fa04	Calculus III	MAC 2313	12	Fa04 (3.6)
Fa04, Fa05, Sp06, Sp08, Fa08	Foundations of Mathematics	MHF 2191	Fa04 (8); Fa05 (3); Sp06 (4); Sp08 (11); Fa08 (17)	Fa04 (4.6); Fa05 (4.3); Sp06 (4.8); Sp08 (4.9); Fa08 (3.6)
Sp05, Sp06	Discrete Math	MAD 3107	Sp05 (11); Sp06 (12)	Sp05 (4.5); Sp06 (4.3)
Fa04, Fa05	Abstract Algebra I	MAS 4301	Fa04 (7); Fa05 (6)	Fa04 (4.4); Fa05 (4.8)
Sp06	Topics in Abstract Algebra II	MAT 5932	Sp06 (3)	Sp06 (4.3)
Fa05, Sp06, Fa07	General Math	MGF 1107	Fa05 (28); Sp06 (20); Fa07 (23)	Fa05 (4.2); Sp06 (4.2); Fa07 (4.9)
Su08	College Algebra	MAC 1105	Large Lecture—55	Su08 (4.4)

STEPS TO IMPROVE TEACHING

While these ratings indicate a very positive overall assessment, I pay greater attention to the individual responses. For example, in the spring 2007 semester when I was teaching two sections of Calculus I, I felt that the traditional method of lecturing most days, with a day or two of problems before an exam, was not exposing the students to enough practice. After speaking on many occasions with Dr. Jose Barreto, professor of chemistry, who instituted the group approach in General Chemistry and Organic Chemistry with resounding success, I was willing to try the **group method**. So in the middle of the semester, I changed methods, lecturing for half the class and breaking up into groups of three for solving problems on worksheets. (See Appendix F.) The results were astounding. Calculus I is a traditional "weed-out" class. Shockingly, I received a 5.0 overall assessment in one section and student comments indicated a very positive response to this change (see Appendix C):

- *"I really thought the new way of teaching helped a lot! The only problem was when we switched up groups, I learned less because I was not comfortable with the new people in my group. Overall this class was very tough but the teacher was very helpful in trying to get us to understand the material as best as he could!"*
- *"The new way of teaching has really helped me learn the material. . . . Also, you make calculus fun."*
- *"I really like the new format of lecturing less and doing more problems in class. I think this method helped me understand the material better. I like working in groups because we can help each other to better understand the problem if some of us don't understand. I have worked in study groups for calculus outside of class."*

The class averages went from 69.0 in summer 2005 and 69.8 in fall 2006 to 73.1 and 77.0 in spring 2007.

The fall 2008 semester, however, saw a marked drop in assessment scores. After reading the individual comments, I found that I was rushing too quickly through the lectures in order to leave more time for the group work. The students expressed a desire for more explanations before they attempted the newly introduced material in their group work. I have taken these comments and applied them to the spring 2009 semester.

CLASSROOM OBSERVATION

During my first year at FGCU, Dr. Beatty, chair of the division, evaluated my classroom teaching in MAS 4301 Abstract Algebra I (see Appendix D):

- "He guides students who are solving problems in front of the class without letting them hang or short-circuiting the discovery learning potential."
- "He was obviously well-prepared to lecture."
- "The students are engaged and obviously respect Rick's knowledge and intelligence."
- "All in all, his teaching performance is credit to the math program."

Remaining Up-to-Date

Every year I attend the Joint Meetings of the Mathematical Association of America (MAA) and the American Mathematical Society (AMS), the two premier math organizations in the country. Besides attending many presentations on new developments in pedagogy, I always take one or two "mini-courses." For example, I have taken mini-courses from Don Saari, Gil Strang, Bonnie Gold, Edward Keppelmann, and Ellen Maycock. From Michael Starbird's and Edward Berger's mini-course, Teaching the Heart of Mathematics, I use a technique on discovering *Cantor's Diagonalization Argument.* This is a difficult concept about different cardinalities of infinite sets, usually discussed at the upper or graduate level. I can now present it to my general education classes, and they fully understand it.

In the fall 2006 semester, I presented a talk on the use of the SMART Board at a seminar sponsored by the Whitaker Center, a collaborative project of the College of Arts and Sciences and the College of Education with a vision and mission focused on improving science, mathematics, and technology education at all levels.

As chair, I have instituted a new colloquium series. To date, we have had five faculty speakers and eleven outside speakers. I strongly encourage my students to attend and have found that many students thank me for the opportunity to hear the speakers. In addition, it exposed the faculty, including me, to new ideas. (See Appendix H.)

As Program Leader for Math, I have taken the faculty on two retreats to address common issues of pedagogy and curriculum. By all accounts, it successfully met the goals of the retreat.

Maximum class sizes were reduced to thirty-five and loads were fixed at nine credits for ranked faculty and twelve credits for instructors per semester. All work above those limits is now paid at the overload rate. In addition, a framework for the new Master's degree was established. (See Appendix I.)

GOALS (ONE TO TWO YEARS)

• Request Dr. Barreto to review my teaching and make suggestions to improve my utilization of the *group method* in the fall 2009 semester. Currently, some of the very best and very worst students occasionally leave when we break into groups. Dr. Barreto has offered to make suggestions to keep all students engaged and to generally improve the class.
• Organize retreats for the chemistry and math faculty in September 2009 to discuss issues of pedagogy and curriculum.
• Present a paper at the winter meetings.
• Update my teaching portfolio every year.

APPENDIX

A. Course Syllabi
B. Student Assessment of Instruction
C. Letters and Comments from Students
D. Peer Assessment of Instruction
E. Sample Assignments/Exams
F. Sample Group Worksheets
G. Sample Projects
H. Colloquium Speakers
I. Retreat Agenda and Minutes

CHAPTER NINETEEN

COMMUNICATION AND PHILOSOPHY

Mary Pelak Walch

Department of Communication and Philosophy
Florida Gulf Coast University
Spring 2010

CONTENTS

TEACHING RESPONSIBILITIES

I came to Florida Gulf Coast University as a communication generalist. In my first year, I taught a wide range of courses, and then I developed the curriculum for a new public relations concentration in our communication major, and focused my teaching in that area. I developed and taught four classes required for this concentration: PUR 3004 Principles of Public Relations, PUR 3100 Public Relations Writing, PUR 4800 Public Relations Campaigns, and PUR 3600 Public Relations Strategy. Currently, my teaching is focused on rhetorical communication. I frequently teach PHI 3106 Principles of Rhetoric and Argumentation, which is required for all communication majors; COM 3343 Rhetorical Criticism; and SPC 2023 Public Speaking, a general education course. All eleven of the courses I have taught at FGCU are listed in the next table.

Course #	Course Name	Role in Curriculum	Total # of Students
PHI 3106	Rhetoric and Argumentation	Com. major requirement	141
COM 3343	Rhetorical Criticism	Communication Studies concentration requirement	34
SPC 3721	Interracial/ Intercultural Com.	Com. major requirement	220
PUR 3004	Principles of Public Relations	PR concentration requirement	165
PUR 3100	Public Relations Writing	PR concentration requirement	82
PUR 3600	Public Relations Strategy	PR concentration requirement	29
PUR 4800	Public Relations Campaigns	PR concentration requirement	27
IDS 3300	Foundations of Civic Engagement	Interdisciplinary Studies course; CAS requirement	29
IDS 2110	Connections	Interdisciplinary Studies course; CAS requirement	49
SPC 2023	Public Speaking	Required by several majors	121
SPC 3360	Interviewing	Performance course	19

TEACHING PHILOSOPHY

My teaching philosophy is based on several core beliefs and values.

1. I believe in the transformational possibilities of education. The pursuit of lifelong learning greatly enhances students' lives personally and professionally, and it equips them to participate more fully as citizens in a democracy.
2. I believe that our ability to communicate distinguishes us as humans. I believe that the study of communication needs to address both communication skills (presentational speaking, writing, group communication, mediated communication) and bodies of knowledge based on these communication contexts.
3. I value theoretical frameworks for their capacity to help us to reach beyond the realms of our own direct experience.
4. I likewise value the marriage of theory and praxis, and its potential to bring ideas to life by making them tangible and meaningful to students.

TEACHING OBJECTIVES, STRATEGIES, METHODOLOGIES

In order to convince students of the transformational potential of education, *my first objective is to provide students with a classroom environment that is conducive to active learning, open discussion, and civil discourse.* I start many of my classes with a simple model of human communication that represents how messages are transmitted from a speaker to a listener through some medium of communication. The basic model of communication is commonly bound by a rectangle that represents the setting or context of communication. In communication studies, context refers to both the physical environment of any human interaction and the relationships between the communicators. As a professor, it is my responsibility to provide leadership and to set the tone for the type of interaction that occurs in the classroom.

In order to nurture relationships with my students and establish an atmosphere conducive to learning, I am very respectful of students and make myself available to them outside of class. Many student comments on my Student Assessment of Instruction [SAIs] forms demonstrate their appreciation:

> She was beyond great as far as making the classroom a comfortable environment in order to give presentations. She was very strong in ensuring that students were respectful and attentive. (Public Speaking, Spring 2008)

> She remembers so much about her students and picks up on little things said. I really felt like a student not a number or a product in this class. (Rhetoric & Argumentation, Fall 2008)

> Dr. Walch is a great teacher who cares about her students. She was always available and willing to help. I would strongly recommend her as a teacher. (Principles of Public Relations student, Fall 2006)

In several of my courses, I use the acronym "WIIFM"—What's In It For Me?—a short phrase that reminds communication students to empathize with designated audiences when developing public messages. It is similar in the classroom; as I prepare for class I imagine students asking "Why should I care about this class?" *My second objective, therefore, is to stimulate students' interest in the subject matter, to make them care about the class by (1) being enthusiastic, (2) inviting them to bring in examples and topics for class discussion, and (3) designing assignments that will actively engage them in the subject we are studying.* Students' written comments on our SAIs confirm my ability to stimulate interest and make learning enjoyable:

> Dr. Walch has transformed what was once my least favorite subject into something I now find very interesting. I have struggled with Rhetoric over the years here at FGCU. I have attempted the class twice with different professors and never quite seemed to grasp the concept. Dr. Walch's class was challenging, yet I felt comfortable with the material and learned something new each class session. She is an outstanding professor of Rhetoric. (Principles of Rhetoric and Argumentation, Spring 2008)

Dr. Walch is a wonderful instructor and is definitely one of my favorite throughout my entire college career. She is extremely intelligent and compassionate about what she does. She makes learning a joy. (Rhetoric and Argumentation Student, Fall 2008)

Very good teacher; has great enthusiasm for the coursework. Encourages student participation, and conducts class in a very comfortable atmosphere. (Interracial/Intercultural Communication Student, Spring 2007)

Many of my courses require students to read the newspaper, and I strongly encourage students to share materials (newspaper articles, speeches, Web sites, and advertisements) pertinent to our class. This strategy democratizes the classroom, and it lets students know that I want us to address issues that are meaningful to them. Providing students with these types of opportunities helps them connect rhetorical theories to their day-to-day lives. (See Appendix A.)

During the spring 2007 semester, a Principles of Rhetoric and Argumentation student showed our class a speech that made it one of our most memorable class meetings. It was Jon Stewart's first opening monologue on *The Daily Show* after September 11, 2001. In the days following these devastating attacks, many comedians didn't feel that it was appropriate to make people laugh. When *The Daily Show* resumed, Jon Stewart's typically sarcastic opening monologue was replaced by a very tender, personal, and spontaneous response to the horrors faced by the people of New York. Despite all of the other 9/11 speeches we watched, a speech discovered by a student and given by a comic most poignantly captured the manner in which people came together, put aside differences, and shared a powerful sense of community and compassion. Stewart ended his speech with a hopeful image of our shared future when he described the view from his Manhattan apartment. Before September 11, 2001, his apartment faced the Twin Towers. Today, his view is the Statue of Liberty, representing the dream and the enduring promise that is America. It was profoundly moving to the students. Our class talked about why it was so special. In a world of slick, highly controlled, carefully edited media messages, Stewart's stuttering, his awkward pauses, and brief tears made his words much more genuine than if they had been polished to perfection. Students didn't just recognize theoretical concepts, such as Aristotle's *pathos*, the emotional appeals of the speaker, or George Lakoff's work on framing theory; students thought through *how* and *why* the speech moved us. (See Appendix G for a transcript of the speech and the student's paper.)

Another way that I strive to bring theories to life for my students is to weave campus and local events into my classes. For example, during the 2008 election, students in my Rhetorical Criticism and Principles of Rhetoric and Argumentation courses wrote response papers and engaged in lively class discussions about vice-presidential candidates Joe Biden and Sarah Palin, who had both visited our area. In 2009, during his first fifty days in office, President Barack Obama came to Fort Myers because we had the dubious honor of having the nation's highest rate of foreclosures. Although we could not all attend Obama's speech, students analyzed a transcript of this speech on an exam two days after his visit, and we watched and discussed it several days later. (See Appendix C.) My classes have also attended art exhibits and theater productions to examine how rhetoric influences many aspects of our lives. For example, two Rhetorical Criticism students who had served in the military were upset by *Home of the Brave: Politics, Propaganda, & Patriotism*, an art exhibit our class attended on campus. One of these students channeled his anger into developing a well-argued critical analysis of the ideology presented by one of the artists. (See Appendix G.)

Another way I engage student interest in my classes is by designing assignments that will actively engage them in the subject we are studying. Students' written comments on our SAIs confirm my ability to stimulate interest and make learning enjoyable:

> I thoroughly enjoyed the last paper (#3) where we were able to choose our own topic. Being a senior and about to graduate, it really made me critically assess the challenge of media and their use of rhetoric. (Principles of Rhetoric and Argumentation, Fall 2008) (See Appendix B.)

I feel the last essay assignment was a great assignment. It made students have to really think about what they want to do with their lives. I also liked when we worked in groups and discussed case studies. It really gave us a chance to hear other opinions and develop strategies for solving cases. (Principles of Public Relations, Fall 2007) (See Appendix B.)

I enjoyed this class greatly! I especially enjoyed the variety of media used in the lectures. (Rhetoric & Argumentation, Fall 2008)

I want my students to be as fascinated with the study of communication as I am, and many of my classroom practices and activities support this goal. Fortunately, students demonstrate their mastery of the theories by means of communication (presentations, class discussions, papers, essay exams) so they are gaining experience and feedback for both their understanding of the course material and their skill at expressing their knowledge. Following are several examples of classroom strategies I often use:

- *Classroom Discussion* is the lifeblood of my classes. A significant portion of a student's grade (10–15 percent) is based on the quality and frequency of his or her contribution to class discussion. (See Appendix A.) It is important to students because it validates their experience and ideas, and it helps me to gauge whether students understand and internalize fundamental concepts in class.
- *Short Response Papers* serve as another opportunity for students to demonstrate their understanding of their readings and their ability to "think with" the theoretical and analytical frameworks presented in class. This is particularly successful in Principles of Rhetoric and Argumentation. (See Appendix A.)
- *Experiential Learning* helps students step out of their comfort zones to do things that will actively involve them in the issues and theories presented in class. For example, in Interracial/ Intercultural Communication, students perform mini-ethnographies by observing or participating in activities with another culture. (See Appendix B.)

- *Service-Learning Projects* provide exciting opportunities for students to apply what they are learning for the benefit of others in our community. This was particularly successful in Foundations of Civic Engagement, which focuses on what it means to be a citizen, and public relations writing. (See Appendix A.)
- *Preprofessional Assignments*—One of the best means of bridging theory and praxis occurs in upper-level public relations classes in which students complete assignments for clients in our community. Students in public relations writing find a client that needs public relations support and produce seven documents that culminate in the completion of a professional portfolio at the end of the course. In Public Relations Campaigns and Public Relations Strategy, students worked in groups to complete major projects for clients such as the FGCU Ecology Club, the FGCU Athletic Department, and the American Red Cross. (See Appendix G.)

DESCRIPTION OF COURSES

Principles of Rhetoric and Argumentation explores the history of rhetoric from ancient Greece to contemporary postmodern and feminist theories. It is required for all communication majors. Students are introduced to the writings of many great thinkers who have contributed to the understanding of how humans influence each other, including Aristotle, Plato, Cicero, Vico, and Burke. The development and structure of arguments is highlighted throughout this historic survey. Student assignments and activities are primarily written and include short response papers, papers, and essay exams. (See Appendices A and B.)

Rhetorical Criticism introduces students to several methods of rhetorical criticism, including Neo-Aristotelian, Cluster, Feminist, Ideological, and Metaphor Criticism. These approaches to research become our "critical toolbox" as we examine a variety of communication artifacts—from political speeches to contemporary music and advertising. Students develop analytical writing and speaking skills through classroom discussions, presentations, and written assignments. (See Appendices A and B.)

Interracial/Intercultural Communication is both a theoretical and applied course that examines the challenges and opportunities of communication between different cultures. Students work to develop a more diverse perspective and increase their competence in intercultural communication. Students take mixed-format exams and write several papers that are experiential. (See Appendices A and B.)

Principles of Public Relations introduces students to the history and the range of practices and specialties that exist within the field of public relations. It serves as a gateway course that introduces students to topics addressed in greater depth in other public relations courses in our curriculum. This class is taught in a combination lecture/discussion format, and public relations professions and instructors guest-lecture in this class. Students' understanding of course materials is evaluated by examinations. (See Appendices A and B.)

Public Relations Writing is a writing-intensive course that gives students helpful feedback and guidance as they develop several promotional documents for a client that they secured on their own. After several drafts have been edited by their professor and their peers, students develop a professional public relations portfolio. (See Appendices A and B.)

Efforts to Improve Teaching

Innovations in Teaching

I believe that teaching is an evolving process, and one of the ways that I grow as a teacher is to listen to my students. I pay very close attention to student evaluations at the end of the semester, and I often solicit anonymous feedback during the semester. (See Appendix E.) On the last day of class, I will informally ask how much they learned from individual assignments and what they thought of the readings, and I will solicit other feedback from students.

In order to keep track of what kinds of lectures, activities, and assignments are most beneficial and well received, I keep a teaching journal each semester. It helps me determine the participation scores of students at the end of each semester, and it provides a way for me to record my reflections about each class. It is a useful habit and a way to record the ephemeral joy of a great teaching day. For example, one class that particularly delighted me was an interracial/intercultural communication course that integrated a lecture by Mikhail Gorbachev on our campus. Students read about former president Gorbachev and his current projects with the Green Cross, and I lectured about his role in the peaceful end of the cold war in class. Students were well prepared for his message, and I was elated to hear them talk with great excitement at the class that followed his lecture. One bright yet contentious student, who was resistant to many of the core values of our course, was so moved by Gorbachev's words that he had memorized portions of Gorbachev's speech and shared them in our class discussion. Several students clearly articulated the essence of his message about peace and the environmental impact of war. They got it. They really, really got it, and I could not have been more pleased.

Keeping a teaching journal has also helped me to learn from my mistakes. During my first semester at FGCU, I enthusiastically assigned Daily Eye-Openers, which required students to write a short response for each of their readings. Although these assignments were meant to be a tool to keep students accountable for their readings, it produced diminishing returns. Students treated these as busywork rather than a means of focusing on key aspects of their readings. I read over seven hundred Eye-Openers while teaching five classes during my first semester, and only a fraction of them demonstrated critical engagement with their readings. I have adapted that assignment into more narrowly focused response papers (assigned three to five times per semester), which require students to answer a specific question about their reading in a thorough and thoughtful essay. (See Appendix A.)

As a faculty member at a young and rapidly growing institution, I have been researching strategies that other professors have used to increase the level of civility in the classroom. Student feedback and collaboration with other faculty members at FGCU confirmed my concerns about the disrespectful behavior of students in the classroom. After reading Delaney Kirk's book, *Taking Back the Classroom*, I made several changes in my classroom practices, including adding a page to my syllabi that addresses what I can expect from my students and what they can expect from me. Five years ago, I never would have thought that I would need to lay out my expectations in such detail, but it has improved students' behavior in my classes. In my estimation, this generation of students strongly prefers very detailed directions on assignments and taking the time to clearly establish expectations on the first day of class has been quite successful.

Teaching Conferences/Workshops

- Completed two preconference workshops on teaching public relations courses at the National Communication Association's annual conference in Miami, FL. (2003)
- Developed a teaching portfolio at the workshop led by Peter Seldin, Clement Seldin, and Elizabeth Miller in 2007 and mentored other faculty at this workshop in 2008.
- Engaged in the Seldin, Miller, and Seldin workshop on academic portfolios and a faculty dialogue about civic engagement with Paul Rogat Loeb, author of *Soul of a Citizen* (2009).
- Other activities that keep me constantly involved in improving my teaching include inviting supervisors and peers to evaluate my teaching and mentoring other faculty.

STUDENT ASSESSMENT OF INSTRUCTION

Course #	Course Name	Total # of Students	# of Student Responses	Avg. Student Assessment*
PHI 3106	Rhetoric and Argumentation	141	121	4.52
COM 3343	Rhetorical Criticism	34	27	4.50
SPC 3721	Interracial/ Intercultural Com.	220	162	4.44
PUR 3004	Principles of Public Relations	165	125	4.38
PUR 3100	Public Relations Writing	82	59	4.58
IDS 3300	Foundations of Civic Engagement	29	20	4.80
SPC 2023	Public Speaking	121	91	4.84

*Scale: 1–5, with 5 high

SHORT-TERM AND LONG-TERM GOALS

The following are my goals for continual improvement as a teacher:

- Invite colleagues to visit my classes and provide a written peer evaluation of my teaching. (annually)
- Coordinate a teaching cell with colleagues that meets at least three times per semester. (2010)
- Discover opportunities for improving my teaching, such as reading specific periodicals and books, and attending teaching conferences. (2010)
- Revise my teaching portfolio annually. (ongoing)
- Contact former students and gain feedback about the most and least helpful aspects of their education and use this information in a systematic way in curriculum decisions. (ongoing)

APPENDIX

A. Course Syllabi
B. Assignment Sheets
C. Examinations
D. Curriculum Development
E. Feedback from Students
F. Letters of Thanks
G. Student Work

CHAPTER TWENTY

ENGLISH AND COMMUNICATION

Margaret Loring

English and Communication Department
Doña Ana Community College
Spring 2009

CONTENTS

TEACHING RESPONSIBILITIES

Since coming on board full time at Doña Ana Community College in the fall of 2007, I have taught most of the English classes we offer, usually at full or nearly full capacity. My primary teaching location is at our main campus, but I have also taught some classes at the Gadsden and White Sands Missile Range campuses.

Descriptions of Courses Taught

- **Effective Communication Skills (CCDE 105)** *[4 credits]* is our first level of developmental English, focusing mainly on reading, locating main ideas, and writing summaries and responses. Toward the end of the class, students begin learning how to construct argumentative essays.
- **General Composition (CCDE 110)** *[4 credits]*, the second level of developmental English, focuses on basic argument. Students learn critical thinking skills in finding and evaluating sources, and begin to use APA [American Psychological Association] documentation style.
- **Rhetoric and Composition (ENGL 111)** *[4 credits]* is the college-level basic composition class required for most college majors. It gives students skills they will need to succeed in their college classes that require research and writing.
- **Writing in the Humanities and Social Sciences (ENGL 211)** *[3 credits]* is a class that I have designed on the specific topic of disability autobiography. Each section has a focus chosen by the instructor, but all students learn how to evaluate what they read, how to research a topic, and how to write a formal report.
- **Technical and Scientific Communication (ENGL 218)** *[3 credits]* focuses on writing in technical areas, including memos, letters, instructions, visual presentation of data, and formal reports.

TEACHING PHILOSOPHY

Engagement is the core of my teaching philosophy. I tell my students two things at the beginning of the semester: they will have more fun in English class than they ever had before, and they will learn things that will help them in their other college classes. I believe teaching should be enjoyable and useful. In order to accomplish these goals, students must be engaged in the class.

I have enjoyed this class far more than I expected to.
—Student in General Composition, December 2008

I engage with my students through effective communication. I start the semester off with readings and lively discussions of controversial topics. Sometimes we talk as a class and sometimes in small groups. My goal is to have everyone engaged in the conversation so they will feel more a part of the class. Shy students will speak out in a smaller group and develop more confidence. ESL students struggling with English might be reluctant to speak in class but can be dynamic leaders of a small group. They all learn to appreciate each other's differences and strengths.

Thanks to you Margaret for being patient and understanding on teaching the whole class and myself. I have noticed that even the way I speak around my peers and co workers is very different. I explain myself as if I am writing an essay. . . . what you taught me in paper I can also use in conversations. . . . My friends, family and co workers tell me I speak very differently since I have started going to school.
—Student in Effective Communication Skills,
November 2008

I want to instill in my students a love of lifelong learning. Many of them don't ever read for pleasure, and some have never read a book before. Through reading assignments and class discussions of them, students become engaged in the topics they will write about. They explore areas they might never before have considered.

I'm really glad I did the book project, because it gave me an excuse to sit down and get lost in a piece of literature that interested me. . . . Actually, now I am reading more books because I really enjoyed reading during that time.
—Student in Effective Communication Skills, April 2009

Critical thinking is often underdeveloped in beginning college students, particularly in developmental classes. Discussing assigned readings helps students see how to evaluate and compare different points of view. Ultimately this helps them write their own coherent opinions on controversial topics. It also helps them appreciate the multicultural diversity that surrounds us and to develop tolerance of difference in our human family. I believe this is a vital element in a college education.

Since this class has started, I was asked to think outside of what was normal to me. I gave it a shot, and I can honestly say that it broadened my horizons.

—From a student who, early in the semester, resisted any discussion on an essay about gay marriage by pointedly putting on iPod earphones and turning up his music until the discussion was over

This class made me contemplate a few issues that I had overlooked most of my life. . . . In the end, the class was successful at allowing me to see the current issues from a new perspective.

—Student in Writing in the Humanities and Social Sciences, December 2008

I want to thank you for helping me overcome my ignorance.

—Student in Writing in the Humanities and Social Sciences, December 2008

TEACHING OBJECTIVES, STRATEGIES, AND METHODOLOGIES

Student Input

At the beginning of this semester, I asked the students in my two General Composition classes about the topics they like to read and write about. I told them that I would change their assignment calendar so that the readings would reflect their interests. They were very open to the idea that they would have a role in structuring the class. One of their interests was writing about true events, particularly important influences in their lives. Accordingly, I assigned a narrative essay as their first assignment (see **Appendix A** for assignment sheet) and changed the first readings from essays on keeping a notebook to examples of student narrative essays. **Appendix A** contains a portion of the revised syllabus after student input, with changes highlighted.

Groups

Groups are used extensively in class, for buddies, for discussion, and for peer editing. Students choose "buddies" to contact if they have questions or miss a class, which helps them feel responsible to each other.

Groups are often used for initial discussion of a new topic. After groups report their results to the class, they are prepared for a livelier discussion, and more students become involved. This has the added benefits of encouraging the shy students to talk more and helping all students get to know each other better.

Students also serve as **peer editors** of each other's work. In asking for feedback and suggestions, they learn to analyze their writing more critically and often improve it. They also begin to understand more fully the challenging concept of **revision**. Many students say they want to learn the "correct" way to write an essay. Some also think that when they turn in a paper, it is "finished," and they can stop thinking about it. Using group work and peer editing reinforces my role as professor. To see that there are many ways to write and that their writing is never "perfect" is an ongoing task. **Appendix B** has a copy of the rubrics used in each composition class and sample peer editing guidelines.

Another thing that has helped me in my essay is when we have the group revisions. I like this strategy because you get to hear your class-mate's suggestions and how to improve your essay.

—Student in General Composition,
December 2008

Working in groups was the best experience in the class. The individuals within my group helped and taught me more than I can explain and thank them for.

—Student in Effective Communication Skills,
April 2009

Student Feedback

Teaching is dynamic, and every class is different. I ask students periodically during the semester what is helping them learn and what is not working. Students feel that their ideas are valued, and I have quick and accurate feedback on what is not going well so I can make changes while there is time for the current class to benefit from them. See **Appendix C** for the Midsemester Evaluation feedback form.

I believe Margaret Loring helped me exceed my beliefs of how learning should be taught. Mrs. Loring is a great teacher and I appreciate the opportunity I got to be taught by her.
—Student in Effective Communication Skills,
December 2007

Discussion

Students want their ideas to be acknowledged, and they appreciate a good argument. Discussion challenges them to back up their ideas logically and to explain them to someone who does not share them. Often they find that their ideas are based on what they have been told and just accepted as true without a solid basis in fact. Their prejudices are broken down and their critical thinking skills are improved when they look up information and analyze it for themselves.

REPRESENTATIVE DETAILED COURSE SYLLABI

Syllabi for 100-level English classes are a product of faculty consensus and are now printed in the custom text that was compiled by the department, but I have freedom to choose how I will teach the material and what I will have my students read and write during the semester. **Appendix D** contains my detailed assignment calendars for these courses.

I developed a syllabus for an ENGL 211 course, Writing in the Humanities and Social Sciences, with the subtitle Disability Autobiography. I also developed the syllabus for the Technical and Scientific Communication class I taught in the summer of 2008. These syllabi, including detailed assignment calendars, are in **Appendix D**.

EVIDENCE OF STUDENT LEARNING

Students learn over the semester, through the process of peer editing and revision, how to make their writing clearer and more detailed. This example is from one of the developmental writing courses, General Composition. The paragraph is from a student essay written at the beginning of the semester, on 9/9/08:

> It's so ironic how a child could change your life. Ethan has changed my life in every aspect that I could ever imagine. He change my way of thinking now I think in a totally different way than I used to think. I never thought that my child would be my life chaining experience, an experience that I will live for the rest of my living years.

This revision of that paragraph was written on 12/2/08:

> It's so ironic how a child could change your life. My son Ethan has change my way of thinking. Before I had my son I would only think of myself and in my own good, but now that I have him I only think in his own good. He has also change my freedom of going out. Before I could go out without worries, and now I don't. I worry because I'm scared that he is not going to be well taken care of or that he is not going to be comfortable. Even though my mother takes care of him I still worry because Ethan is not used to be with my mother.

While it can still use a lot more work, this paragraph shows quite a bit of improvement over the original.

Appendix E contains examples of student papers at the beginning and end of the semester. The examples are both of excellent papers and those still needing work. Grading comments are included.

STUDENT EVALUATIONS

I am especially pleased with the high student evaluations I have regularly received throughout my twelve years as an adjunct, which have continued during my full-time tenure. **Appendix F** contains evaluations from the last two years. My mean ratings since becoming full time, summarized in **Table 1**, are consistently at or above those of the college as a whole.

TABLE 1. OVERALL STUDENT EVALUATIONS BY COURSE AND SEMESTER

Semester	Course Number	Course Title	Overall Rating	College Average
Fall 2007	111–6	Rhetoric and Composition	4.7*	4.3*
Fall 2007	110–4	General Composition	4.5*	4.3*
Fall 2007	110–29	General Composition	4.3*	4.3*
Fall 2007	105–3	Effective Communication Skills	4.4*	4.4*
Spring 2008	111–2	Rhetoric and Composition	3.8**	3.5**
Spring 2008	110–15	General Composition	3.5**	3.5**
Spring 2008	110–15	General Composition	3.8**	3.5**
Spring 2008	105–10	Effective Communication Skills	3.8**	3.5**
Summer 2008	218–2	Tech & Scientific Communication	N/A	N/A
Fall 2008	211–2	Writing in Humanities & Social Sciences	3.6**	3.4**
Fall 2008	110–7	General Composition	3.6**	3.4**
Fall 2008	110–8	General Composition	3.6**	3.4**
Fall 2008	105–2	Effective Communication Skills	3.6**	3.4**
Fall 2008	105–3	Effective Communication Skills	3.7**	3.4**

*Mean ratings on a 5.0 scale, with 5.0 being the highest score.
**Mean ratings on a 4.0 scale, with 4.0 being the highest score.

CCDE 110 [General Composition] has given me the confidence in my writing that I needed. It has also helped me [be] more organized and focus in the development of my essays. But most of all it has taught me the importance, and the passion someone can have when it come to writing. I now see writing in a more mature perspective.
—Student in General Composition,
December 2008

Overall I really enjoyed the class and I would add that you are a great instructor, I felt comfortable speaking my mind and discussing the readings; I usually don't get that from English instructors.
—Student in Writing in the Humanities and Social Sciences,
December 2008

The writing I've done for the class has really brought out a deeper part of me. . . . I have you to thank for that. I'm sure not all instructors are trained in the art of drawing people out, but you did.
—Student in Effective Communication Skills,
April 2009

CLASSROOM OBSERVATIONS BY FACULTY PEERS AND ADMINISTRATORS

Classroom observation (see **Appendix G**) on April 23, 2008, by my supervisor, Assistant Professor Greg Hammond, Department Chair of English and Communication, resulted in positive comments:

The class has a relaxed atmosphere that the students obviously appreciate. They are attentive but jovial. . . . The classroom is well-managed and conducive to student learning. . . . Assessment of student learning/ understanding is occurring on a regular basis with responsiveness to students' needs.

Dr. Paul Mason, associate professor in the Math and Physical Sciences Department, has chosen me as his subject for observation for the Gaining Retention and Achievement for Students Program (GRASP), which helps faculty mentor each other in areas of teaching, assessment, and retention of students. He observed one of my Effective Communication Skills classes on a weekly basis during the spring semester of 2009. **Appendix G** contains his in-class observations.

I implemented many of Paul's suggestions right away, particularly using students' names in and outside of class. I found it much easier to remember names when I made a point to use them regularly. The result is that my students and I seem to feel more of a connection.

REVIEW OF TEACHING MATERIALS BY COLLEAGUES

Course Syllabus

In consultation with Sheila Black, assistant professor of English at New Mexico State University, I developed the Writing in the Humanities and Social Sciences class on Disability Autobiography. She suggested the books *Autobiography of a Face* by Lucy Grealy and *The Hospital Poems* by Jim Ferris, and several essays from the book *Disability Studies Reader* edited by Lennard J. Davis. She also had favorable comments on a book I had already chosen, Nancy Mairs' *Waist-High in the World.* Sheila had already taught a similar class, so her input was particularly valuable to me in developing mine. **Appendix D** contains copies of the syllabus and assignment sheets.

Assessment Material

In consultation with Professor Susan Wood, our assessment coordinator, I am developing assessment material, including pre- and posttests, on teaching APA documentation style to my General Composition classes. See **Appendix H** for copies of drafts and other materials that I am using to develop assessment instruments to get an accurate evaluation of student learning on this difficult topic.

Teaching Recognition

In 2008, I was honored to be among the five finalists, chosen by a vote of the student body of Doña Ana Community College, for the **Donald C. Roush Excellence in Teaching Award**. This award, highly regarded by faculty, is given annually in recognition of exceptional teaching, one in each of the five colleges of New Mexico State University.

She is a great instructor. I just wish we had more like her. I have learned a lot from her class.
　　　　　—Student in Rhetoric and Composition, December 2007

The instructor was passionate about the students. She talked to the student individually if they needed it.
　　　　　—Student in General Composition, December 2008

TEACHING IMPROVEMENT

Conferences

I regularly seek ways to increase my knowledge base. Attending conferences helps me connect with colleagues from around the country to share teaching ideas. I use information from conference workshops to make my teaching more effective, often immediately, as well as in planning for the next semester.

Workshops Attended

- "Teaching Portfolio Workshop," Teaching Academy, Peter Seldin, Elizabeth Miller, and Clement Seldin, January 30–February 2, 2009. In helping me to write my teaching portfolio, this workshop has increased my awareness of areas in which I can improve my teaching effectiveness.
- "Teaching Scholars Workshop," Teaching Academy, Tara Gray and Jean Conway, spring semester 2008. Besides valuable networking experience with colleagues, this workshop helped me write and more effectively implement my teaching philosophy.
- "Be All You Can Be—Teach!" Teaching Academy, Tara Gray and Jean Conway, October 26, 2007. I was able to utilize some of the materials from this workshop immediately in my classes, particularly the midsemester assessment.

TEACHING GOALS

In the next one to three years, I plan to accomplish goals in the following areas:

- *Assessment:* Create or adapt assignments for my General Composition classes that will include pretests and posttests, designed to assess students' knowledge of APA documentation style, one of the departmental Student Learning Outcomes for this class. APA style is a challenge for most of our students, and mastery of it is essential to their college success.
- *Feedback:* Administer at midterm anonymous student evaluations to implement instructional development plans tailored to increase student learning in each class. Also, continue to find more effective means of providing feedback to students.
- *Teaching Performance:* Continue to attend Teaching Academy workshops to improve my teaching and learn from my peers.
- *Development of Teaching Materials:*
  - Sustainability curriculum: Work with the Learning and Curriculum Team of the Sustainability Council at New Mexico State University to develop materials that incorporate sustainability concepts into my course assignments.
  - Nongendered language: Create materials to convey to students the importance of their choice of words, since language is an important medium to discover identity and to break down misunderstandings and prejudice. Gendered language and careless epithets offend and exclude people.
  - Lecture files: Create PowerPoint lecture notes that can be used for teaching both online and face-to-face classes to assist visual learners.

APENDICES

Appendix A: Student Feedback
Appendix B: Rubrics and Peer Editing Guidelines
Appendix C: Midsemester Evaluations
Appendix D: Class Syllabi and Detailed Assignment Calendars
Appendix E: Examples of Student Papers
Appendix F: Student Evaluations
Appendix G: Evaluations by Supervisor and Peers
Appendix H: Assessment Materials

CHAPTER TWENTY-ONE

FAMILY AND CONSUMER SCIENCES

Esther L. Devall

Family and Consumer Sciences Department
New Mexico State University
Spring 2010

CONTENTS

TEACHING RESPONSIBILITIES

While at New Mexico State University, I have taught twelve different courses (five undergraduate, seven graduate) and numerous independent study courses. For most of my career, I had a 75 percent teaching appointment. Typically, I taught six different courses per year. During the past five years, I was awarded several large grants and reduced my teaching load to one graduate course per semester. Currently I teach three graduate courses in family and child science and one interdisciplinary graduate seminar in alcohol and drug counseling (see the next table). The syllabi for these four courses are included in **Appendix A**.

Course #	Course Name	Level	Class Size	Role in Curriculum
FCS 546	Adolescent Development and the Family	Graduate	15–20	Human development course for students in Family and Child Science and Marriage and Family Therapy
FCS 583	Parenting and Child Guidance	Graduate	15–20	Human development course for students in Family and Child Science and Marriage and Family Therapy
FCS 589	Family Crises	Graduate	15–20	Required for Marriage and Family Therapy students; optional family course for other Family and Child Science students
MSW 597	Seminar in Alcohol and Drug Counseling	Graduate	8–10	Required for students in the Interdisciplinary minor in alcohol and drug counseling

TEACHING PHILOSOPHY

As a young child, I always wanted to be a teacher. Even in elementary school, I could tell when another student was having difficulty and could explain the concept in a way he or she could understand. I loved helping people learn and decided that teaching was my calling in life. During my career, I have taught at the preschool, elementary school, community college, and university levels. Regardless of whether my students were 3 or 63, I found that the qualities of a good teacher were the same.

- *Good teachers care about their students and get to know them in ways that extend beyond the classroom.* Teachers need to understand their students' background and situation to present information in a meaningful way. Students are willing to put forth more effort when they feel accepted and valued. I make a point to learn students' names, find out about their life situation, and determine their hopes and plans.
- *Good teachers take on many roles with their students.* They act as a guide to help students navigate the educational system. They act as an advocate for students who are experiencing difficulties and roadblocks. They are a consultant, helping students figure out their goals and how to achieve them. And they are a cheerleader, believing in students who do not believe in themselves. I take on these roles, and more, with my students.
- *Good teachers know their subject matter.* To stay abreast of changes in my field, I read scholarly publications, attend professional conferences, and network with colleagues. To keep courses interesting for the students and myself, I change textbooks and experiment with different learning activities. I engage in scholarly activities that enhance my expertise, and help students see the link between research and teaching.
- *Good teachers involve students in the learning process.* I see myself as a partner in learning rather than as a dispenser of wisdom. My job is *not* to fill students' heads with what I know. Instead, I try to communicate a passion for the subject matter and a sense that we are on a knowledge journey together. My responsibility is to create a situation where learning can occur

and to encourage each student's contribution to the learning process. My goal is a busy, noisy classroom where students are engaged in learning.

- *Good teachers help students learn how to use the knowledge they acquire.* Instead of just memorizing material for an exam, I want students to internalize the concepts and know how to apply the concepts in their work. If students made an A in my class but did not know how to use their knowledge to improve the quality of life for children and families, I would consider myself a failure as a teacher.

I am fortunate to have had many good teachers in my life, and I want to touch people's lives the way they touched mine. Of course, there are days when I feel inadequate as a teacher. Rather than discouraging me, this challenges me to try even harder. Just as every student has the potential for success, every teacher has the potential to excel in the classroom.

TEACHING METHODOLOGY, COURSE ASSIGNMENTS, AND MOTIVATIONAL TECHNIQUES

A variety of methods are used to actively engage students in the learning process and to help students apply knowledge instead of just memorizing it. I try to show students the purpose of learning the material and how they would use it in both their personal and professional lives. Some of the methods I use include:

- PowerPoint presentations—I give mini-lectures enhanced by PowerPoint slides. I post the slides on WebCT, even when I don't lecture, so students can review the key points.
- Role plays—couple having an argument; parents disciplining a child; adolescents with differing identity statuses.
- Case studies—comparison of parent education approaches; treatment plan for a family in crisis.
- Debates—Should pregnant women using cocaine be jailed for child endangerment? Should gay couples be allowed to marry?

- Small group discussions—stereotypes and strengths of ethnic families; ethical dilemmas related to assisted suicide.
- Panel discussions—adult children caring for aging parents; transition to parenthood; couples married fifty or more years.
- Guest speakers from community organizations—National Alliance for the Mentally Ill, Parents and Friends of Lesbians and Gays, and La Casa Domestic Violence Shelter.
- Field trips—arranged for students to observe teen drug court in session and to meet with the judge afterwards.

Course Assignments

Student assignments are developed to encourage critical thinking, oral and written communication, and application of course concepts. The assignments include:

- *Using Novels to Analyze Families:* Students select a novel that describes a family problem. They evaluate the family's functioning using two conceptual models, and then specify the areas they would focus on in therapy with the family.
- *Case Studies:* The midterm in one class consists of three case studies, each with ten questions. They select two of the three cases, and then answer five of the ten questions for each case. They have three weeks to analyze the case studies. The midterm is presented in **Appendix B**.
- *Observation Paper:* Students observe and interview two adolescents who differ by gender, age, ethnicity, or social class. They compare and contrast the adolescents' development, looking for patterns as well as unique differences.
- *Program Evaluation:* Students select an evidence-based parenting education program and prepare a thirty-minute presentation with PowerPoint slides and informative handouts. They describe the program and evaluate it on specific criteria such as the qualifications of the developer, the research supporting program effectiveness, and the quality of the materials provided.

- *Book Critique:* Students compare and contrast two books about parenting written for a lay audience. The students determine the intended audience of the books and then evaluate the books based on theoretical approach and the appropriateness of the methods described.

Motivational Techniques

A variety of techniques are used to motivate students and help them succeed:

- Before the first day of class, I send students a personal e-mail, welcoming them to class; reminding them of the day, time, and location of the class; and encouraging them to purchase the textbook.
- I get to know the students personally. I greet them as they enter class, and I call on them by name during class. When they share important events in their lives, I follow up later by asking questions such as, "How is your mother recovering from surgery?" or "How did your job interview go?"
- To encourage students to come to class, I try to make class interesting and engaging by interspersing activities with mini-lectures.
- I tell stories, sometimes from my own life, to illustrate key learning concepts. Students tell me they remember the stories for years.
- In-class activities are developed on the premise that students have read the required reading before class. This encourages students to come prepared.
- To relieve anxiety about memorizing large amounts of material for an exam, I let students bring a 3 × 5 card with notes to each exam. I also give them a three-minute "Magic Moment" to look in their notes during the exam. This encourages students to organize their notes and to clarify their thinking about what is important.
- Students receive bonus points for good attendance and class participation, but there are no penalties for absences.
- Instead of giving extra-credit assignments, I occasionally give a bonus question on an exam or do an in-class activity that will earn extra points on the next exam.

EVALUATION OF TEACHING

PERCENT OF STUDENTS WHO STRONGLY AGREE OR AGREE

Item	FCS 546 N = 18 Spring 2007	FCS 583 N = 15 Spring 2008	FCS 589 N = 17 Fall 2008	MSW 597 N = 8 Fall 2008
Class sessions were organized	100%	100%	100%	100%
Presented in an understandable manner	100%	100%	100%	100%
Appropriate examples used	100%	100%	100%	100%
Stimulated interest in course material	91%	100%	93%	100%
Knowledgeable about subject matter	91%	100%	100%	100%
Concerned that students learn the material	91%	100%	100%	100%
Stimulated student participation	100%	100%	100%	100%
Receptive to new ideas and others' viewpoints	91%	100%	100%	100%

Representative Student Comments

- *"Class was very well organized and kept my attention."*
- *"I always felt comfortable sharing my opinions."*
- *"She allowed for learning through participation."*
- *"The assignments really related to what we were doing and helped me grasp the concepts better."*

Complete documentation related to student course evaluations is presented in **Appendix C**.

Peer Evaluation

Dr. Brenda Seevers, professor in agricultural and extension education, observed me in the FCS 589 (Family Crises) class. She evaluated my teaching in five areas: clarity, variability, enthusiasm, task-oriented behavior, and student opportunity to learn material. These five areas were chosen based on effective teaching behaviors associated with student achievement. Her comments were very positive. She concluded the evaluation by stating:

> *It was a pleasure to observe Dr. Devall in the classroom. She is passionate and enthusiastic about her profession, the topic, and her students. Additionally, she has mastered the organization and delivery required for effective teaching. Finally, she exhibits a genuine care and concern for each student.*

The complete peer evaluation is included in **Appendix D**.

HONORS RELATED TO TEACHING

I feel fortunate to have been nominated for teaching awards at the college, university, and national levels and to have been chosen a recipient for some (see the next table). Evidence related to these awards is presented in **Appendix E**.

Date	Title	Awarded By	Level
2009	NMSU Regents Professorship (nominated)	New Mexico State University	University
2002	Food and Agricultural Sciences Excellence in College and University Teaching Award (nominated)	National Association of State Universities and Land-Grant Colleges	National
2000	Distinguished Teaching Award	College of Agriculture and Home Economics, NMSU	College
1998	Who's Who Among America's Teachers	Who's Who Among America's Teachers	National
1997	Donald C. Roush Award for Teaching Excellence	New Mexico State University	University

TEACHING IMPROVEMENT ACTIVITIES

Attending workshops on teaching keeps me energized and excited about my chosen profession. For example, I attended a workshop in 2008 on team-based learning. We were taught how to motivate students to work together and increase student responsibility for learning material prior to class. I recently tried some of the methods in a graduate class. The class was divided into three equal groups and given several learning activities to complete individually and as a team. The activities started off with simple concepts and then got progressively more difficult. The final activity required the teams to apply several theories to four vignettes. For each activity, students received points based on their individual score and team score. Students were very focused on learning the material and helping each other grasp the key concepts. They enjoyed the team competition and evaluated the class period positively. See **Appendix F** for documentation related to this and other teaching improvement activities.

ADVISING RESPONSIBILITIES AND COMMITTEE WORK

Instead of relying on staff or an advising center, faculty members in the Family and Consumer Sciences Department advise our own undergraduate and graduate students (see the next table). I take a personal interest in students and develop a mentoring relationship that extends far beyond what classes to take. We discuss career plans, internship and job opportunities, scholarships, and participation in professional development.

Year	Undergraduate Students	Graduate Students (Chair)	Graduate Students (Committee Member)
2009	53	10	18
2008	48	9	17
2007	52	8	20
2006	45	12	22
2005	40	18	29

Committee Memberships

I have served on many committees related to teaching and student learning. At the department level, I was a member of the curriculum committee for many years. I helped restructure the undergraduate curriculum in family and child science to meet course requirements for the Certified Family Life Educator credential in my profession. At the college level, I served on the advising committee that developed a handbook and a workshop for new faculty. At the university level, I serve on the outcomes assessment committee. We evaluate how departments use direct and indirect measures of student learning to improve their instruction. At the national level, I was a member of the committee that reviewed portfolios for those wishing to obtain the Certified Family Life Educator credential.

STUDENT ACHIEVEMENT

Year	Student	Award	Given By	Level
2009	Noel Martinez	Student Unit Scholarship	New Mexico Association of Family and Consumer Sciences	State
2008	Terri Gutierrez	Outstanding Graduate Student	Gamma Sigma Delta Honor Society	College
	Terri Gutierrez	Dean's Award of Excellence for Graduate Students	College of Agriculture and Home Economics, NMSU	College
	Ashley Martin	Dean's Award of Excellence for Undergraduate Students	College of Agriculture and Home Economics, NMSU	College
2007	Christine Ross	Outstanding Student in Family and Consumer Sciences	College of Agriculture and Home Economics, NMSU	College

Year	Student	Award	Given By	Level
2007	Masey Doss	Mary Gillespie Scholarship	New Mexico Association of Family and Consumer Sciences	State
2005	Erica Velez	Student of the Year	New Mexico Association of Family and Consumer Sciences	State
	Erica Velez	Merit Scholarship for Graduate Assistants	Graduate School, NMSU	University

Documentation related to student awards is included in **Appendix G**.

Recent Advisee Accomplishments
- Nicole Cuzzola finished her bachelor's degree in family and child science, and then obtained two graduate degrees simultaneously in social work and public health administration.
- While pursuing her master's degree in marriage and family therapy, Terri Gutierrez also completed requirements to become a Certified Child Life Specialist. Within six months of graduation, she took and passed the required national exams in both areas.
- Merranda Marin completed her master's degree in marriage and family therapy, and then went on to complete a Ph.D. in counseling and educational psychology. She was recently hired to teach at the University of Texas–El Paso.

Comments from former students:

- *"Dr. Devall is a devoted educator who puts student learning as her top priority."*

- *"The Family and Consumer Sciences Department would not be what it is today without the committed efforts of Dr. Devall."*
- *"Dr. Devall has been a wonderful mentor to me. . . . I have found her professionalism to be truly inspiring."*

MOST SIGNIFICANT TEACHING ACCOMPLISHMENTS

Although I am honored by the recognition I have received for teaching, what means the most to me is having made a difference in someone's life. James was a burly middle-aged construction worker who started his bachelor's degree after being injured on the job. He had never considered going to college because he had been told repeatedly that he was not college material. I was his teacher in his first college course. He was anxious about his ability to succeed. However, I saw great potential in James and told him so. He gained confidence, became a leader among his classmates, and was elected president of the student club in the department. He went on to graduate with honors in family and child science, and then to complete a master's degree in our field. Today he is a respected professional. He told me that my belief in him turned his life around and that he tries to do the same for the clients he serves.

Another accomplishment was promoting the major of family and child science and increasing its visibility on campus and in the community. When I came to NMSU in 1991, there were ten undergraduates and two graduate students in the major. The only other faculty in my discipline was the department head, who taught only one graduate course per semester. I realized that if I did not grow the major, I might soon be out of a job! The only way for one person to teach all the courses in the undergraduate major was to offer them on a rotating basis. So, I taught six different classes my first year and six completely different classes the second year. I worked very hard to be an engaging teacher in the classroom, to recruit students into the major, and to publicize the field. By 1994, I had increased the number of majors to 110 undergraduates and 38 master's students. By 1997, there were over 200 undergraduate and 50 graduate students. In 2005, the department was able to hire two more faculty members in the major.

APPENDICES

Appendix A: Course Syllabi
Appendix B: Examinations
Appendix C: Student Course Evaluations
Appendix D: Peer Evaluation of Teaching
Appendix E: Teaching Awards
Appendix F: Teaching Improvement Activities
Appendix G: Student Achievement

CHAPTER TWENTY-TWO

FISH, WILDLIFE, AND CONSERVATION ECOLOGY

Wiebke J. Boeing

Department of Fish, Wildlife and Conservation Ecology
New Mexico State University
Spring 2010

CONTENTS

1. INTRODUCTION

Since 1997, I have taught college-level classes in fisheries, natural resources, and biology. I have been an assistant professor in the Department of Fish, Wildlife and Conservation Ecology at New Mexico State University since 2004.

I am a passionate and enthusiastic teacher, and although teaching requires an enormous amount of energy, I find it very energizing at the same time. In my opinion, 5 percent of students will do well in a class and 5 percent poorly—independent of the quality of the teacher. However, for 90 percent of the students, we as teachers have significant impact. This portfolio has been created as an effective way of documenting and communicating my efforts to improve my teaching by implementing different teaching methods that enable our diverse student body to not just pass tests but to truly learn. This will help to ensure the success of our students and provide our workforce with capable individuals.

Below are five key elements of my teaching portfolio:

- Promoting critical thinking and effective oral and written communication
- Multiple teaching strategies engaging students
- Student evaluations in the two highest ratings in all categories
- *William H. Gates Teaching Award* for Excellence in Freshman Instruction
- *USDA Higher Education Challenge Grant* to place students from collaborating New Mexico institutions in internships throughout the world

2. TEACHING RESPONSIBILITIES

COURSES TAUGHT AT NMSU, 2005–2008

Class	Credits/Frequency	Students	Average Enrollment
Principles of Natural Resource Management (WLSC 255)	3-credit lecture; once a semester	Majors and nonmajors; required	26

COURSES TAUGHT AT NMSU, 2005–2008 (*continued*)

Class	Credits/Frequency	Students	Average Enrollment
Techniques of Natural Resource Management (WLSC 355)	3-credit lecture/ lab; once a year; cotaught	Majors, required	24
Ichthyology (WLSC 482)	3-credit lecture/lab; once every other year	Majors, elective	27
Undergraduate Seminar (WLSC 402)	1-credit seminar; once every third year	Majors, elective	12
Graduate Seminar (WLSC 515)	1-credit seminar; once every third year	Majors, elective	12

At New Mexico State University (NMSU), I teach three undergraduate classes each year with approximately twenty-five students per class. Two are required core classes in natural resource management, and one is an elective ichthyology (fish ecology and taxonomy) class. Two of those classes include a laboratory. In addition, our faculty rotates teaching the undergraduate and the graduate seminar, and I advise approximately thirty undergraduates and two graduate students each semester in both academic and personal issues.

3. TEACHING AND ADVISING PHILOSOPHY AND OBJECTIVES

The mind is not a vessel to be filled, but a fire to be ignited.
—PLUTARCH (CIRCA 45–125 A.D.)

My primary goal is to spark my students' interest in the intriguing and exciting world of ecology and science and turn them into capable and thoughtful natural resource managers. Our students obtain jobs all over the country, and thus it is impossible to provide them with all the facts to manage the diverse natural resources, especially in the face of an ever-changing environment. A contribution to society at large is to educate students who are able to assess problems pertaining to natural resource management—students with the capability to choose the best option with the most likely positive outcome and then share their analysis with others. Therefore, my focus is on teaching my students critical thinking and effective written and oral communication skills. This is best accomplished by creating a safe environment.

- *Encourage Critical Thinking:* This is an essential tool for evaluating information and independently finding solutions. Although some concepts are crucial, critical thinking is more important than memorizing mere facts. A thinking student will often be able to reconstruct concepts even after facts and figures have been forgotten. However, teaching an abstract concept is easier said than done, and students exhibit different levels of thinking when they attend our classes. My role is to be a facilitator and guide and to provide *all* students with a safe environment and to expose them to various perspectives that are not wrong or right, just different (*see Teaching and Advising Strategies and Methodologies*).
- *Build Communication Skills:* Such skills are necessary to be effective in natural resource management. Even the greatest ideas just stay ideas if they cannot be communicated and implemented. Our students need to be able to correspond with natural resource stakeholders and be able to convincingly convey the information that is in the best interest for the sustainability of the natural resource and for all entities involved. Next to national issues, our students also need to be versed in international issues, since natural resource issues extend across borders. Refined communication skills are also key to successful job applications. Both oral and written communication are fundamental parts of my classes (*see Teaching and Advising Strategies and Methodologies*).
- *Create a Safe Environment:* This encourages participation and open dialogue among students and also with me. My intention is to create an environment where any student with the interest to learn can do so. Therefore, it is my responsibility to set the tone and atmosphere in the classroom. I have learned that students are best approached with honesty, respect, and a sense of humor. If we as educators invest the time in our students and encourage them to raise their own bar of achievement, they will. Therefore, I make every effort to spend time with them and attempt to connect with them on a personal level. In doing so, I have seen them excel in my classroom.

- *Promote Active Advising:* The system that supports my teaching also serves as a foundation for my advising. I maintain an open-door policy and take as much time to listen and advise students as they need. I advise students on academic questions (what classes to take), career opportunities (internships, jobs, graduate schools), and personal issues (time management, family problems). To accomplish constructive advising, it is my responsibility to be familiar with resources available on campus, in the community, nationally, and even internationally, and I need to be able to assess when to send a student with emotional issues to our professional counselors.

4. TEACHING AND ADVISING STRATEGIES AND METHODOLOGIES

> *Tell me and I will forget.*
> *Show me and I might remember.*
> *Involve me and I will understand.*
> —CHINESE PROVERB

Research has shown that an **active learning environment is key to success**, especially for minority and nontraditional students. By using multiple approaches, *all* students with different learning styles can grasp important concepts. To implement my teaching objectives (*see Teaching and Advising Philosophy and Objectives*), I use a variety of methods in my classes, including *traditional lectures, teamwork, assignments*, and *student presentations*. I also incorporate *field trips* in the curriculum and see it as a very effective method in bringing a multisensory approach to learning. In all classes I use multiple methods to help students learn (*see Appendix A, Representative Syllabus*).

- *Traditional Lectures:* I design my lectures to twenty minutes or less, which is the time span students can follow in a concentrated manner. Typically I have PowerPoint presentations and will frequently switch to the Internet to show a short movie or so on. I utilize the board for complex concepts. This slows the pace down and gives students more time to process information. Throughout my lecture, I ask questions to strive to keep the students engaged and challenged.

- *Teamwork:* Students within teams develop a bond and often friendships. These connections provide a support system for each student. It also creates natural competition that challenges them to do their best. The teamwork pushes the students to evaluate information, listen to different opinions, and argue their own side, which promotes critical thinking as well as communication skills. For example, in my Principles of Natural Resource Management (WLSC 255) class, I place students into diverse teams of five to six students. We choose controversial issues and discuss them in class, whereby I assign what side of the topic each team has to argue. This allows students to argue more freely (since it might not represent their actual opinion). When taking quizzes, students first take the quiz individually and then as a team. This results in students teaching each other.

- *Assignments and Student Presentations:* Students often have to complete homework to keep them thinking about the subject outside of class. For example, in Principles of Natural Resource Management (WLSC 255), as a major class assignment, each student has to develop a management plan. The topic is left intentionally broad so students can work on something they are passionate about, which typically leads to more enthusiasm and a better end product. The format of the management plan follows the professional scientific writing norm, and students have to include six citations, four of which have to be peer-reviewed articles. At the end of the semester, students present their management plan using PowerPoint. Initial concerns are usually replaced by pride in their achievement.

- *Field Trips:* In my classes, all students are required to attend field trips. For example, we go to the Mescalero Tribal Fish Hatchery for a day and get hands-on experience handling fish and provide needed labor to a fish hatchery that is run by only two people. In subsequent classes, we discuss the experience and think about impacts of fish stocking on natural ecosystems.

- *Independent Research:* Next to graduate students, I also support and advise up to ten undergraduate students in independent research projects. I encourage students to come up with their own ideas for their research or provide them with ideas depending on comfort level. I some cases, the undergraduates coauthor peer-reviewed publications. All undergraduates who complete their research give a poster presentation at a scientific meeting. My student Justin Mapula won the prize for best student poster at the New Mexico/Arizona American Fisheries Society meeting.

5. STUDENT EVALUATIONS

Students evaluate instructors at the end of the semester in eight different categories on effectiveness, attitude, and fairness. Overall scoring occurs in five ratings, where the lowest rating is "unsatisfactory" (0–20) and the highest is "very commendable" (80–100). I am gratified that students in my classes have consistently placed me in the top two levels and my ratings are always above 78 (*see Appendix B, Student Evaluations*). In the next table, I summarize my scores in my different classes. For WLSC 255 and advising, the weighted average of both semesters each year is presented.

STUDENT EVALUATIONS OF TEACHING AND ADVISING

Class	2005	2006	2007	2008
WLSC 255	81	85.5	84.5	84
WLSC 355	78	83	79	80
WLSC 402		95		
WLSC 482		86		81
WLSC 515	92			
Undergraduate advising	93.5	86	79.5	97
Graduate advising	90	80	80	100

Typical written remarks from students: *(see Appendix B, Student Evaluations)*:

Wow! Overall, the best class I've had this semester.

I love Dr. Boeing as an instructor; she made me see things differently and look at things in a new perspective.

Wiebke is a fantastic teacher. She is very knowledgeable, enthusiastic, helpful and wants her student to do well. Very reasonable and fair. Excellent humor.

6. PROFESSIONAL DEVELOPMENT, SERVICE, AND PRESENTATIONS

The scientific world is fluid, and there are constant discoveries and new views to be accepted, questioned, or reinforced. It is my responsibility to stay informed and keep up to date with the latest peer-reviewed literature and to keep my lecture material current. Similarly, teaching methods need to be tested and refined in order to become the most effective teacher possible and to continue my professional growth.

- *Classroom Observations by Peers:* For constructive feedback on my teaching, I regularly invite faculty to observe my classroom (*see Appendix C, Letters from Peers*). Thereby, I purposefully include peers from different disciplines who have previously won prestigious teaching awards or recognitions. My observers praise my efforts to have students participate and use active learning methods:

  In my opinion, most students remained engaged in the discussions, which I believe reinforced their learning of the key concepts that Wiebke wanted to teach in that session.

  —Dr. Octavio Ramirez
  (Two Awards as Outstanding Professor of the Year)

  I thoroughly enjoyed my visit to Wiebke's class and am pleased to report that she is an excellent teacher and motivator and that her students were fully engaged in learning.

  —Dr. April Ulery (Three Teaching Awards)

- *Professional Development:* I regularly attend workshops on different teaching methods as well as skills dealing with diverse students at the NMSU Teaching Academy and have over 150 hours of documented professional development during the past five years (*see Appendix D, Teaching Academy Attendance*).

- *Undergraduate Curriculum:* I also actively participate in improving student learning at NMSU. I was the chair of the undergraduate curriculum in the Department of Fish, Wildlife and Conservation Ecology when we developed our new undergraduate curriculum. One of the crucial changes we made was to require an internship for all our students. This hands-on experience will help our students and increase their motivation, experience, and networking abilities as well as benefit the natural resource agencies (*see Appendix E, Internship Opportunities*).
- *Teaching Conferences and Presentations:* Since 2005 I have attended three teaching conferences (*see Appendix F, Teaching Conference*). These include the Academic Programs Committee on Organization and Policy (ACOP) Western Regional Teaching Symposium at Colorado State University in 2005 and the Sun Teaching Conference in El Paso in 2006. Additionally, I was a committee member of the ACOP Western Regional Teaching Symposium in Las Cruces in 2008 and was responsible for organizing the poster session. I also contributed a poster presentation to the symposium with the title *"Combining Scholarship and Teaching with Recruitment—How to Kill Two Birds with One Stone."* In 2008, I also gave an invited career presentation for about two hundred high school students titled *"Professional Dreaming."*

7. TEACHING RECOGNITIONS, AWARDS, AND GRANTS

I was honored to receive the William H. Gates Teaching Award for Excellence in Freshman Instruction in 2001 from Louisiana State University as the best teaching assistant (*see Appendix G, Grants and Awards*).

In 2008, I received a USDA Higher Education Challenge Grant for $475,889 for three years with the title "Student Experiential Learning in the Natural Resource Sciences through Summer Internships and Professional Mentoring—a Joint Project Proposal." The grant is a large collaborative effort among ten co-principal investigators (PI), whereby I am the leading PI (*see Appendix G, Grants and Awards*). The grant allows us to place students from multiple institutions across New Mexico into natural resource internships around the world, as well as form student teams to conduct independent research. These are valuable hands-on experiences for students that will help them succeed.

8. TEACHING GOALS

As a teacher I am constantly looking for ways to improve student learning and am seeking ongoing challenges. The four following teaching goals that I am currently pursuing and plan on implementing this year are:

- Use cards with names and call on randomly drawn students to repeat important concepts that were covered in that particular lecture.
- Find other field trip opportunities that offer hands-on experience for my students; in particular, I want to make better connections with the Mesilla Bosque State Park just outside Las Cruces.
- Document student learning, comparing student test results at the beginning versus the end of the semester using a test with twenty identical questions.
- Develop a log in order to identify a successful student advising system.

9. APPENDICES

A. Representative Syllabus
B. Student Evaluations
C. Letters from Peers
D. Teaching Academy Attendance
E. Internship Opportunities
F. Teaching Conferences
G. Awards and Grants

CHAPTER TWENTY-THREE

GOVERNMENT

Nancy V. Baker

Department of Government
New Mexico State University
Spring 2010

CONTENTS

PREFACE

Six years ago, I received an e-mail that captured my sense of wonder and love for teaching. It was from a former student who commanded a group of young Marines in Iraq. During the long boring hours waiting for action, he said he started instructing his men about constitutional law, a class he had had with me. Using chalk on the side of his tank, he tried to explain *Marbury* v. *Madison*, the Supreme Court ruling that established judicial review. Under the best of circumstances, it is not an easy case to convey, but his men got it. He is now back home, in graduate school. And he wants to teach.

His e-mail touched me and made me reflect on my own teaching. I see this portfolio as an opportunity to assess what I do in the classroom, why I do it, and what has worked. In addition to this personal goal, I hope my portfolio can provide guidance to others both in teaching and in constructing their own portfolios documenting their achievements.

TEACHING PHILOSOPHY AND STRATEGIES

The relationship between professor and student is ancient and much more profound than the contemporary view that teachers are the purveyors of an educational product and students are the consumers. I believe that the obligations of a teacher are much more complex and compelling than that. As a professor, I seek to:

1. Impart knowledge
2. Strengthen critical thinking skills and the ability to apply information
3. Build communication skills
4. Support the development of an active citizenry
5. Model professional and ethical behaviors
6. Inspire a lifelong joy of learning

I approach each student with the optimistic expectation that she or he is as passionate to learn as I am to teach, and this expectation has been met more often than not. I experience genuine pleasure in the iterative process of learning and teaching. Finally, I feel privileged to be teaching about politics, because I believe that understanding politics empowers every individual and enriches society as a whole. To meet the six goals delineated above, I employ certain strategies that have become guiding principles:

1. **To impart information**, I strive to be thoroughly versed and current in the subject that I am teaching, even in classes taught a dozen times. Yet knowledge alone is not sufficient; I also have to be well organized and clear. I am cognizant of different learning styles, so I supplement lectures with class simulations, political games, and discussions, and I incorporate newer technologies such as PowerPoint and Blackboard. I have found Web-based tools useful even for the traditional classroom, to communicate with students and post additional readings. Prior to each of my freshman classes, I post an outline of the upcoming lecture online, including visuals and links to current news stories. Students at all levels comment on the relevance of course material. One freshman wrote, *I liked the incorporation of news events and analysis of how those events affect the world.* A senior added, *Baker did a wonderful job of incorporating a lot about the modern presidency, which I've missed out on in the past.*

2. **To strengthen critical thinking skills and the ability to apply the information**, I aim to be rigorous and challenging because I believe students are poorly served when we lower expectations. To foster learning, I give timely and extensive feedback, provide review sheets that require students to synthesize material, and pose hypothetical political and legal scenarios on exams. Said one student, *The tests really made me have to learn.* Simulations also develop critical thinking, particularly the mock trials. As one student wrote, *Mock trials were a great way of testing our knowledge, critical thinking and writing skills.*

3. **To build communication skills**, I require writing assignments in all upper-division and graduate classes, as well as class presentations, simulations, essay exams, and discussions at all levels. Students in my graduate seminars must orally present their papers to each other for constructive criticism prior to the final draft. In the process, students learn how to explain their work; other students give them useful

feedback; and, by reading a peer's work, their own editing skills are enhanced. To target graduate student writing problems, I created a workshop to cover everything from basic grammar to research questions. Writing and public speaking are important for those who plan to work in the public sector, but they can trigger student anxiety so I try to foster a comfortable environment. This graduate student noted: *The conversational atmosphere—which was intimidating at first—became an important part of the learning process. It taught me how to take a different perspective and apply or analyze it for myself.*

4. **To support the development of an active citizenry**, I use assignments and extra credit opportunities to encourage students to become engaged in politics—from registering to vote to working on a campaign. In addition, I supervise student internships with public officials and nonprofit agencies. As one student said, *Dr. Baker encourages us to take what we learn and put it to practical use.* I want to give students the tools to think critically and use reasoned argument when they debate public issues. To promote student engagement, I keep my own political preferences to myself (except insofar as my values inform who I am as a person). This is particularly difficult yet important to do in a class on politics. Students from the introductory through the graduate level have commented on this. One freshman observed: *Prof. Baker was completely unbiased. I still don't know what her views are or what party she supports.*

5. **To model professional and ethical behaviors**, I treat students with respect. I guard against arbitrary treatment by writing clear syllabi and policies and then following them. I respect student time by not missing meetings or canceling class. I seek to be patient and caring, yet never patronizing. This is critical because students often feel overwhelmed. One freshman wrote, *She talked to me many times and helped me through rough spots.* Others said they felt comfortable asking questions; one wrote, *I never felt like the idiot that I know I am when I asked a question or didn't understand.* I pay attention to all students, not just high achievers or class talkers, and am interested in their aspirations and the obstacles they face. I also recognize that women in my field remain the anomaly, although less so

than when I started to teach. So I am conscious of modeling the role of a female professor. One student explained what it meant to her: *She has a wonderful intellect and serves as a female role model in higher education for me.*

6. **To inspire a lifelong joy of learning for its own sake**, I seek to create an engaging classroom experience. I use voice modulation, eye contact, humor, and energy to capture and hold students' attention. I never just read from my notes or the book, except for direct quotes. I want to communicate my passion for the field and for learning. Students have remarked, *She made it a fun course,* and *Fun & hard!* (See Appendix A.)

TEACHING RESPONSIBILITIES

My formal teaching load is three courses per semester, usually a lower division, upper division, and master's. In addition, I supervise independent studies, internships, experiential learning, and thesis work for graduate and undergraduate students. As department head, my load has dropped to one/two, although I still supervise a lot of independent student work. Since coming to NMSU in 1989, I have taught nineteen different courses: three lower division (one in the Honors College), nine upper division (one in Honors), and seven at the graduate level. All but two were new preparations. I also created two one-credit workshops: Scholarly and Professional Writing, and Preparing for the Law School Admissions Test. (See Appendix B.)

Current Course Rotation

- *Govt 596 International Law:* explores sovereignty, jurisdiction, and human rights
- *Govt 550 Seminar in American Politics:* examines institutions, actors, and policy challenges
- *Govt 501 Scholarly and Professional Writing:* covers graduate research and writing
- *Govt 397/593 Law and Sex:* studies sex discrimination, sexual harassment, same-sex marriage, and other legal issues related to sex and gender
- *Govt 394 Civil Liberties:* explores case law and political context of key constitutional rights

- *Govt 344 American Presidency:* examines the office, its history, powers, relations to other political actors, and impact on domestic and international policy
- *Govt 110G Introduction to Political Science:* explores the entire field, from political concepts and ideologies, to comparative political systems and international relations

Research Supervision

I have chaired eighteen master's theses/research projects in government, and served on 116 master's committees and 2 Ph.D. committees (in other departments). In addition, I have supervised twenty-one graduate independent studies and directed readings. Many former students have gone on to doctoral programs, and some are now colleagues at NMSU and other universities.

I believe strongly in research opportunities for undergraduate scholars as well, and have supervised twenty undergraduate honors thesis students and two Ronald McNair scholars. I have directed 88 independent studies and supervised 103 internships. I regularly serve as a judge or moderator of the Undergraduate Research Symposium held on campus each spring. One year, as acting director of the Honors Program, I organized the symposium.

Campus and Community Outreach

Much student learning occurs outside the classroom. Recognizing the value of less formal venues, I have presented dozens of talks to campus organizations through the years, as well as more than a dozen guest lectures, generally on aspects of U.S. law or politics.

Beyond the campus, I consider community presentations and media publication as part of the broad educational role of faculty at a land grant institution such as NMSU. I have given dozens of public talks—more than twenty-five since 2001—that focus on legal issues, elections, and my presidency research. I have been invited to speak by various organizations, such as the Academy for Learning in Retirement, local chapters of the American Civil Liberties Union, and the Las Cruces Rotary. Statewide, I have spoken before the New Mexico League of Women Voters and Press Women of New Mexico, and lectured at a continuing education seminar put on by the state bar association. Nationally I have given public addresses at the Woodrow Wilson Center in Washington, D.C., and Loyola Marymount University, among others. During one sabbatical leave, I gave guest lectures at Istanbul University and Bogazici University, Istanbul.

My research on the U.S. attorney general has brought multiple media interviews, including with the *New York Times*, National Public Radio Weekend Edition, the *Economist*, the *Los Angeles Times*, and CBS-News, among others, as well as campus and local print and broadcast outlets. I have published opinion pieces with NMSU, Las Cruces, and El Paso newspapers. These efforts reflect my commitment to share my scholarship with a wide audience.

TEACHING EFFECTIVENESS

I gauge my effectiveness in the classroom through teaching-related honors, teaching-related activities and publications, student responses on course evaluations, and feedback from alumni. (See Appendix C for documentation in this area.)

TEACHING-RELATED AWARDS AND HONORS (SINCE 2000)

NMSU Regents Professorship	2009
Highest academic honor at the university	
Westhafer Award for Excellence in Teaching, NMSU	2005
Top teaching recognition at the university, given only every two years	
Outstanding Teaching in Political Science	2005, 2001, 1999
American Political Science Association and Pi Sigma Alpha, political science honor society	
Donald C. Roush Award for Teaching Excellence, NMSU	2000, 1992
Recipients selected in part by graduating seniors	
NMSU Pi Sigma Alpha Government Professor of the Year	2001, 2000

Selected Publications and Presentations

"The Provocative Classroom: Challenging Students to Challenge Their Assumptions." NMSU Teaching Academy, 2006

"In Praise of Provocation: Professors, Democracy and the Public University." Westhafer Address, NMSU Awards Ceremony, 2005

"Teaching Law to Undergraduates: The Value and Limits of Interdisciplinary Pre-law Studies." Western Association of Pre-law Advisers, Albuquerque, 2001

"Using the Socratic Teaching Method with Undergraduates." Invited presentation. NMSU Center for Educational Development, 2000

"Oyez, Oyez, Oyez: The Trials of Teaching the Supreme Court." *PS: Political Science and Politics,* June 1994.

Student Assessments

I have consistently received high student evaluations at every level. From 1998 to 2008, for example, my average student evaluation at the lower-division level was 3.8 on a 4.0 scale (4.0 is the highest); my upper division was 3.93; and my graduate 3.9. The next table provides a breakdown of student responses to questions pertaining to *Attitude toward students, Knowledge of subject,* and *Overall, how would you grade the teaching in this course?*

	Fall 2005	*Spring 2006*	*Fall 2006*	*Spring 2007*
Attitude				
Intro to P.S.	3.94	3.9	3.9	3.8
Upper division	3.94	4.0	4.0	4.0
Graduate	3.86	3.9	4.0	4.0
Knowledge				
Intro to P.S.	3.97	4.0	4.0	3.9
Upper division	3.94	4.0	4.0	4.0
Graduate	4.0	4.0	4.0	4.0
Overall				
Intro to P.S.	3.6 (n = 32)	3.94 (n = 31)	3.7 (n = 41)	3.7 (n = 44)
Upper division	3.94 (n = 17)	4.0 (n = 29)	4.0 (n = 20)	4.0 (n = 17)
Graduate	4.0 (n = 7)	4.0 (n = 10)	3.8 (n = 6)	4.0 (n = 8)

Since becoming department head, I have taught fewer classes but maintained high evaluations. For example, in fall 2007, students rated my upper-division class overall as 3.94 and my graduate as 3.9. In spring 2008, my graduate seminar was given a 4.0.

The most valuable component of the evaluations are the open-ended questions. This is where I learn that I speak too quickly (which I try in vain to address) and that students disagree with one another on the value of class discussions. Overwhelmingly, though, student remarks are encouraging. Said one graduate student: *She leads the discussion well by asking provocative questions. She is knowledgeable and enthusiastic.* Another wrote, *She walked us through theory and attached it to current reality.* Undergraduates remarked, *She always encouraged us to 'think outside the box';* and *So many of those who attain a PhD. lose touch with the 100 & 200 level of teaching, but Dr. Baker did not.*

Selected Alumni Feedback

I have been fortunate to maintain contact with scores of former students, initially through letters and visits, and now e-mail. In 2008, I decided to facilitate that process by joining one of the social networking Web sites, Facebook. In six months, I reconnected with 110 former students, primarily more recent graduates. Among their comments are several reflections on my classes:

- *I really miss your midterms.*
- *I would LOVE to be in your Presidency class this semester.*
- *Dr. Baker! Every time I read about some juicy cases before the Supreme Court I think of you.*

Several have told me that a class of mine changed their career plans. Wrote one who is now himself a professor: *Did I ever tell you that your civil liberties class cemented my decision to be a poli sci major? You injected life into legal doctrines and constitutional jurisprudence.*

I am especially delighted when alumni share their good news: *You'll be proud to know that I have taught my very own American government course at Baruch College.* From another, *You will be pleased to hear that I got an A- in my first year constitutional law class last semester!*

INSTRUCTIONAL MATERIALS

I employ a variety of assignments to encourage critical thinking and higher-level synthesis. Writing legal briefs, students learn how to critically read a case, draw out the major points, and present that information in a clear and concise manner. Essay questions on exams are designed to trigger deeper reflection and synthesis of course materials, not rote memorization. Even in my large lower-division classes, I assign one essay exam to expose freshmen to this testing style and foster more critical engagement with the material. In my prelaw mock trials, I require a paper outlining both sides of the argument, and an in-class oral argument with students portraying attorneys or Supreme Court justices. Both my presidency class and graduate seminars require research papers ranging in length from 15 to 25 pages. Students in several of my classes are assigned to lead class discussions on the readings. (See Appendix D.)

STUDENT LEARNING

Student work is the ultimate gauge of classroom effectiveness. Students learn not only through lectures, activities, and readings, but also through written feedback on assignments and exams. For it to have an impact, feedback must be timely, so I return graded work within one week.

I see improvement most dramatically on legal briefs, since I customarily assign two or three in the course of a semester. Those who have gone to law school reiterate the value of this exercise, for both writing and critical reading. Even the ability to answer essay exams improves with feedback, as students begin to understand what a good answer entails. For research papers, students submit annotated bibliographies and drafts. I provide them with explicit grading criteria to guide them in polishing their work. Their final products evince stronger organization, deeper research, and better command of the English language and style. (See Appendix E.)

CURRICULUM DEVELOPMENT

I have participated in several invitation-only conferences and seminars. Three seminars—exploring Asian, Southeast Asian, and Islamic issues—expanded my knowledge of subjects often unexplored in undergraduate classes in the United States. I used this material to revise my courses in Introduction to Political Science, International Law, and Women and Politics.

I also have attended conferences to improve my undergraduate prelaw advising. These working sessions led to the revision of the Law and Society program while I was director. I also created a course on Preparing for the Law School Admissions Test and established Law Day, to bring law schools, attorneys, and students together on campus. (See Appendix F.)

LESSONS I'VE LEARNED

Like many professors, I first entered the classroom knowing my academic field but without any training to teach. As a student, I had learned from poor instructors what not to do (read directly from the textbook, for example), and I had a vague sense from the great ones what to try to do (capture the student's imagination). Intuition guided me more than expertise. In the two decades since, I have learned a lot from students, peers, articles and workshops, and self-reflection. I include a few of those lessons here.

First, I have heard colleagues express the belief that as educators, we are faced with a stark choice: to be engaging and flexible, with high enrollments and course evaluations; or to be challenging and principled, with lower enrollments and evaluations, but alumni thanking us years later. The institutional rewards attach to the first model, the sense of professional integrity to the second. I have come to see this as a false dichotomy. Students respond well to environments that are both engaging and challenging. Indeed, they often express that preference on teaching evaluations, giving high "popularity" ratings to classes they also rank as "difficult" or "more difficult" than others of the same level.

Admittedly, course policies must be followed to ensure against arbitrary decisions that benefit or burden only certain students. Due process is an important value. However, a just outcome is an important value as well. The *spirit* that drives the rule cannot be ignored in our quest to enforce the rule without exception. Students at NMSU often have to accommodate work and family demands that those elsewhere do not face; I recognize the need to be flexible in those circumstances. That does not mean providing opportunities or deadlines not available to others. It does mean making equitable adjustments to ensure a level playing field for all to learn.

A second lesson I have learned is this: that the act of teaching is inherently creative. We can unleash that part of ourselves that yearns to paint, to act, to make music, to sculpt, to play. Consider this: a faculty member teaching a 3/3 load must research, write, produce, direct, and perform nine hours of theater each week. That part is easy; the real challenge is that the students are not the audience but costars. The faculty member must bring them into the production and be willing to release enough control to permit those rare but priceless sparks of improvisation, when students take the class to an even higher level.

The third lesson is a brief one. Teaching is work but it is also joy. Even when we are buried under a hundred student papers, we must not forget that.

Table of Appendices

Appendix A   Evidence of teaching strategies
Appendix B   Evidence of teaching responsibilities
Appendix C   Evidence of teaching effectiveness
Appendix D   Samples of instructional materials
Appendix E   Evidence of student learning
Appendix F   Curriculum development activities

CHAPTER TWENTY-FOUR

JUSTICE STUDIES

Heather A. Walsh-Haney

Division of Justice Studies
Florida Gulf Coast University
Spring 2010

CONTENTS

1. Teaching Responsibilities and Syllabi
2. Teaching Philosophy
3. Teaching Strategies
4. Teaching Objectives
5. Curricular Revisions
6. Student Course Feedback and Teaching Evaluation Data
7. Professional Outreach as Evidenced by Presentations, Publications, and Expert Testimony
8. Student Publications and Presentations as Evidence of Student Learning
9. Goals
10. Appendices

TEACHING RESPONSIBILITIES AND SYLLABI

My teaching responsibilities are twofold: (1) to teach courses as required under my Florida Gulf Coast University contract and (2) to ensure that my course content is in keeping with standards of the American Anthropological Association and the American Academy of Forensic Sciences' Forensic Science Education Program

Accreditation Commission. I teach a minimum of three lecture-based and two field-based courses per semester as well as providing at least one practitioner-based seminar (forty contact hours in one week) per semester. I was the instructor of record for eleven courses during the academic year (Table 1). As noted in Table 1, my teaching responsibilities focus on teaching forensic anthropology and human osteology and both undergraduate and graduate-level courses. Enrollment ranged from two to forty-two students for the graduate and undergraduate courses, respectively.

I concurrently chair eleven master's committees. As chair, I guide my students through the development of their quantitative research projects. Indeed, each master's project builds off of my expertise as a physical anthropologist with topics that range from skeletal size and shape differences between males and females, to health status among modern and ancient peoples, to cellular analysis of skeletal age, and tooth loss to establish when an individual died (Table 2).

General Course Responsibilities

My primary course responsibilities are the same no matter the class or education level of the student (undergraduate versus graduate versus practitioner). All of my courses are designed to bring together multiple learning formats (lecture, class discussion, laboratory exercises, oral presentations, films, and group projects) so that I may reach a wide spectrum of student learners, which may broadly include those students who want to learn and those who are unmotivated to learn but are capable. I meet my general course responsibilities through the following methods:

- Present the students with meaningful material that covers new trends and technologies that are tethered to established standards and theories
- Ensure that my class objectives can be integrated into the broader context of the course
- Elevate critical thinking and deemphasize rote memorization
- Teach course information in an enthusiastic manner
- Communicate effectively by defining terms with simple language

TABLE 1. WALSH-HANEY FALL AND SPRING TEACHING LOAD, NUMBERS OF STUDENTS

Course	Course #	Credits	Undergrad vs. Graduate	Semester	Enrollment
Forensic Anthropology	ANT 3520	3	Undergrad	Fall	42
Human Osteology	CCJ 4933	3	Both	Fall	21
Physical Anthropology	ANT 2511	3	Undergrad	Fall	35
Human Identity Practicum	CJE 6748	3	Graduate	Fall	3
Master's Independent Research	CJE 6749	3	Graduate	Fall	2
Bugs, Bones, and Botany	CJE 6629	3	Both	Spring	19
Forensic Anthropology	ANT 3520	3	Undergrad	Spring	41
General Anthropology	ANT 2510	3	Undergrad	Spring	43
Human Osteology	CCJ 6935	3	Both	Spring	16
Human Identity Practicum	CJE 6748	3	Graduate	Spring	3
Master's Independent Research	CJE 6749	3	Graduate	Spring	2
Bugs, Bones, and Botany	CJE 6629	3	Both	Spring	19

TABLE 2. WALSH-HANEY SPRING 2009 MASTER'S STUDENTS
AND CORRESPONDING THESIS TOPIC

Master's Student Name	Project Topic
Anderson, Jennifer	Fluctuating Asymmetries Among African and European Americans
Butler, Alyssa	Mandibular Bone Morphology and Body Mass Indices
Gibson, Laura	Skeletal Anemia in Prehistoric Floridian Hunter-Gatherers
Herrick, Christen	The Origin of Syphilis as Evidenced by the Gautier Collection
Iliopoulos, Minas	Bone Density Fluctuations and Artificial Hormone Delivery Systems
Kish, Chad	TBA
Klienfelder, Deanna	Anterior Tooth Loss as a Tool for Estimating Times Since Death
Roberts, Victoria	TBA
Amanda Pogel	TBA
Shepherd, Katy	Fibular Histology and Age Determination
Webb, Nicole	Cranial Suture Fusion in Tarsiers
Zajilka, Valerie	Air Bag Related Skeletal Injuries in Southwest Florida

- Guarantee the course is organized and begins on time
- Provide hands-on laboratory work and field experience

Graduate and Practitioner Course Responsibilities
My graduate and practitioner course responsibilities involve providing the students with knowledge of the values, history, standards, and practices of the field of forensic anthropology. In so doing, I meet my graduate and practitioner course responsibilities through the following methods:

- Provide grantsmanship opportunities with timely feedback and editing

- Provide research opportunities by honing student interests rather than spoon-feeding hypotheses
- Provide publication opportunities that further the field of forensic anthropology while ensuring sound empirical scholarship
- Provide field experience in a safe, Socratic environment
- Provide teaching assistant opportunities with in-class observations and feedback
- Help the student to become a member of scholarly associations, such as the American Academy of Forensic Science, American Anthropological Association, and American Association of Physical Anthropologists
- Help the student progress through the program in a timely fashion that culminates in graduation, a job, and/or acceptance into a Ph.D. program
- Help the student to obtain funding from within the university and outside funding sources
- Provide postgraduation mentoring for scholarly purposes, job prospects, and strong letters of recommendation

TEACHING PHILOSOPHY

My teaching philosophy is based on my firsthand experiences with my major advisors, Drs. Susan C. Antón of New York University (formerly of the University of Florida) and William R. Maples of the University of Florida. I began my teaching career modeling their styles and behaviors both in and out of the classroom (with regard to fieldwork, research, grantsmanship, publications, etc.). Although I still strongly evidence the training I received during my fourteen years of tutelage under Antón and Maples on a daily basis, I have morphed my teaching philosophy to fit my personality, needs of FGCU's practitioner-based criminal forensics program, and the scholarly requirements necessary for students to be accepted into Ph.D. programs at level 1 research institutions.

In three words my teaching philosophy is *kind, meticulous,* and *scholarly.* For my graduate students, my teaching philosophy has the addition of one word: *access* (to me, my professional colleagues, funding resources, field experience, and skeletal and archival research materials).

My teaching philosophy enables me to instill **intrinsic-thought** and **extrinsic-physical processes** within the student so that he or she will be able to recognize, interpret, and critique scholarly works, forensic cases, and the world in which they live. The following is an example of the **intrinsic-thought process** the student would go through when presented with a 10 mm bone fragment from a femur during a Human Osteology laboratory practical. I expect the student to think in the following manner in order to identify the bone:

1. Is the bone human?
2. If human, is it cranial or postcranial?
3. What side of the body is it from?
4. What anatomical landmarks are present (e.g., gluteus maximus muscle)?
5. Is the muscle insertion size and robusticity consistent with a male or female?
6. What was the age of the decedent?
7. What markings on the bone were caused by environmental changes that would suggest the bone is archaeological?

The techniques used to conduct archival research, collect nonmetric and metric skeletal data, and behave when on a forensic cases are the **extrinsic-physical processes** (Appendix A). The **extrinsic-physical processes** the students have manifested were evident when they participated in the filming of *America's Most Wanted*, their work during the Forensic Science Education Conference, and the thank-you letters (Appendix B) I received from law enforcement agencies, such as the Florida Department of Law Enforcement (FDLE) regarding student participation in forensic casework.

TEACHING STRATEGIES

My courses tend to be offered in three-hour blocks, one day per week. I use multiple formats to keep the students interested for three consecutive hours. Specifically, I use quizzes, classroom lectures, films, discussion sessions, laboratory assignments, and team field projects to help each student to discover why the topic of study is important, help them to meaningfully integrate new knowledge with information culled from their other major required courses, and to stimulate critical thinking through class participation via the Socratic method. My teaching philosophy is transparent as I include my pedagogy in all course syllabi (Appendix C).

I strategically begin each class with a quiz. These daily quizzes encourage the student to come to class prepared because approximately 60 percent of the questions cover material from the previous class, while the remaining questions cover key reading terms for the current day's lecture. I post the answers to the quiz on my office bulletin board immediately after class. The answer key corresponds to my PowerPoint slide numbers and/or text page numbers (Appendix D). During lecture I also ask open-ended questions, calling on students by name, and providing extra credit and/or class participation points for those students who correctly answer.

Lectures are developed in PowerPoint and are available up to twenty-four hours before class via my class Web site, which is hosted by the university. This Web site, Angel, includes all lecture notes, PowerPoint presentations, real-time interactive discussion boards, and ancillary Web links to interesting Web pages and newspaper articles. Strategically, my lectures tie the assigned readings to the materials that I present only in lecture (Appendix E). The additional lecture-only materials may come from my own forensic case/research experiences, current events, video/film footage, or comments that arise during classroom discussions. For example, I show a five-minute clip of the film *My Cousin Vinnie* during my forensic anthropology module that covers the federal and state rules governing expert witness testimony.

I usually end each class with hands-on laboratory projects. The students are placed into groups of four or five to facilitate movement between stations and to provide opportunities for the students to work together to fill out their laboratory worksheets (Appendix F). Before these students begin the exercise, I discuss each station and its expectations. While the students work, two graduate assistants and I circulate through the room and help the undergraduates complete the laboratory assignment.

I motivate the students to think about the course objectives and content through projects that they complete outside of class periods. Since many of my students were attracted to the study of forensics, in general, and/or forensic anthropology, in particular, because of popular television shows like *CSI* and *Bones*, I created a project that merged pop culture with scholarly research. Working in groups of three, I ask the students to select a favorite episode from *CSI* or *Bones* and to watch the episode on their own time. The students must research the methods, technologies, and findings presented in the show to determine whether the science actually exists or if it was used properly. Each group critique must be linked to current scientific journal articles. Their research culminates in a PowerPoint presentation that covers the show's content (3 minutes), scholarly findings (6 minutes), and alternate show endings (4 minutes).

Many of my class lecture and reading topics focus on the manners of death, which include murder, genocide, war, mass fatality, or disease, and the cultural practices associated with burial, cannibalism, body donation, and scientific racism. As such, my teaching strategies also involve evidencing genuine care and concern for my students by knowing my students' names, aspirations, and how and when forensic science has touched their lives. I gain this knowledge by requiring each student to create a Web-based Angel profile that includes their answers to the following questions:

- Have you been touched by death in your family?
- Have you endured forced immigration?
- Have you been the victim of violence?
- Do you or have you worked with a law enforcement agency, medical examiner, or hospital?

This knowledge prepares me for understanding the various student viewpoints that I may encounter during the course (from practitioner to precocious student, to those who need to fulfill a graduation requirement) and readies me to handle the emotional personal experiences the students may reveal during class. Additionally, I provide my students with my Angel profile, curriculum vita, and my personal experiences with death and crime. Furthermore, I am always prepared to debrief any student outside of the class period should the content of the course be too graphic or emotional.

Because I mentor at least eleven master's graduate students per year (all of whom are volunteer teaching assistants), I involve them in the preparation of my syllabi, lectures, laboratory exercises, and one-on-one meetings with the undergraduate students. I counsel each graduate student on lecture methods, teaching styles, grading, and how to interpret the TA student assessment of instruction forms (Appendix G). I accomplish this goal by having these graduate students prepare one or two slides with lecture notes on a topic that I assign (for the day's lecture). I also have them submit five questions per quiz and exam with answer key. We have weekly meetings to discuss undergraduate student progress; design or redesign laboratory exercises, quizzes, and exams; and go over upcoming classroom expectations.

The forensic anthropology major is time intensive for both mentor and student as fieldwork within a medical examiner's office (at autopsy) or on a crime scene (recovering skeletal remains) occurs at all hours of the day. Each skeletal case provides an opportunity for me to allow my master's students to assist me in the processing and analysis of the skeletal remains by performing technical tasks (for example, note taking, photography, radiography, metric assessment, mapping, and rendering). Indeed, the students and I worked on eighty cases this academic year as evidenced by my casebook entries (Appendix H).

I also require my master's students to provide me with thesis topic précis, annotated bibliographies, institutional review board submittal reports, and data collection sheets by having them meet research writing milestones (for example, introduction, materials and methods, results, discussion, and conclusions). Drafts of these documents flow back and forth between the students and me as the work product is edited and foci change (Appendix I).

I also motivate my master's students to attend professional meetings with me. As such, I help to pay for student hotel rooms as long as they agree to present at the meeting. This process affords them the chance to meet their peers as well as my colleagues. These meetings also foster critical thinking skills and build their curriculum vitae (Appendix I). This process has culminated in the publication of one graduate student article in the *Journal of Forensic Sciences* and six poster presentations at three professional conferences (Appendix J).

TEACHING OBJECTIVES

The strength of my teaching lies in parsimonious objectives, which include:

- Select books and supporting documentation that help the students learn the course material.
- Provide study aids and how-to guides.
- Present lecture material in simple and cohesive manner.
- Use appropriate testing methods to gauge the student's retention and understanding of the material.
- Facilitate completion of the course and degree requirements.

I also teach the students how to prepare for intensive courses by requiring that reading and chapter note taking occur before class. I further recommend that they take notes during lecture and merge their study and lecture notes at least eight hours after class. My main objective then becomes providing feedback to the students that evidences that through good study habits, active listening, and class participation, they will be able to apply what they have learned to their course practicals, report writing, and research projects—and that these habits will carry on into other parts of their lives.

CURRICULAR REVISIONS

My curricular revisions have included bringing to light the legal reasons that experts in this field would have human skeletal remains in their care, custody, and control. To this end, I include a reading on ethics in forensic anthropology with a chapter that I coauthored and current state (such as, Florida Statute 406.11) and federal statutes (for example, the Native American Graves Protection and Repatriation Act, NAGPRA) that outline why specialists in this field are entrusted with human remains and what their access to those remains means. My courses now include my coauthored books, *The Forensic Anthropology Laboratory* (2008) and *The Nonhuman Skeletal Identification Guide* (2010), which further elaborate on this theme.

For my graduate students, I have also taken steps to make sure that they clearly understand health exposure risks associated with forensic anthropology. As such, I have added Occupational Safety and Health Administrations (OSHA) recommendations for the safe handling of human remains and suggest that the students receive hepatitis A and B vaccinations or titers.

My revised graduate curriculum also includes information concerning the sensitive and privileged information they will receive concerning active cases and the health of victims they will analyze. With this in mind, I created a confidentiality agreement for each student to sign with a witness (Appendix K).

Student Course Feedback and Teaching Evaluation Data

The student feedback for my courses has been superlative. Handwritten student comments from all of my courses have included the following (Appendix L):

- She is a wonderful instructor and role model. I will definitely recommend her to other students pursuing a forensic degree.
- All of her quizzes and tests are relevant . . . she can hold the classes attention for the whole time . . . all of her assignments were interesting.
- She is the most articulate lecturer I've ever been fortunate enough to hear. I only wish she taught more classes. She has raised the bar at FGCU.
- I have been privileged to feed off of your love, dedication, and heart felt information that will not only help us in the field but in a way help us to become closer cohorts in the program.
- Of all of the professors I have had at FGCU you have taught with the most passion and I learned the most from you.

My teaching evaluation data have also been strong and are presented in simple tabular form (Tables 3–5), with the raw data presented in Appendix L.

In addition, to the written student assessment of instruction data, I distributed and evaluated pre- and posttest scores for Human Osteology; Bugs, Bones, and Botany; and Forensic Anthropology, and conducted statistical analyses. Significant differences between the scores of the pre- and posttests were noted

TABLE 3. STUDENT ASSESSMENT OF INSTRUCTION OF HUMAN
OSTEOLOGY, FALL 2009

		Excellent	Very Good	Good	Fair
1	Objectives and assignments	75%	13%	12%	
2	Communication of ideas and information	63%	37%		
3	Expression of expectations	88%	12%		
4	Availability outside of class	63%	25%	12%	
5	Respect and concern for students	88%	12%		
6	Stimulation of interest in course	100%			
7	Facilitation of learning	75%	13%	12%	
8	Overall assessment of instructor	88%	12%		

for all three classes. These findings suggest that the students understand and retain the integral course material and that I am presenting the material in a manner that is conducive to learning.

As part of my effort to shed light on my teaching effectiveness, I invited two faculty members into my classroom. Specifically, Dr. Duane Dobbert observed my teaching style and read over my course materials for Human Osteology and Dr. David Hall did the same for my Bugs, Bones, and Botany course. Dr. Dobbert's review culminated in his "highest unconditional recommendation" for the 2008–2009 teaching award. Dr. Hall's written review was exemplary, indicating that I was "thorough, methodical, and patient" in my teaching (Appendix M).

TABLE 4.   STUDENT ASSESSMENT OF INSTRUCTION OF BUGS, BONES,
AND BOTANY, FALL 2009

		Excellent	*Very Good*	*Good*	*Fair*
1	Objectives and assignments	80%	20%		
2	Communication of ideas and information	100%			
3	Expression of expectations	100%			
4	Availability outside of class	100%			
5	Respect and concern for students	100%			
6	Stimulation of interest in course	100%			
7	Facilitation of learning	100%			
8	Overall assessment of instructor	100%			

PROFESSIONAL OUTREACH AS EVIDENCED BY PRESENTATIONS, PUBLICATIONS, AND EXPERT TESTIMONY

I have presented various aspects of forensic anthropology to several elementary schools (Appendix N) as well as forensic practitioners (e.g., Bugs, Bones, and Botany; Bahamian Forensic Science Convention; Bermuda Forensic Science Convention (Appendix O) with my master's students in tow. These opportunities provide my students with examples of how to alter lecture content based on the education and culture of the audience. Indeed, these lecture and laboratory exercises have also allowed the master's students chances to interact as an instructor and meet practitioners. It has also been my privilege to mentor a recent Innocence Project exonerate, Mr. Dwayne Dail, through the application process at FGCU (Appendix P).

My practicum field-based teaching has also culminated in over eighty forensic anthropology reports this academic year, many of

Table 5.   Student Assessment of Instruction for Forensic Anthropology, Fall 2009

		Excellent	Very Good	Good	Fair
1	Objectives and assignments	100%			
2	Communication of ideas and information	91%	9%		
3	Expression of expectations	91%	9%		
4	Availability outside of class	82%	10%	8%	
5	Respect and concern for students	82%	18%		
6	Stimulation of interest in course	100%			
7	Facilitation of learning	100%			
8	Tests/assignments require problem solving and/or creative thought	100%			
9	Uses a variety of instructional materials/ methods in course	91%	9%		
10	Instructor conducts class in an organized way	91%	9%		
11	Assignments helped me understand subject	82%	2%	16%	
12	Instructor is a confident presenter	100%			
13	Instructor is prepared	100%			
14	I recommend this instructor	100%			
15	I was always prepared for class	82%	2%	16%	
16	Instructor encourages student participation	91%	9%		
17	I learned a great deal about the subject	91%	9%		
18	Graded work is representative of assigned material	91%	9%		

which have led to expert witness testimony in Broward, Lee, and Duval counties as well as the country of Bermuda (Appendix Q). My students have attended two homicide trials in which I was an expert witness. Not only did they experience firsthand the rules of court and expert witness conduct, but the experience allowed for lively class discussions regarding jury pools, attorney practices, and the Florida judicial system in general.

STUDENT PUBLICATIONS AND PRESENTATIONS AS EVIDENCE OF STUDENT LEARNING

Exemplary proof of the scholarly work my master's students have completed over the past year includes their eight published abstracts for their poster (seven) and oral (one) presentations given at the American Academy of Forensic Sciences Meeting and American Association of Physical Anthropology (Appendix R). My most senior master's student has published in the prestigious *Journal of Forensic Sciences* (Appendix S). Lastly, three master's students received top honors for their coauthored research project during our university's Research Day (Appendix T).

GOALS

My goals for the upcoming year include creating a new course, entitled Introduction to Forensic Science. As this is an auditorium lecture course that may contain approximately two hundred undergraduate students, I plan to use weekly Web-based laboratory exercises to underscore and operationalize the material presented in lecture. In addition, I hope to create a summer field school for my master's and upper-division undergraduate students. This field school would stem from my work with Fijian skeletal remains in the Fijian National Museum. This field school would highlight the Fijian culture as well as data collection methods.

APPENDICES

Appendix A: Teaching Philosophy as Evidenced by Student Projects
Appendix B: Thank-You Letters as Evidence of Teaching
Appendix C: Teaching Strategies as Evidenced by Course Syllabi

Appendix D: Teaching Strategies as Evidenced by Quizzes and Exams

Appendix E: Teaching Strategies as Evidenced by PowerPoint Presentations

Appendix F

Teaching Strategies as Evidenced by Laboratory Exercises

Teaching Strategies as Evidenced by Graduate Student Research Papers

Appendix G: Student Assessment of Instruction Forms as Evidence of Teaching

Appendix H: Forensic Anthropology Casebook as Evidence of Teaching

Appendix I: Teaching Strategies as Evidenced by Graduate Student Précis

Appendix J: Teaching Strategies as Evidenced by Graduate Student Curriculum Vitae

Appendix K: Curriculum Revisions as Evidenced by Confidentiality Agreements

Appendix L

Student Feedback as Evidenced by Student Assessment of Instruction

Professional Outreach as Evidenced by Professional Presentations

Appendix M: Faculty Feedback as Evidenced by Letters of Recommendation

Appendix N: Professional Outreach as Evidenced by Thank-You Letter

Appendix O: Professional Outreach as Evidenced by Practitioner-Based Courses

Appendix P: Professional Outreach as Evidenced by Innocence Project Exonerate

Appendix Q: Professional Outreach as Evidenced by Case Reports and Expert Testimony

Appendix R: Evidence of Student Publication via Graduate Presentations

Appendix S: Evidence of Student Publication via Graduate Journal Article

Appendix T: Evidence of Student Publication via Institutional Review Board Research

CHAPTER TWENTY-FIVE

LAW

Marc Jonathan Blitz

Oklahoma City
University School of Law
Spring 2010

CONTENTS

1. Teaching Responsibilities
2. Teaching Philosophy
3. Teaching Strategy and Methodologies
4. Representative Course Syllabi
5. Honors Relating to Teaching
6. Evaluation of Teaching
7. Teaching Improvement Activities
8. Community Outreach Activities
9. Plans for Developing Teaching Skills
10. Appendices

TEACHING RESPONSIBILITIES

As a law professor at Oklahoma City University, I specialize in constitutional law (with a focus on the First Amendment and privacy law), law and technology, computer law, national security law, and evidence. I teach or have taught the courses listed in the next table.

Constitutional Law I (Structure of Gov't)	2005 COURSE NO 7123	70 students	Required
Constitutional Law II (The Bill of Rights)	2006–2008 COURSE NO 7223	50–80 students	Required
Administrative Law	2006–2010 COURSE NO 8243	20–90 students	Elective
National Security Law	2007–2008 COURSE NO 6332	25–40 students	Elective
Law of Alternative Dispute Resolution	2006–2008 COURSE NO 6523	30–50 students	Elective
Evidence	Planned for 2009–2011 COURSE NO 8742	60 students anticipated	Elective
Computer Law	Planned for 2009–2011 COURSE NO 8742	15 students anticipated	Seminar

TEACHING PHILOSOPHY

I believe my primary mission as a law teacher is to prepare every law student for the rigorous analysis and professional commitment that will define their lives as lawyers. Because many will also play leadership roles outside the practice of law, I also try to contribute to their preparation for (i) the service and deliberation about law and policy that many of them will engage in as leaders, and as engaged and responsible citizens of their nation, states, and communities and (ii) for the challenge of developing their own individual view of (and voice on) constitutional powers and liberties and on other aspects of the legal system.

This mission requires me to think long and hard about how to prepare each class in a way that fully engages students' attention and helps them carefully hone their thinking and argumentation skills. I also believe it requires me to design courses in which each student is empowered to *teach themselves* about law outside of class. (They will have to do so throughout their careers as lawyers, leaders, and engaged citizens—since the laws will change dramatically during their lives.)

More specifically, my pursuit of this teaching mission is defined by the following three guiding principles:

Principle 1: A commitment to training students in a core body of knowledge and a core set of analytical skills

While I believe it is essential to respect each student as an individual, and to take account of his or her specific goals, interests, and learning styles, there is a core set of analytical skills and subject matter that every student has to learn if they are to be an effective attorney and an educated member of the legal community. For example, students cannot vigorously and effectively represent their clients—whether that client is a major corporation or a death penalty defendant—unless they are well versed in the core elements of the American legal system and how to navigate that system. Even when they are *not* acting as attorneys, students may well find they have to speak and argue in the "language of law" in order to persuade lawmakers or fellow citizens of their views about bioethics, the war on terrorism, or other subjects that are of tremendous importance in our public life.

Principle 2: A commitment to a certain kind of pedagogical "individualism"—by which I mean a proper appreciation of students' (i) distinctive individual goals and interests, (ii) distinctive learning styles, and (iii) capacity to adapt my courses to their own interests and learning styles, often through out-of-class reading and discussion

Although classes generally meet as groups (sometimes large groups), I believe that there are key elements of my teaching that require taking careful account of students *as individuals,* each of whom brings his or her own distinctive set of passions and interests to the law classroom. One student may want to take the analytical skills and constitutional law that she masters in my classroom and put it to use writing new laws as a legislator or congressional staffer. Another may want to use these skills and knowledge as an advocate in a public interest group. And yet another may wish to defend property rights in a private law firm. Some law students never intend to become lawyers: they simply believe it is valuable for them to have a command of the law—and legal reasoning skills—as background for work as a journalist, a public policy advocate, or a police officer.

They also bring diverse experiences and ideological commitments to my classes—and (not surprisingly) will differ in which visions of jurisprudence and constitutional law they find most appealing. I therefore try to expose them to a wide variety of judicial and scholarly perspectives on each controversial issue we discuss, so they can decide for themselves which vision of constitutional law seems most powerful for them. I do not see it as my role to advocate for any particular view on these issues but rather to present each vision of constitutional law set forth by prominent jurists and scholars, and then let students decide for themselves which they find most persuasive. Students also differ in their learning styles. So I try to provide students with an array of materials beyond the readings so they can find the learning devices that will be most helpful.

Principle 3: A commitment to making every class as memorable and engaging as possible

I strongly believe that even material that likely appears dry and confusing to many students—for example, the administrative procedures that are often a central topic in administrative law—can become both clear and engaging when it is presented in an atmosphere that is dynamic and entertaining, and using teaching technologies and methods that capture students' attention and connect it to concrete experiences. For example, lessons on administrative procedure become more enjoyable and memorable when students can see vivid images of (or hear music related to) the different air bag designs at the center of an administrative dispute (and the possible consequences to ordinary people of adopting one rather than another). Many students also learn effectively by doing, and thus I believe it is up to me not simply to treat them as passive learners, but as active legal thinkers in training who must get plenty of practice in tackling legal problems on their own.

TEACHING STRATEGY AND METHODOLOGIES

In order to fulfill this teaching mission, and do so in a way that works for different students' distinctive learning styles, I use a wide variety of methods and teaching technologies.

Intensive Questioning and Rigorous Discussion

My classes are characterized by the same intensive reading and discussion of cases that is the hallmark of American legal education. Following the example of some of my own very impressive teachers and mentors at the University of Chicago Law School, I make it clear to students that they have to treat the legal cases they are assigned to read not simply as reading assignments, but as raw materials for effective analysis and argument (which often requires reading each case at least twice to gain more than a superficial understanding).

To this end, students must be prepared in my classes for the kind of Socratic questioning that is often used in legal education (and was used with great effect in my own legal education): they must be prepared to be called on to answer difficult and challenging questions about their reading.

Use of Multiple Audiovisual Technologies

Film clips, music, animations, and slides not only help make class more colorful and dynamic—they also provide students with imagery that can help them remember (and understand) what would otherwise be dry, abstract, and unfamiliar ideas. Such visual and audio technology also helps me to reach out to students who have very different learning styles—some who have trouble focusing on traditional lectures, but become very engaged in a class when they can see visual representations of legal concepts. The specific slides and animations include: (1) video of current events in the world of constitutional law—including clips of the Supreme Court confirmation hearings; (2) film, media, music, computer animations to draw analogies. For example, I used teleportation scenes from fantasy and science-fiction movies to stimulate debates about constitutional limits on regulation of e-mail and materials sent almost instantaneously from one part of the country to another on the Internet; (3) interactive diagrams and flowcharts—and subject-matter-specific interactive "museums" in the 3D virtual world Second Life—to help students take advantage of their sense of spatial relationships and spatial memory to better understand the relationship between different concepts.

(See Appendix A2 for examples of some of the imagery I have used during in-class slide presentations, and electronic flowcharts or virtual world "museums.")

Exercise-Based Learning

Many students learn most effectively by doing. They learn how to build a legal argument not simply by watching me build one, but by repeatedly engaging in this task by themselves. To offer such opportunities, I provide students with detailed suggestions for applying familiar legal categories to "hard cases" that do not fit easily (or as obviously) into the conceptual boxes set out by a court-crafted test or a statutory rule. I also ask them to analyze and prepare answers on multiple hypothetical scenarios that help them hone their skills in applying the legal rules they learn from cases and statutes.

REPRESENTATIVE COURSE SYLLABI

Consistent with my philosophy of helping students to teach themselves, I try to use syllabi not just to inform students when they will read what, but rather as a detailed overview of, and road map for, the entire course that they can use to navigate the course materials and put them in context even when they are outside of class. Each syllabus begins with a two- or three-paragraph statement laying out the key concepts of the course and explaining the central skills I expect them to learn. I then provide one or two pages that present what I describe as a "big picture" overview of the course.

This allows students to understand the course not as scattered topics collected together, but as a systematic study, the components of which are all part of a larger whole. (See Appendix B for sample course syllabi.)

HONORS RELATED TO TEACHING

Professor of the Year (2007). This is one of two awards given by law students at Oklahoma City University School of Law to recognize their professors' teaching performance.

Priddy II Fellows (2007–2008). Presented for participation in a learning community dedicated to reflection on teaching and integration of arts in education. (See Appendix C for copies of these awards.)

EVALUATION OF TEACHING

It is impossible to assess whether teaching techniques are working simply from my own reactions. I talk extensively with students about their perspective on my teaching methods. Of course, anonymous and systematic surveys provide information that I cannot hope to get from informal face-to-face conversations. These evaluations have generally been extremely positive and encouraging. For example, in the next table are averages for students' answers for the five classes I taught during 2008. The possible responses for each question range from 1 to 6, with 1 = Very Poor, 2 = Poor, 3 = Adequate, 4 = Good, 5 = Very Good, and 6 = Exceptional. Almost all of the averages are between "Very Good" and "Exceptional":

COURSE	Responses	Knowledge of Course Material	Organi-zation of Course	Choice of Content	In-Class Perfor-mance	Relation-ship with Students	General Overall Teaching Ability
Legal Analysis Fall 2008	48	5.75	5.66	5.54	5.76	5.54	5.72
Constitutional Law II (The Bill of Rights) Spr. 2008	49	5.66	4.71	5.08	4.96	5.60	5.00

COURSE	Responses	Knowledge of Course Material	Organi- zation of Course	Choice of Content	In-Class Perfor- mance	Relation- ship with Students	General Overall Teaching Ability
National Security Law Fall 2008	36	5.79	5.28	5.53	5.67	5.89	5.80
Law of Alternative Dispute Resolution Spr. 2008	24	5.38	5.23	5.74	5.54	5.69	5.31
Law of Alternative Dispute Resolution Fall 2008	69	5.80	5.67	5.74	5.72	5.80	5.74

The following comments in evaluations and e-mails during my time as a law teacher provide illustrations of student reactions to my teaching techniques:

From Anonymous Student Evaluations

Professor Blitz has a strong passion for teaching and developing innovative strategies.

The way the professor tied music into the daily class slides was absolutely brilliant. It made class much more enjoyable. Plus, the professor really seemed like he wanted to be here and wanted to help the students.

Really cared about explaining everything.

From Student E-Mails

Not only do I want to thank you for the help [preparing for the final] . . . but your dedication all semester to making [the class] entertaining and understandable, through music and video and daily PowerPoint. It was all very impressive. You should be commended for your dedication to teaching.

The class you offered us today was one of, if not the best, taught class I've ever received, certainly in law school as a whole, and probably in my whole collegiate life. Regardless of the grade I make or don't make, I really appreciate the life and comprehension you bring to the subject.

(See Appendix D for a sample evaluation and for additional evaluation excerpts.)

TEACHING IMPROVEMENT ACTIVITIES

I am strongly committed to both improving my teaching and adjusting it, where necessary, to developments in educational methods and technology. For example, during the 2007 calendar year, I was a member of the Priddy II Fellows Learning Community and in that capacity frequently met with and learned from other teachers who are passionate about integrating arts into teaching. As part of this community, I participated in significant reflection about my teaching methods and in many teaching improvement exercises designed by Oklahoma City University's Fine Arts Institute and Center for Excellence in Teaching and Learning. I also participated over the 2008–09 academic year in a monthly "Teaching with Technology Faculty Learning Group."

COMMUNITY OUTREACH ACTIVITIES

I have used and honed my teaching techniques not only in the classroom but also by organizing and participating in many symposia, conferences, and panel discussions open to the Law School community, or to a larger civic, professional, or scholarly audience.

Commentator on law-focused Web logs: Contributed numerous postings related to law teaching on Prawfsblawg and the Neuroethics & Law blog. I have also given numerous media interviews on constitutional law issues.

Initiator and organizer of April 2007 symposium on the legal
   framework for America's war on terrorism, cosponsored by
   the Law School and the Memorial Institute on the Prevention
   of Terrorism (MIPT).

Legal and policy expert: One of five law professors invited by the
   United States Department of Homeland Security's Privacy
   Office to participate in a workshop on developing "privacy
   best practices" for use of public video surveillance (December
   2007). (See Appendix E for materials about these community
   outreach activities.)

Plans for Developing Teaching Skills

I have set the following teaching development goals to achieve
over the next two academic years:

- Generate new and more effective ways to demystify the reasoning and argumentation skills that make lawyers into powerful
  writers and effective advocates. To this end, I intend to focus
  more on problems and exercises. In contrast to other assignments, where students are responsible for reading judicial
  opinions they have not seen before, these assignments will be
  reserved entirely for skill development—i.e., for taking the
  substance they have already learned and figuring out how to
  apply it.
- Use technology to find new, more effective ways to help students teach themselves. For example, I intend to provide
  students with self-guided tours where they can see and interact
  with representations of legal concepts. To this end, I intend to
  deepen my understanding of animation software, virtual reality platforms in education, and software for creating interactive diagrams.

Appendices

Appendix A—Sample Teaching Materials
   Appendix A1—Guidance in Reading Cases and Preparing for
      Class Discussion
   Appendix A2—PowerPoint and KeyNote Slides

Appendix A3—Exercise-Based Assignments
Appendix B—Class Syllabi
Appendix C—Honors Relating to Teaching
Appendix D—Sample Student Evaluation and Evaluation Excerpts
Appendix E—Community Outreach Activities

CHAPTER TWENTY-SIX

MUSIC

Stephanie Jensen-Moulton

Conservatory of Music
Brooklyn College of the City University of New York
Spring 2010

CONTENTS

I. TEACHING RESPONSIBILITIES

When I began teaching at Brooklyn College in the fall 2007 semester, I had not yet completed my dissertation and was hired as an instructor. As such, my four and four teaching load in fall 2007 and spring

2008 included two sections of the core music course for nonmajors and one upper-level/graduate seminar in American music. In addition, I received three hours of release time each semester for serving as the deputy director for graduate music studies. In fall 2008, I was appointed as assistant professor of musicology, and my load was reduced by one course to three and four. Thus, the four primary areas of my teaching are academic courses, academic advising, independent work with graduate students, and community outreach.

A. Academic Courses

Each semester, I teach **Core Class 1.3 Music: Its Language, History, and Culture** (CC 1.3 or "core music"). Core music is a required course for all Brooklyn College undergraduates, and classes are populated by approximately forty to sixty students of varied majors. CC 1.3 provides students with a vocabulary for the sound world in which they live and calls on them to listen in new, complex ways to art music, popular music, and world music. Cultural context and interdisciplinary links are at the heart of the course. Though formal writing assignments are few, I give low-risk writing tasks frequently, in addition to assigning an oral presentation, a concert essay, five unit tests, and a final exam. The syllabus for this course may be found in *Appendix A*.

In fall 2008 I taught the new **Core for Music Majors**, an honors section of CC 1.3 that incorporates this core requirement into the rigorous schedules of undergraduate music students, education majors with music concentrations, and music minors. This class differed from CC 1.3 in that students had some ability to read scores and generally used a more complex musical language.

I also teach a graduate and/or upper-level undergraduate seminar for music majors on an American music topic of my choosing. The past three semesters' courses, populated by twelve to eighteen students, have centered on: **Women in American Music** (fall 2007), **American Music from Colonial Times to the Present** (spring 2008), and **Music and Politics in 20th Century America** (fall 2008). In spring 2009, I taught a new undergraduate upper-level history seminar entitled **Opera and Musical Theater in America**, which is cross-listed with American Studies. All of these seminars are reading and writing intensive and center on discussion rather than lecture. I ask for weekly writing assignments, a midterm paper, an oral presentation, and a final paper, in addition to many in-between writing phases. Selected syllabi from these seminars may be found in *Appendix A*.

B. Academic Advising

In my position as deputy director, I am the adviser to all graduate students in the Conservatory of Music (approximately one hundred). This advisement includes the handling of all aspects of course advisement, admissions, graduate school and career mentoring, as well as the administering of the graduate comprehensive exam. I hold between six and eight office hours per week and maintain a continual "virtual office" via e-mail for my advisees.

I meet with every graduate student to plan the next semester's courses, and often career questions become part of the discussion. I am happy to advise students about doctoral work in performance or academic fields of music, and frequently help them make contact with professionals in their chosen field. Admission of new graduate students and recruitment also fall under the umbrella of the graduate deputyship, and include organizing graduate student open houses and orientations, connecting students with faculty in their fields, and reading admissions portfolios and audition results. An applicant checklist which I created to help with the complexities of the CUNY admissions process can be found in *Appendix B*. After students are admitted, I administer a graduate diagnostic exam and the graduate language exam.

Once graduate students have completed most of their courses, they take the Graduate Music Comprehensive Exam (found in *Appendix C*), a four-hour test that covers style criticism, analysis, terminology, and expertise within a student's primary specialization, be it composition, performance, musicology, or music education. I supervise and contribute to the writing of this exam and routinely hold an orientation meeting at the beginning of the semester that helps students to understand the format of the exam and the expectations of faculty.

C. Independent Work with Graduate Students

Graduate independent studies, especially those that prepare students for thesis writing, are also part of my teaching load, both officially and unofficially. I currently have one thesis advisee who is working on Aaron Copland's ballet *Rodeo* and gender dynamics; I have also taken on students with independent studies for credit on blues and popular music, experimental music in the classroom, and vocal chamber music. Unofficially, I have been a first reader on three thesis projects and am currently helping two students who will soon be official advisees choose topics. Although the research topics differ widely, in my approach to independent studies, the student is the designer of the course of research, while I maintain a rigorous set of deadlines to help in completion of the writing project.

D. Community Outreach

Each summer, I teach at Daniel's Music Foundation (www.daniels music.org), and throughout the academic year I serve on the foundation's advisory board. Daniel's Music Foundation provides free music instruction for New Yorkers with disabilities and was founded in 2006 by Daniel Trush and his father. Daniel is the survivor of five brain aneurysms and was a student in three different classes I taught at Hunter College. At the foundation, I have served as the instructor for a music lab, a voice class, and a hybrid class that combines music theory, history, and ear training. I have also referred several Brooklyn College students with interests in music therapy to the foundation as teachers. As an educational adviser, I have written a foundation curriculum based on current course models that can be found in *Appendix D*. My experiences at the foundation profoundly affect not only my Brooklyn College teaching but also my scholarship. In summer 2009, I published an article on teaching disabled students such as Daniel Trush in the journal *Music Theory Online*, which can be found in *Appendix E*.

II. STATEMENT OF TEACHING PHILOSOPHY

"Real Learning"

My overarching goal is to make the classroom an environment in which real learning—as I define it, "real learning" is a voluntary, enthusiastic acquisition of knowledge—takes place because students are truly engaged with the material, the other students, and the professor. The students themselves take the lead in presenting and thus connecting with material; since many minds are greater than my one mind, I can best serve my students as a facilitator and organizer rather than as a lecturer at the center of the classroom universe. From the first day, I communicate to the students the immense value of their own prior knowledge of music, regardless of style.

My emphasis on acknowledging and using students' prior knowledge reflects a deep desire to value each student equally. I define *diversity* not strictly in terms of race, but in terms of gender, nationality, disability, learning style, and beyond. In assignments such as the musical autobiography (found in *Appendix F*), I encourage them to be frank about the music they listen to and how it reflects who they are.

Active Learning: Writing, Presentations, and Organized Minds

In my core class, formal student presentations begin each session, followed by a discussion of material that students have read for class. While I do some lecturing, student participation in discussion and question-and-answer sessions is integral to the way students process and retain information. Likewise, in my graduate seminars, students lead discussion on the readings each week, and I encourage them to be as professional as possible in their presentations by using handouts and/or PowerPoint slides, as well as sound and visual examples.

Writing is a crucial part of my graduate seminars, becoming almost a secondary area of study. I ask students for weekly position papers, early drafts and abstracts, as well as two research papers. I see it as my job to give graduate students and upper-level undergraduates permission to explore and theorize their own ideas, in addition to those they have read in books or periodicals. This helps the students move beyond the expository and into the exciting realms of analysis and critique. Professional development also enters into the seminars as a much-needed aspect of graduate school.

At the undergraduate level, I help students explore ways of learning to study effectively and use their time efficiently. One method of incorporating these skills into the core music course is to discuss time management in a practical way using a worksheet I have developed. (See *Appendix E*.) Part of helping students develop the mental organization to succeed in college is to model clarity. My students enter the classroom with the expectation that I will be creative and spontaneous in my teaching, but that they always know my expectations in terms of assignments and tests. This reflects what I want to see developing in their writing assignments: evidence of both organized thinking and creative thinking.

Finally, I try to use humor as a teaching tool in equal measure with appropriately serious treatment of socially relevant topics. For example, students tend to be intimidated by the twelve-tone serial techniques developed by Arnold Schoenberg in the early twentieth century. In one core class, I linked Arnold Schoenberg with Arnold Schwarzenegger, noting (in character, of course) that Arnold could "pump you up" with his twelve-tone system. We all had a good laugh, but the students remembered, as with a pneumonic device, the name of the composer who developed the system and the number of tones involved in serial composition. Humor has an important place in my life, and as such, it is an integral part of my teaching.

III. Teaching Methods and Strategies

The objective of my core class is to give students a language with which to discuss music and to give them sharper ears with which to discern its many intricacies. I want my students to bring the specificity of listening into the everyday, and incorporate it into the way they choose to support music events and fill their iPods. Student presentations, as well as low-risk writing assignments, address connections between the outside and the inside of their musical worlds. (See *Appendix F.*) In addition to mp3 players, I use and encourage my students to use music-related technologies such as YouTube and Rhapsody in the classroom.

Outside of class, I provide study notes on Blackboard for every unit (*Appendix F*); these notes help students study for the frequent low-risk tests I give so that students don't fall too far behind in reading assignments by midterm. Also, I try to connect each musical work I cover with some overarching theme that relates to music of the twenty-first century, including popular styles. The students reinforce this idea in their own presentations as well, which fosters tolerance and respect for other cultures and musics, and/ or for those local musical styles that may incite strong opinions.

In the graduate classes and seminars, I begin by handing out a time-management worksheet, followed by reading from Anne Lamott's book, *Bird by Bird: Advice on Writing and Life*. I want students to know that great writing doesn't happen in the first draft, but that the first draft has to happen in order to get to great writing. Then I give weekly writing assignments that warm up their writing "muscles" and get the students ready for larger projects. Finally, I give one "conference-style" paper in class each term so that they can see the level of preparation I expect and hear what I am working on in my scholarly life; meanwhile, I entice them with e-mails about upcoming student conferences and forums in which they could potentially present and or publish their work.

IV. COURSE SYLLABI

The syllabi I give my classes at the beginning of the term contain not only the administrative details of the class, but also very specific explanations of assignments and, for the undergraduates, ways to succeed in the course and rules for e-mail communication. (See *Appendix A*.) I am extremely strict regarding assignment deadlines and expectations; I do not give incompletes without documentation of an emergency, and I do not accept late papers. I want students to recognize that beneath the relentlessly positive classroom demeanor is a professor who means business. One unusual aspect of my undergraduate syllabi is that part of each unit's work is the completion of note cards for new terms. (See *Appendix F*.)

V. STUDENT LEARNING

In all of my courses, students write an initial, low-risk musical biography that enables me to establish where a student is "meeting" the material for the course, in terms of writing skills, as well as the student's use of music terminologies and capacity for creative thinking. For undergraduates, this exercise is a timed, speed-writing endeavor, whereas for graduate students, it is a one- to two-page take-home assignment. I have included sample biographies in *Appendix F*. Student learning is also evidenced by students' completion of tasks assigned both in class and on the syllabus. In *Appendix F*, I have included copies of sample index cards that a student gave me after having achieved an A on her final exam by studying with them. I have also included a printout of examples of an online discussion thread that challenged students to define "musical style" in their own terms.

I have included as evidence of student learning the entire scheme of one final project for **Music and Politics in Twentieth Century America**, from abstract to final draft, including my comments (*Appendix F*). A student from my seminar **Women in American Music** was selected to present her final paper on pop singer Jennifer Lopez at the Pizer Graduate Student Colloquium; the program from this event is found in *Appendix F*.

VI. TEACHING EFFECTIVENESS

A. Peer Assessment of Teaching and Mentoring

I have been observed by my peers twice since I began teaching at Brooklyn College, and both reviews have been very positive and have offered suggestions for future teaching goals. Prof. Jonathan Babcock's observation of the core music class states:

> Professor Jensen-Moulton is a dynamic and highly creative teacher. Her lecturing style made complex musical ideas easily understandable to non-musicians. She consistently asked questions of the class, reviewing previously covered topics and vocabulary. She not only demonstrated her mastery of the subject matter, but also her enthusiasm for it.

Prof. Nancy Hagar, observing the core for music majors class in fall 2008, writes:

> Prof. Jensen-Moulton is energetic and outgoing and the students clearly respect and like her. It was evident from the high level of student participation, the poise and self-confidence of the four presenters, and the respectful attention and enthusiastic response of their fellow students that she has created a comfortable yet business-like atmosphere that is conducive to a broad range of learning experiences.

In addition to these formal observations, Prof. Fabio Girelli-Carasi, the 2007–2008 director of the Center for Teaching at

Brooklyn College, wrote the following about a workshop I led on time management in December 2007:

> In your presentation you revealed a deep knowledge of the peda-
> gogical issues that play a role in the learning process, both in gen-
> eral terms and specifically about Brooklyn College. Your insights
> were informative, stimulating and full of brilliant ideas. Your
> presentation offered the ideal point of departure for a lively and
> engrossing conversation that you led with great aplomb and sense
> of humor. We all appreciated your professionalism, competence
> and common sense.

The full text of all peer observation letters may be found in *Appendix G.*

B. Student Assessment of Teaching

In his annual conference report, Conservatory of Music chair Prof. Bruce MacIntyre states: "Prof. Jensen-Moulton's Student Evaluations demonstrate her students' admiration and appreciation for her obvious teaching excellence. In *every* question on the evaluation form, she fared better than the Conservatory's overall average responses." In the fall 2008 report, 90% of students enrolled in my courses stated that they would "recommend this instructor to a friend." Printouts of my averages and those of my department for fall 2007, spring 2008, and fall 2008 may be found in *Appendix H.* I include below excerpts from letters written by students in e-mails and thank-you notes. (See *Appendix I* for complete text and other letters.)

> *Thanks again for everything over the past year. You in particular have been
> an incredible teacher, role model, and support system. You really are making
> Brooklyn College Conservatory a different place; a better place.*
> —Graduate advisee; student in Music 765,
> spring 2008 and fall 2008

> *Arguably the best music professor in the conservatory, brilliant, quirky and a
> fantastic scholar, encouraging and ridiculously helpful.*
> —Student in Music 94, fall 2008

This course has been an amazing experience.... I think you are one of the most inspiring teachers I have ever had. I will remember most of what we learned forever and wouldn't change a thing about the methods you use in class.

—Student in CC 1.3, Spring 2008

VII. TEACHING IMPROVEMENT ACTIVITIES

Improving my teaching is an essential part of my growth as an educator and as a scholar, and I have consistently participated in discussions and panels on pedagogy since I began teaching college courses. Prof. Bruce MacIntyre writes: "Also admirable is Prof. Jensen-Moulton's constant desire to improve her students' learning experiences through her constant reassessment and revising of her courses." (See *Appendix G* for full text.)

As an interdisciplinary scholar, I have been interested in feminist pedagogy for some time. In 2006, I cochaired a full-day conference entitled, "Women, Gender, Pedagogy: Conference on Feminist Pedagogy," at The Graduate Center, CUNY. A program for this event may be found in *Appendix E*. During the summer of 2008, I participated in the NYU Faculty Enrichment Seminar entitled "Women's Studies in a Global World: Pedagogies of Transformation" led by Professors Beverly Guy-Sheftall and Chandra Talpade Mohanty.

I have also led several workshops for the Roberta S. Matthews Center for Teaching at Brooklyn College, including two on time management, and two workshops on prior knowledge. In spring 2009, I received the Center for Teaching's Fellowship for Research and Publishing in General Education Pedagogy. Materials pertaining to these activities can be found in *Appendix E*. I also routinely attend many of the enrichment workshops and activities sponsored by the Center for Teaching.

In February 2009, I served for the second time as a faculty participant in the proseminar on Teaching Music History at the Graduate Center, a course designed for doctoral students who will soon begin teaching fellowships at CUNY's senior colleges. The proseminar is a wonderful opportunity to continue developing my teaching philosophy and strategies in the company of my former professors.

Finally, as part of the panel "Diversity and Inclusion in the Music Classroom" at the annual meeting of the American Musicological Society, I presented a paper entitled "Music Fundamentals: Three Classes with Daniel Trush." The paper may be found in *Appendix E*. I continue to seek out opportunities to connect with other scholars with interests in new and interdisciplinary methods of pedagogy.

VIII. FUTURE TEACHING GOALS

Central goal: continue sharing my love of music history with students to the degree that they maintain a lifelong interest in music, but more important, a lifelong interest in learning.

By the end of spring 2010: implement new strategies for grading writing and oral presentations more effectively and efficiently so that I can integrate more writing into my larger classes.

By spring 2011: revise Blackboard pages and use them more effectively for group discussions.

IX. APPENDICES

Appendix A. Sample Course Syllabi
- CC 1.3 Music: Its Language, History, and Culture (Fall 2008)
- Music 49.3/American Studies 60 (draft of syllabus)
- Music 94/765 Women in American Music (Fall 2007)
- Music 94/765 Music & Politics in 20th Century America (Fall 2008)

Appendix B. Graduate Student Handbook and Graduate Applicant Checklist

Appendix C. Sample Graduate Comprehensive Exam

Appendix D. Curriculum Document from Daniel's Music Foundation

Appendix E. Sample Teaching Improvement Materials
- Time Management Sheet
- "Teaching to Their Strengths: Prior Knowledge in the Core Classroom" as presented on Brooklyn College Faculty Day, May 2008
- Prior Knowledge Faculty Worksheet
- Invitation to serve as a faculty mentor, Teaching Music Proseminar, The Graduate Center, CUNY

- "Music Fundamentals: Three Classes with Daniel Trush" as presented at the annual meeting of the American Musicological Society, November 2008
- "Women, Gender, Pedagogy: Conference on Feminist Pedagogy" Program
- "Fellowship for Research and Publishing in General Education Pedagogy" materials

Appendix F. Evidence of Student Learning
- Sample Musical Biographies from CC 1.3 and Music 765
- Notes from other professors asking for sample materials
- Sample note cards from CC 1.3 student
- Sample Unit Study Notes from CC 1.3
- Final paper abstract, first draft, and final draft by Lindsey Eckenroth for Music 765, Music and Politics, Fall 2008
- Student Conference Announcement for Pizer Graduate Forum

Appendix G. Peer Observation Letters
- Prof. Jonathan Babcock, CC 1.3, Fall 2007
- Prof. Nancy Hagar, CC 1.3, Fall 2008
- Prof. Fabio Girelli-Carasi, Center for Teaching Workshop, December 2007
- Prof. Bruce MacIntyre, Report on Teaching from Annual Conference, 2007–2008

Appendix H. Student Evaluations of Faculty, Brooklyn College 2007–2008

Appendix I. Thank-You Cards and E-Mails

CHAPTER TWENTY-SEVEN

NURSING

Vicki D. Lachman

Department of Nursing
College of Nursing and Health Professions
Drexel University
Spring 2010

CONTENTS

1. Teaching Responsibilities
2. Teaching Philosophy
3. Teaching Strategies and Methodology
4. Syllabi, Assignments, and Responses to Students' Work
5. Evidence of Teaching Effectiveness
6. Awards/Honors
7. Professional Outreach
8. Future Teaching and Professional Development Goals
9. Appendices

TEACHING RESPONSIBILITIES

I became a full-time clinical associate professor in the College of Nursing and Health Professions on January 5, 2004. For the first two and a half years at the university, I taught ethics, psychiatry and leadership in the Physician Assistant (PA) Department. On July 1, 2006, I transferred to the Nursing Department; therefore, this portfolio will focus on the courses I am currently teaching.

I still teach three ethics classes and three psychiatry classes for the PA Department, but my primary focus in nursing is on teaching an online ethics course for master's students and an in-class ethics course for doctoral students.

I am also the track coordinator for **Innovation and Intra/ Entrepreneurship in Advanced Nursing Practice** and teach core courses—Intra/Entrepreneurship and Consultant, as well as Capstone I, II, and III. This track was started in fall 2006 and is one of only two such master's programs in the United States. Since the inception of the track, the number of students has increased by 25 percent each year, with the first nine graduates of the program occurring in 2009. My responsibility includes overseeing curriculum, marketing the track, and mentoring the students in development of their business plans and in the implementation and evaluation in Capstones.

An example of entrepreneurial and intrapreneurial Capstone projects I mentored will give you a flavor of the innovation track: Herritt Medical Technologies' premier product is a disposable, one-patient use, alarmed fluid delivery system, TUR-CUE, to be used during urology surgery as well as for postsurgical treatment therapy. Herritt Medical Technologies' business concept paper was voted best-written paper in the universitywide competition, achieved third-place win in "Elevator Pitch Contest"; this second success gained the student access to the venture capital community she needed.

An intrapreneurial student led a team that developed The Competency and Assessment Process Portal. This portal is an electronic information management system, providing a single point of access to a variety of competency tools and guidelines for the leaders and employees of the hospital's sixty-eight departments.

The master's ethics course is titled **Advanced Ethical Decision Making in Health Care** and is one of the first required courses in our master of science in nursing curriculum. I designed this three-credit course and teach the course two or three times a year with approximately twenty-five students in each class. It includes three synchronous classes, weekly Blackboard discussion, analysis of a case study, and a final paper on some clinical ethical topic of the students' choosing.

The doctoral in-class ethics course, **Clinical and Applied Ethics in Nursing Practice**, is a required three-credit course with twelve to fourteen students per class. I have taught it once in Philadelphia and twice in London as part of a two-week international program for our doctorate in nursing practice (DrNP) students. As I also have responsibility to coordinate this two-week program, I have had the opportunity to bring to our students professors from Kingston University, St. George's University of London, Center for International Nursing Ethics, Royal College of Nursing, and University of Bedfordshire. In London the course is taught from 9:00 A.M. to 12 noon four days a week, and I teach four of the eight classes. Since my primary appointment is as a doctoral faculty, I also act as chair or member of qualifying and comprehensive exams, serve on dissertation committees, and advise students in the clinical nurse executive track that I coordinate.

Teaching Philosophy

I believe great teachers help people see the world contextually, experience the world empathetically, and even possibly live a better life. The following are my core beliefs about teaching:

1. The learning process begins with a self-assessment of present knowledge and practices. This self-assessment helps the learner recognize present strengths and areas for development.
2. Knowledge is built through logical sequential education, and repetition of information leads to learning.
3. The learner must understand the relevance of the information in improving the clinical care of patients.
4. Teaching needs to engage the learner to use all senses; therefore, visual and auditory presentations need to be interesting, and, where possible, kinesthetic involvement is needed.
5. Learners' minds need to be engaged in the process; therefore, I ask questions constantly rather than present the answers (Socratic method).
6. Most people find change difficult; therefore, the need to change beliefs and habits must be compelling, and the learner

needs to actually experience a different way of believing or acting.

7. People must understand the consequences of changing and of not changing if they are to be motivated to risk change.
8. Use of positive feedback and a focus on students' strengths preserves self-esteem and furthers joy in learning.

Teaching Strategies and Methodology

With these beliefs in mind, my actions have always focused on helping students apply knowledge in a practical way. Prior to coming to the university, most of my experience has been in teaching adults employed in the health care field. These were all continuing education events in organizations or at local and national conferences. Therefore, these experienced health care workers came to learn a better way to manage a clinical, ethical, or leadership problem and/or learn the most current, evidence-based knowledge.

Nursing students, educated in applied physical and social sciences, desire the ability to apply knowledge. Therefore, my teaching strategies focus on helping students answer questions. In our online ethics course synchronous sessions, I ask, *"What would you say in this situation?"* In my role as Innovation and Intra/ Entrepreneur track coordinator, my questions focus on, *"What is a business idea you may want to develop that will improve one or more of the following—patient care, community health, patient safety, or employee satisfaction?"*

I use six primary strategies:

1. **Clinical Cases:** I use a multitude of clinical cases I have experienced in my thirty-three years as a practicing clinician and/or consultant, or use cases from books to illustrate the didactic points. I have received consistent feedback from the students as to how this makes the didactic information easier to remember and integrate.
2. **Experiential Activities:** I always include some experiential exercise in every class since I believe students need to be active in their learning to retain information. In one Intra/Entrepreneur

and Consultant class, the students pick seven consultant Web sites to evaluate from a list of fifteen. They are expected to demonstrate critical analyses of sites and list their concerns with the sites and the characteristics they will include on their business Web site. Also, as part of their final project for Capstone III, they need to create a fifteen-minute video designed to sell their business plan.

3. **Role Playing:** I use the strategy of role playing, since my students need to have crucial conversations with patients, families, and other health care professionals on a variety of ethical topics or to sell their innovative ideas. Using the clinical examples they bring to the online discussion of ethical issues, I ask students to give examples of the next steps in the dialogue with the individuals involved in the dilemma. Over the week I offer, "What would you say if they said this?" Though not the same as one-on-one role playing, it provides practical guidance for difficult conversations.

4. **Self-Assessments:** In The Nurse as an Intra/Entrepreneur and Consultant course, they take three self-assessments—Are You an Entrepreneurial Type? Management Skills Assessment, and What Is Your Credit Score? They place their learning and what actions they plan to take in Blackboard discussions. For example, several students found they scored low on the management skill of delegation. This led to an interesting discussion on strategies to increase delegation that other students have used.

5. **Contemporary Content:** It is essential to provide the most up-to-date content to the students. Because I believe that students need current evidence-based knowledge, I do not rely on textbooks for the doctoral ethics course. Before each course, I spend hours researching on the Internet and electronic journal articles that I believe will provide a balanced view of the issue. For example, in this course, I present pro and con readings and lecture information on physician-assisted suicide.

6. **Critical Thinking:** Critical thinking deliberately evaluates the quality of one's thinking. I want students to consider in a thoughtful way the problems they experience in clinical or leadership situations and apply logical inquiry and reasoning.

For example, when discussing ethical issues, I encourage students to find two resources that support their opposite points of view. In both the master's and doctoral ethics courses, they do a case analysis and are asked to reason through the legal and ethical issues. I want my students to know the joy and the responsibility of their role as clinicians or business owners. I want them to have practical skills to deal with and provide ethical justification for alternative solutions to the difficult situations they will encounter daily.

I want my voice to be instilled in their thinking as they problem-solve complicated situations. I also want them to look back on what I taught them and remember to stop, listen, and critically think through the problem, but never hesitate to ask for help. Examples of Blackboard questions in assignments to stimulate critical thinking for ethics and Innovation courses are in Appendix A, and one example is below:

> I utilize the American Nurses Association (2001) *Code of ethics with interpretive statements* as a required book in both the master's and doctoral ethics course. Unfortunately, I have been repeatedly struck by the fact that so few nurses are aware of ethical obligations outlined in our Code. Therefore, with each case we analyze or when we are discussing the reading, I ask for relevant Code provisions. This provides the opportunity to cement the obligations in practical applications, introduce ethics committees as a place to ask for help, and discuss the duties nurses owe their patients, colleagues, profession, and community.

SYLLABI, ASSIGNMENTS, AND RESPONSES TO STUDENTS' WORK

Each of the syllabi gives an overview of the course—description, objectives, assignments, as well as brief descriptions of relevant university policies with links to university sites. The syllabus lists the rubrics for the major assignments and the percentage of the assignment that will count toward the final grade. It also includes the dates and times of the Wimba (synchronous sessions) and virtual office hours. The course evaluations at the end of the quarter are taken seriously, and changes in syllabi, rubrics, course content, and workload are examined.

For example, the evaluation **Advanced Ethical Decision Making in Health Care** triggered a change in percentage of the grade designated to Blackboard discussion, which I believe now more accurately reflect the workload. The most recent syllabi for all the courses I teach are in Appendix B.

Examples of feedback to students are included to indicate the depth and breadth of feedback I believe is crucial for the development of graduate students. In Appendix C, there are four examples of feedback given to students: written feedback on an ethics paper, e-mail feedback on an ethics paper, feedback to doctoral students on their ethics presentation, and feedback on Blackboard assignment of the creation of mission and vision statements for business plans.

Evidence of Teaching Effectiveness

I determine effectiveness in teaching in two ways: student evaluations and feedback from peers. The next table shows an example of evaluations in some of the areas for ethics, master's, and doctoral courses, as well as for The Nurses as Intra/Entrepreneur and Consultant (I/E & C) for most recently taught courses, except for the I/E & C course. The 2009 evaluation for this course was an aberration in evaluations of my teaching, as it has been for the other professor who teaches this cohort in the track. This evaluation is included in Appendix D with changes to course, message to students, and follow-up example that was instituted with each student. I have included an example of an end-of-course summary evaluation with recommendations for change for Advanced Ethical Decision Making in Health Care.

In the next table, I have included six specific questions from the seventeen questions asked on each Drexel professor's evaluation to give a flavor of the evaluation questions and responses. Responses in other arenas are equally positive. I have also included three student comments from these courses that are relevant to my teaching philosophy or strategies.

	Ethics (Master's) Spring 09	Ethics (Doctoral) Fall 08	I/E & C Spring 08
	Percentage Who "Agree" or "Strongly Agree"		
Course helped me think critically	91%	100%	94%
Course was well organized	95.2%	100%	93.7%
Instructor gave timely feedback on assignments	95%	91.6%	82.4%
Instructor appeared knowledgeable about subject matter	100%	100%	100%
Instructor explained the material well	98.2%	91.6%	95.7%
Overall, I would rate course as well above average or above average	75%	75%	93.7%

Very thought provoking course. Dr Lachman is a very tough task master but in a good way as she gets the student thinking on how to improve themselves throughout the course.

—Ethics (Master's)

I learned so much this semester. It made me realize how insufficient my knowledge of ethics was. I now feel that I have a much better understanding of ethical principles and the importance of applying them to practice. I feel that Dr. Lachman is incredibly knowledgeable, enthusiastic about teaching and really provided all of us with a foundation of ethics that will always be with us.

—Ethics (Doctoral)

Dr. Lachman has a wealth of knowledge which she readily shared with the class. She was extremely accessible to us by phone, email and discussion board. In a word, she is "fabulous," a real treasure. I consider it a privilege to be her student.

—I/E & C

Evaluations from 2008/2009 from students for each course I taught are in Appendix D. In Appendix E, I have included samples of e-mails and cards from students and peers that validate my teaching strategies and supportive interpersonal style with students.

Several professors have observed me teach. The most common feedback I receive is, *"Lively presentation of material, with great clinical examples, stimulating questions to the students and practical strategies to manage the problem situations."* A letter of recommendation for a teaching award is in Appendix D, as well as several letters and e-mails from professors with comments about my teaching. I was also selected as one of a dozen best classroom professors to form a "Master's Guild" in the college. The invitation e-mail is in Appendix D. Below is a quote from the letter and an example of feedback from a professor in the PA department:

> *Dr. Lachman is a committed teacher and scholar. She is deeply dedicated to her students and takes great care to provide knowledge, guidance, and support. Her courses are impeccable and her interactions with students are both engaging and professional.*
> —Dr. Mary Ellen Smith Glasgow, associate dean of MSN programs, undergraduate programs and continuing nursing education

> *I wanted to thank you for doing such a great job with counseling/delivering bad news. . . . Your expertise and insight continue to be invaluable to the PA program and to me personally.*
> —Professor Rebecca Buckley

AWARDS/HONORS

I am proud to report acknowledgment from my colleagues inside and outside the university and from my dean. First, in 2005, I received the **President's Award** for mentorship of leaders within the organization from the International Society of Psychiatric-Mental Health Nurses. In 2007, I received the **Drexel University Physician Assistant Program's Nathaniel Alston Service Award** for recognition of my numerous contributions to the development of physician assistant students and exemplary support of the Physician Assistant Program and its mission. In 2008, I was selected by the American Nurses Association (ANA) to be the Mid-Atlantic Representative to the **Center for Ethics and Human Rights**. We author position statements and place relevant ethics information on the ANA Web site. In 2009, my dean selected me to be the **CNHP Baidia Fellow Representative** to the university committee. This group will develop entrepreneurship interdisciplinary courses and research opportunities.

PROFESSIONAL OUTREACH

There are several methods I use to improve my teaching and simultaneously reach out to the professional communities of psychiatry, ethics, and leadership. In Appendix F is the table of contents from my 2005 book, *Applied Ethics in Nursing*, and from my 2009 book—*Ethical Challenges in Healthcare: Developing Your Moral Compass*. Springer Publishing is the publisher for both of these books. Also in this section are examples of four ethics articles I wrote; three are from a column I write in *MedSurg Nursing* entitled "Ethics, Law and Policy." I have also included an article that will appear in *Nursing Administration Quarterly* in 2009, entitled "Teaching Innovation."

My ethical focus is on the dilemmas of end-of-life. I am ELNEC (End-of-Life Nursing Education Consortium) trained and provide classes on communication and ethical issues modules. I serve on the ethics committee for Chestnut Hill Healthcare and Hahnemann University Hospital and provide four educational sessions for a hospice organization yearly. I attend the hospice and palliative care conferences every year and have presented the past two years at the Rutgers University ELNEC conference. I have placed in Appendix F brochures to provide examples of presentations in each of these arenas I did at national conferences and several evaluations of these presentations.

I continue my health care consulting practice, where 80 percent of my time is spent on leadership development, performance coaching, team building, and conflict resolution at the board, executive, and frontline management arenas. I also present a one-day course entitled Nurse Executive Exam Preparation five times a year. This course enables nurse executives and nurse managers to pass the American National Accrediting Commission Credentialing exam. Several evaluations of this course are in the last section of Appendix F. My service on the board of Chestnut Hill Hospital since 1996 and on the Quality Improvement Committee keeps me abreast of the many issues facing hospitals today.

Future Teaching and Professional Development Goals

To continue to achieve excellence in teaching, my goals for 2009–2010 are the following:

1. Convene a designated committee of faculty teaching in course to revamp Advanced Ethical Decision Making in Health Care.
2. Determine how to integrate LeBow College of Business Baiada Entrepreneurial Business Competitions (concept, pitch, and plan) into Innovation and Intra/Entrepreneurship track assignments.
3. Continue participation in development of two doctoral courses, entitled Legal and Ethical Issues for Nursing Faculty and Administrators and Philosophy of Science, for our Ph.D. degree, which will be launched in fall 2010.
4. Integrate learning from acting as doctoral department chair from September 21, 2009, to March 13, 2010.
5. Utilize the College of Nursing and Health Professions peer evaluation system to gain master teacher feedback in winter quarter 2010.
6. Prepare documents for application as a Fellow in the American Academy of Nursing and promotion to clinical professor in 2010.

On an ongoing basis, I plan to do the following:

1. Act as second author on at least two doctoral student papers per year.
2. Support master's and doctoral students who want to write publishable papers by being second author or referring to other faculty who have interest in the subject.
3. Attend one conference on teaching strategies each year.

LIST OF APPENDICES

Appendix A: Samples of assignments and presentations

Appendix B: Syllabi and sample of assignments

Appendix C: Examples of feedback to students

Appendix D: Student evaluations, recommendations for change in course, and letters/e-mails from peer professors

Appendix E: Letters, e-mails from students

Appendix F: Examples of invited and peer-reviewed presentations, articles, and book table of contents

CHAPTER TWENTY-EIGHT

PATHOLOGY

Peter G. Anderson

Department of Pathology
University of Alabama at Birmingham School of Medicine
Spring 2010

CONTENTS

1. Statement of Teaching Responsibilities
2. Reflective Statement of Teaching Philosophy
3. Analysis of Methods, Strategies for Enhancing Student Learning, Curricular Development, and Use of Technologies
4. Efforts to Improve Teaching
5. Examination of Student Ratings and Diagnostic Questions
6. Teaching Goals: Short and Long Term
7. Appendices

1. STATEMENT OF TEACHING RESPONSIBILITIES

I am involved in a broad range of education-related activities:

- I am director of pathology undergraduate education, and in this capacity, I oversee all of the pathology department teaching activities for medical, dental, and graduate students. I am responsible for managing the pathology teaching office, and I supervise the program coordinator and a senior instructional design specialist. Our office provides logistical support, curricular development assistance, and technology support for all pathology faculty involved in educational endeavors.

- I developed and manage the Pathology Education Instructional Resource Web site (http://peir.net), which is an online resource for health sciences educators. This Web site contains a searchable database of over forty thousand digital images appropriate for health professions teaching. We have also developed a variety of self-study educational programs with formative quiz features. Our Web site receives thousands of hits per day from all over the world.
- For sixteen years, I was course director for the second-year medical pathology courses that ran for the entire second year of the medical school curriculum. The General Pathology course in the first semester provided background instruction in the basics of pathology. The second-semester course, Correlative Pathology, comprised nine units representing major organ systems. Each of these nine units had one or more unit leaders. I worked closely with each of these content expert unit leaders to assist them in their teaching activities and to help ensure continuity throughout the entire semester.
- In 2006–2007 I was responsible for developing an implementation plan for a new integrated medical curriculum comprising the first two years (preclerkship years) of the medical curriculum. In 2007 when we rolled out this new curriculum, I became coordinator of the preclerkship curriculum and am responsible for overseeing and assisting the module leaders and support staff who are involved in this new curriculum.
- I am also course director of the Biology of Disease course for second-year pathology Ph.D. graduate students and graduate students from other departments. I developed this course in 1996 and have led it ever since. This course is designed to expose graduate students to disease and some aspects of clinical medicine in order that they will have a better understanding of the disease issues they are investigating in their research.
- I also participate as a lecturer and facilitator in my own as well as other pathology courses for medical, dental, and graduate students.
- I mentor graduate students and serve on graduate committees, as well as mentor medical students who rotate through my laboratory for a summer research experience.

- Outside of my teaching duties in the department of pathology, I also give lectures on technology-enhanced learning to various departments at UAB, and I also give presentations on copyright issues as part of the Web design instruction series given by our UAB Instruction Technology group.
- I have also taught pathology review courses for medical students preparing for Step 1 of the United States Medical Licensing Examination (USMLE) certification examination.
- I have been a member of the Pathology Examination Committee for the USMLE Step 1 since 2002. As a member of this committee, I wrote and reviewed pathology questions that are used in the Step 1 medical licensing examination. I am currently chair of this committee. I am also a member of the USMLE Step 1 Interdisciplinary Review Committee, which reviews examination items that are in the "live bank" of questions available for the Step 1 examination each year. And I also participate on the committee that reviews the final version of the new USMLE Step 1 examination form that is prepared each year. I have also been appointed as the Test Committee Representative to the National Board of Medical Examiners and I am currently serving as the chair of the NBME Pathology Committee.
- I also lead faculty development workshops and chair course director workshops at various national and international meetings on topics of technology-enhanced learning and copyright and fair use issues.
- I have been a long-time member of the UAB School of Medicine Curriculum Committee and have chaired various curriculum review committees both internal and for external accreditation bodies.
- For a listing of specific teaching-related activities, see **Appendix A**.

2. REFLECTIVE STATEMENT OF TEACHING PHILOSOPHY

My main philosophy of teaching is an extension of my personal philosophy that you must always remain open and receptive to new things, new information, and new ideas. My teaching philosophy centers on the idea that we need to learn how best to access the flood of new information coming at us every day and process that information in a manner that makes it useful and usable to us.

My goal is to strive to make my students effective learners, not just learned professionals with heads full of facts that were obtained out of context and may soon become outdated. Of course, I also hope that my students will be learned as well— but the main theme of my teaching philosophy is to help students gain the background knowledge, the skills, and the desire to search out, evaluate, and comprehend new information. I feel that these knowledge-seeking behaviors and skills are the tools that will most likely make a good physician ready to practice the medicine of the twenty-first century.

Since most of my students are either professional students or faculty, I think it is important to utilize adult learning methodologies and approaches to education. In the context of health sciences education, I think the best approach is to use clinical cases where we provide a framework by which my (adult) students have enough background information to get them started, but also let them explore and dig deeper into whatever additional information they need to solve the case.

My approach to education is a hybrid of constructivism theory (build the knowledge base sequentially), cognitive psychology (learners as active processors of information), and adult learning principles (relevance, experiential learning). Thus, educational activities must be directed and structured to a point, but they must also allow learners to explore, interpret, and analyze for themselves in a relevant context.

A natural adjunct to my basic philosophy of teaching is that technology can be utilized to facilitate many of the activities and approaches needed to provide an instructional environment that will encourage lifelong learning in my students. Technology can be utilized and manipulated to perform a variety of functions that augment the instruction/learning process. Computers are infinitely patient taskmasters for students involved in drill and practice activities that are an integral part of the constructivism and the formative learning processes. Technology and the Internet are also wonderful tools for obtaining new information and for honing knowledge-searching behaviors that are key to the lifelong learner. My bias as a pathologist and a health professions educator is that the ability of technology to display images, sounds, motion, and, in some cases, tactile stimulation provides a perfect environment for health professions students to experience many aspects of their future profession without putting patients at risk. Thus, technology-enhanced learning is a major component of my education armamentarium, and the appropriate exploitation of technology forms an integral part of my teaching philosophy.

3. ANALYSIS OF METHODS, STRATEGIES FOR ENHANCING STUDENT LEARNING, CURRICULAR DEVELOPMENT, AND USE OF TECHNOLOGIES

Because of my varied roles in education I have a variety of teaching situations that require different objectives. Subsequently I have diverse methods for trying to achieve these objectives.

Director of Pathology Undergraduate Education

As director of pathology undergraduate education, my main goal is to provide an infrastructure and support system that facilitates innovative curricula and teaching methodologies. First and foremost, we try to make teaching easier for busy faculty members. We provide logistical support, scheduling room assignments, syllabus development, and so on, and we serve as the front for student questions and specific needs. We also provide instructional design support, most notably in the area of technology-enhanced learning activities. I also provide faculty development for young faculty involved in teaching and assist them with developing materials for their promotion and tenure process. For a list of faculty development seminars that I have given both at UAB and as invited presentations nationally and internationally, see **Appendix B**.

Webmaster—Pathology Education Instructional Resource

We have developed an extensive Web-based repository for pathology educational materials that is used by our faculty and by outside faculty. Review of server logs demonstrates that thousands of people from all over the world log onto our Web site every day and download instructional materials or review our online instructional programs and formative quiz modules. We also license access to our instructional materials to various publishers that use our images in educational publications. Because of our expertise in this area, we are often called on to assist other faculty in developing Web sites to meet their educational needs for residents, fellows, health-related professional students, and others. We have developed and maintain numerous Web sites for a variety of faculty here at UAB as well as a national pathology education group; see **Appendix C**.

UAB School of Medicine Preclerkship Curriculum Coordinator

As coordinator of the first two years of the medical curriculum (preclerkship curriculum), I manage large team-taught modules that run for approximately five to eight weeks each. These modules have a module director and a clinical codirector, as well as a module advisory group. I am responsible for overseeing the curricula and planning the implementation of this entire series of modules. In this regard, my main goal is to provide support to the module leaders to help them develop a stimulating and rigorous learning environment for our students that encourages development of independent thinking and lifelong learning skills. In the first few modules of our curriculum (the "fundamentals" modules), we have a curriculum that is directed and fairly linear. We provide a few lectures as a thread throughout the module and then add to this thread a variety of reading assignments, self-study case presentations with formative and summative computer quizzes, case presentations, and periodic summative examinations that are computer-based assessments designed to mimic the format of their medical national board examinations. This structure is designed to guide students but also to challenge the students to seek out information and develop lifelong learning behaviors. My role as coordinator overseeing the entire eighteen months of this curriculum is to provide support and guidance to the faculty educators serving as module leaders and to ensure continuity throughout the preclerkship curriculum. I try to provide assistance and advice when asked and I offer suggestions, but I try not to be too overbearing as coordinator. I try to empower each of the module leaders and their management group so they feel responsible for that module. This involves some juggling of control versus freedom, but, all in all, the modules run smoothly, and this new curriculum is well received by the students. For performance data on National Board examinations and sample student course numeric evaluations and comments, see **Appendix D**.

UAB School of Medicine Preclerkship Curriculum Module Director

I am also the module leader for one of the modules in our pre-clerkship curriculum. In this module, we present the fundamentals of pathology, microbiology, and pharmacology. This is a team-taught course with a variety of experts who present overview lectures. We also extensively utilize self-study computer-based instructional materials, case studies, team-based learning exercises, and other modalities to provide an effective learning environment for our adult learners. For performance data on National Board examinations and sample student course numeric evaluations and comments, see **Appendix E**.

Lecturer and Content Expert in Health Sciences Education

As a lecturer and participant in other courses, I am primarily responsible for delivering content via lectures or as a small group case facilitator. To this end, I try to utilize effective communication skills to provide classic lecture-type presentations in a way that captures the attention of the students and motivates them to be engaged. This is primarily accomplished by using clinical examples and trying to make the issues and material relevant to the students. I also endeavor to engage the students to participate in the process. For sample student course numeric evaluations and comments, see **Appendix F**.

4. EFFORTS TO IMPROVE TEACHING

It may sound self-serving, but in fact I am continually trying to improve my teaching. As stated in my philosophy statement, I feel it is important to continue growing and trying new things. For my own personal growth and intellectual enrichment, I am always on the lookout for new ideas and new strategies to enhance education. Below are some of the approaches that I have initiated.

Pedagogical Experiments

• As we have developed more and better Web-based instructional materials, the students have embraced the concept of self-study, and now we find that large numbers of students rarely, if ever, attend lectures or participate in review and/or discussion sessions with faculty. One way to get better student involvement is through small group discussion sessions. However, in a bustling academic medical center, it is difficult to find faculty who have time to serve as facilitators for the large numbers of small groups. Thus, we developed a team-based learning exercise for our course. We also designed it such that the cases we presented involved not only pathology but also microbiology and pharmacology—thus, we called these *integrated case studies*. With cooperation from the microbiology and pharmacology course directors and with grant funding that I obtained, we have developed online cases that the students can study and review. After they review the case the students write an essay (fewer than one thousand words) answering a question we posed about the case. In this essay, they are also required to list three references and give a rationale for how they chose the references and how they evaluated the quality of each reference. The entire class is then scheduled to meet and participate in the team-based learning exercise. The students are divided up into groups and are seated in their groups. When they enter the classroom, each student takes a five- or six-question multiple-choice quiz. After they turn in their answer sheets, each group discusses the quiz questions and comes to a consensus about the answers. They then submit a single answer sheet for each group. A faculty discussant then reviews the case and is encouraged to ask questions of the groups during the discussion session. After the case discussion is completed, a final multiple-choice quiz is handed out, and the students again work in their groups to come up with consensus answers to each question. The students' grades are the sum of all three quiz grades (individual and two group grades). Student response to this exercise has been mixed. If we have a dynamic case presenter who engages the students, the reviews tend to be fairly high. If we have a less dynamic case presenter, the student evaluations are less enthusiastic. By and large, the essays have been of fairly high quality, and since we do these on WebCT, we can also check them for plagiarism. In addition, our requirement that the students use references and also justify the quality of the references has been an effective teaching and learning tool. This was designed to coincide with an effort by our medical library staff to teach our medical students about how to find reputable reference sources. For a sample case, student course numeric evaluations and comments, and assessment comments from library personnel, see **Appendix G**.

- As stated in my teaching philosophy, I feel that technology can be an important adjunct to the curriculum. To this end, I have been active in developing computer-based and Web-based instructional materials and programs. One such program is the Interactive Pathology Laboratory (IPLab; http://IPlab.net). The IPLab offers an interactive, case-based approach for learning the concepts of general pathology as taught in today's medical schools. The program contains one thousand digitized photomicrographs and gross photographs supplemented by text written for a general pathology course director. The program has been designed with groups of cases organized into laboratory modules to complement any general pathology textbook. This program is employed as a peripheral learning instrument in addition to traditional text and laboratory slides. It can expand a student's exposure to an unlimited variety of pathological diagnostic interpretations. This extended access to photomicrographs and photographs can expose students to rare pathological conditions for which specimens are unavailable. For a sample case and student evaluations, see **Appendix H**.

- Due to my interest and expertise in the topic of technology-enhanced learning, I was asked to present a faculty development workshop for the International Association of Medical Science Educators. Each year prior to the start of the main meeting, I give a faculty development workshop for fifteen to thirty health science educators (depending on how many computers are available in the classroom). I have recruited two instructional design experts to help me with this workshop. The title or main topic of our workshop is Web pedagogy. We try to demonstrate various ways to utilize technology in a pedagogically sound manner to facilitate their instructional activities. This is a hands-on workshop where participants create case modules, author formative quiz programs, develop online surveys, and utilize resources readily available on the Web. This workshop has been repeated for the last five years, has received excellent reviews by the participants, and is usually sold out each year. For course outline and participant comments, see **Appendix I**.

Faculty Development Activities

• Early in the birth of the Internet, I became interested in using digital images for developing Web-based instructional programs. At the time, almost all pathology images were in the form of Kodachrome slides. I undertook a project, with the help of numerous collaborators (most of whom were medical students and work study students), to scan all of the teaching slides used in our pathology teaching program and put these slides into a Web-accessible database. The Pathology Education Instructional Resource Digital Library (http://peir2.path.uab.edu/pdl) contains a searchable database of over forty thousand digital images appropriate for health professions teaching. This Web site receives over a thousand hits per day on average and is utilized by health professions teachers all over the world. We also license our image database to publishers, which then use these images in their educational publications. For a sample image search, see **Appendix J**.

• In addition to designing and leading faculty development workshops at various venues, I also try to regularly participate in workshops to learn new things and hopefully come away with new ideas to improve my teaching. One example is the team-based learning conference that I recently attended. This conference is organized by the Team-Based Learning Collaborative (TBLC), which is a group of health professions educators dedicated to using team-based learning to further medical and allied health education. The main purpose of the TBLC is to support other faculty implementing team-based learning, to share teaching resources, and to promote evaluation and scholarship on team-based learning in medical education. Although I have used team-based learning in my pathology courses, I wanted to learn new things and experience many of the exciting new methodologies that educators are using across the country and around the world. For a listing of all faculty development workshops and activities that I have attended, see **Appendix K**.

5. Examination of Student Ratings and Diagnostic Questions

UAB has an extensive student ratings program that collects data on all instructional activities. These data can be extremely important for analyzing trends and getting a feel for students' feelings about the instructional process. However, in my opinion, it is always important to remember that the students are novices to the health professions education process, and their opinions are not necessarily that well informed. Things they may complain about as second-year medical students may become extremely important to them when they are working in the clinics. However, our job as educators is to provide an environment that demonstrates the relevance of all our educational activities, although it is not always possible to please everyone!

The UAB School of Medicine has an extensive student evaluation program with massive documents cataloguing all student comments over the last ten to fifteen years. I have included representative information from these medical student evaluations, as well as dental and graduate student evaluations; see **Appendix L**.

6. Teaching Goals: Short and Long Term

My teaching goals are commensurate with my overall philosophy of teaching in that I will strive to continue learning new things and try new experiments as they relate to teaching and learning. Although I have achieved some success in the area of education, I am always interested in improving my own teaching abilities and helping others improve as well. If I can continue to increase my understanding of the whole teaching and learning process I can use this knowledge to improve my own teaching and share this knowledge with colleagues who may look to me for guidance and support in their educational endeavors. To help guide this process I have the following short- and long-term goals:

Short-Term Goals

- Continue experimenting with team-based learning in the medical school curriculum. This modality, when paired with clinically relevant cases, makes for a powerful tool/process to help students learn new material in a clinically relevant

context and develop team-building skills. Our main obstacle
to date has been training of discussants who facilitate the exercises. I plan to work with specific faculty over the next year to
help them develop skills in this area.
- Over the next two years, I would like to refine the curriculum
in the medical and graduate courses to enhance learner-
centered exercises. We have begun and will continue to tie
the course objectives directly to our specific learning exercises
and to the examination questions.
- Update and refine current computer-based instructional materials and utilize new technologies to improve and update our
instructional materials.
- Continue to avail myself to faculty development activities and
literature related to improving education.

Long-Term Goals

My main long-term goal is to serve as a resource person or mentor
to junior faculty who are interested in teaching. I will continue to
use my experience and knowledge of academia to help faculty utilize their educational activities as a source of pride and as a useful
tool for academic advancement. It is my belief that an effective
way to improve the educational experience of our students is to
provide a strong support system for our faculty, thus helping all of
our faculty to become better educators. Knowledgeable, engaged
faculty will do a good job teaching, and this will result in a much
better educational environment/process for the students. Thus,
my main goal is to improve faculty development, and the net
result will be a better educational environment for our students.
In short, my long-term goal is to continue to improve in my own
teaching and to facilitate the improvement of my colleagues.

7. APPENDICES

A. Catalogue of teaching activities
B. List of faculty development presentations to UAB Pathology
faculty and residents
C. PEIR Web site information and usage data
D. General Pathology course syllabus, national board scores, stu-
dents' evaluations

E. Correlative Pathology national board scores, students' evaluations
F. Student evaluations and teaching awards
G. Sample integrated case, sample student essays, and student evaluations
H. Sample IPLab case and student evaluations
I. Faculty development workshop outline and participant evaluations
J. PEIR Digital Library examples and usage statistics
K. Listing of faculty development courses/activities attended
L. Representative student evaluations: Medical, dental, and graduate students

CHAPTER TWENTY-NINE

PHYSICAL THERAPY

Kimberly Tarver

Physical Therapist Assisting Program
Elgin Community College
Spring 2010

CONTENTS

PURPOSE STATEMENT

The purpose of my teaching portfolio is to improve my teaching, to serve as a model and legacy for my department, and to demonstrate my work in a format conducive to sharing with my peers in formal and informal settings. The process provides opportunity to document my teaching as I transition into a new role in the emerging Physical Therapist Assistant Program at Elgin Community College, which admitted its first class of students in the fall of 2007. While I also teach courses in the Physical Education-Health area, the content of this portfolio will primarily focus on my Physical Therapist Assistant Program teaching responsibilities.

TEACHING RESPONSIBILITIES

My primary teaching responsibilities lie in the Physical Therapist Assistant (PTA) Program with secondary responsibilities in the Physical Education-Health area. Graduates of the PTA program earn an associate of applied science degree, which qualifies them to sit for the state licensure examination. Physical therapist assistants work with patients in hospitals, clinics, rehabilitation settings, and school systems under the direct supervision of a physical therapist. PTA program courses are taught once per year with a cap of twenty students. The PTA program courses include both lecture and laboratory sessions and are concurrent with clinical practicum course work. This approach provides students opportunity to integrate and apply academic concepts by demonstration and practice of skills and techniques in the classroom and in the clinic. All PTA program courses are required and must be taken in sequence. The next table summarizes my teaching responsibilities reflecting my transition from the Physical Education-Health area to the Physical Therapist Assistant Program.

Course #	Course Title	Brief Description of Course	Semester Offered	Students per Section
PTA 120	Physical Therapist Assisting I	Introduces student to basics of patient care steps, legal and professional issues, fundamental skills, and vital signs	Fall 2007 (first time offered)	20

Course #	Course Title	Brief Description of Course	Semester Offered	Students per Section
PTA 122	Physical Therapist Assisting II	Builds on PTA 120; emphasizes pathophysiology, treatment interventions, and data collection skills	Spring 2008 (first time offered)	20
PTA 231	Physical Therapist Assisting III	Builds on previous course work; emphasizes orthopedics, wounds, and geriatrics through problem-based/ case study approach	Fall 2008 (first time offered)	20
PTA 241	Physical Therapist Assisting IV	Builds on previous course work; emphasizes neurologic, pediatric, and cardiopulmonary case studies	Spring 2009 (first time offered)	20
PTA 250	Physical Therapist Assistant Seminar	Explores current issues in health care; prepares students for licensure, employment, and development of lifelong learning plan	Spring 2009 (first time offered)	20

TEACHING PHILOSOPHY

As I have grown professionally and personally over my twelve years of teaching at Elgin Community College, I recognize three main areas that are critical to my success as an instructor. They are the foundation of my instruction in the Physical Education-Health area and have a significant influence on the Physical Therapist Assistant Program curriculum which I have helped to develop:

1. *Provide a fundamental base of knowledge on which to build and develop lifelong learning.* I strive to help students create a base of knowledge on which they can build throughout their lives. It is critical to me that they accept personal responsibility and are able to provide a rationale for both the actions they take and decisions they make. I am often heard saying, "You should always know why you're doing what you are doing, and if you don't, then maybe you shouldn't be doing what you're doing." Progression of the PTA Program curriculum reflects an ongoing process of accessing and reviewing new information, acquisition and practice of skills, and implementation of decision-making strategies. All courses I teach require students to practice accessing information and integrating it with course content.

2. *Provide opportunities to practice skills and apply knowledge.* I provide multiple opportunities for students to apply knowledge and practice skills. I want students to be prepared for the clinical setting. I want to create "aha!" moments in which they link knowledge gained with the skills they've learned and things become "real" rather than textbook examples they struggle to conceptualize. The classroom is an opportunity to "fly on the trapeze with a net" before going live in the real world where the stakes may be high and mistakes may result in serious consequences. Practice in the classroom provides students an opportunity to progress from an environment where they receive a high degree of supervision with support and cues to independent and confident practitioners. Experiential opportunities in the classroom build confidence, support future success in the external environment, and encourage retention of knowledge and skills over time.

3. *Create ethnic and cultural awareness and a climate of respect for the attitudes and beliefs of other groups and individuals.* I believe this may be the single most important thing I can do to prepare my students for success in the workplace and to positively impact the community in which we live. I recognize and

acknowledge my own limited perspectives and biases and the impact they have had on my own experiences with patients in the clinical setting and students in the classroom. Many of the students I have worked with also have limited experience and exposure to other cultures. Creating awareness, fostering positive attitudes, and dispelling myths and stereotypes are critical to achieving one of ECC's goals "to prepare students to learn, live, and work in a globally diverse society." It is also critical for health care providers to have a basic understanding of cultural characteristics regarding time, communication, the role of family, religion, and gender, health and health-care-related practices and beliefs as they impact the quality and delivery of patient care. This concept is also relevant to students taking courses in the Physical Education-Health area, as a majority of them are pursuing degrees in education, emergency response, and health care.

TEACHING METHODOLOGIES AND INSTRUCTIONAL MATERIALS

My philosophy is reflected in the variety of teaching methods I use to provide a fundamental base of knowledge on which to build and develop lifelong learning. They include lecture, collaborative activities, experiential learning activities, access to evidence through literature and technology, and integration of general education course content to build a foundation of knowledge and support development of lifelong learning skills. I also require activities through an online course management system. Syllabi include a course description, textbooks and readings, course objectives, grading criteria, course requirements, skill competencies, assignments, course policies, and a syllabus quiz. A course schedule provides a weekly breakdown of topics, readings, and important dates. Each topical unit includes a guide that identifies general and specific learning objectives linked to state and professional standards, learning resources, required equipment, key terms, summary of content, application and evaluation methods, lecture handouts, and lab activities. Students are encouraged to use the units to prepare for class, study, and review and as a study guide for examination. (Items referred to in this paragraph are available in Appendix A.)

My philosophy is also reflected in provision of opportunities to practice skills and apply knowledge through laboratory sessions utilizing demonstration, guided practice, paper patients or case studies, guided questions, worksheets, and role playing. Lab exercises and activities rely on students working in pairs or small groups with two lab instructors circulating to assist and address questions. A detailed rubric is issued to students for specific skills. It is utilized in lab activities to demonstrate and instruct students, serves as a peer and self-assessment tool, and is used later as a formal evaluation tool. Supplemental lab activities are voluntary and provide additional opportunities to practice outside of scheduled lab time. Lab problems or patient examples encourage critical thinking by requiring students to deviate from "normal" or standard procedures. (Samples representative of practice opportunities are found in Appendix A.)

My philosophy of creating ethnic and cultural awareness and a climate of respect for the attitudes and beliefs of other groups and individuals is addressed through modeling the behaviors and attitudes I hope my students will embody by seeking to understand, appreciate, and acknowledge similarities and differences of other groups and individuals. I encourage students to explore the cultural characteristics and values of groups to which they belong and compare them to those of other groups. The activities rely on reflection and discussion both online and in the classroom. The online segments provide students time to consider thoughts carefully before sharing them with others. Lecture and discussion provide an overview of a variety of cultural groups focusing on time, communication, the role of family, religion, and gender, health and health care related practices and beliefs. (Activities that are representative of my efforts are found in Appendix B.)

EVIDENCE OF STUDENT LEARNING

Evaluation and assessment of student learning and performance include written examinations, problem-based lab examinations, written work, classroom participation, online course contributions, self-assessment of skills, interventions, data collection skills, and self-assessment of professional behaviors. Evaluation of student learning is multidimensional and distributed among these activities. Written examinations are primarily in a multiple-choice format as items are intended to resemble licensure examination items. Exams also include short-answer and/or essay questions. Practical examinations are administered in pairs; students self-select their partner. (Samples of student performance work including in-service presentations, annotated bibliographies, modality charts, generic abilities assessment, and sample short-answer responses to specific test items are found in Appendix C.) A brief description of each item follows.

- In-service presentation handouts prepared by students demonstrate retention of student learning over time, communication skills (a critical element of patient care), and application of knowledge and skill in a new context. The ability to educate others is an entry-level expectation in many fields. This activity progresses knowledge along a continuum in which they must synthesize previously learned material, organize it into a presentation requiring they demonstrate and explain the material, and prepare handouts for the audience. This process provides opportunity to link knowledge to performance and apply it in a different context.

- Samples of the annotated bibliography assignment reflect the ability to access, describe, and interpret physical therapy–related research in PTA 122. Students self-select a topic of interest that they have been exposed to in the clinic or classroom. The activity provides opportunity to practice accessing literature to provide a rationale for the selected technique. Findings either support or negate the efficacy of the technique. This knowledge is considered in the decision-making process of whether the activity is warranted. Students become independent, lifelong learners as they discover they are able to find the answers to clinical questions without assistance.

- The modality chart activity is designed to help students prepare and study for written examination, review content prior to licensure examination, and serve as a reference tool in the clinical setting in PTA 122. This activity serves to create "aha!" moments as students recognize patterns relating to various modalities. The criteria permit each learner to organize the content into a format that makes sense to him or her. As this challenging content is organized and categorized, learners recognize patterns and make relational connections within the content. Anecdotal feedback from students includes: "I am so glad I did this before the exam!" "I wish I had done this before the exam." "I used this in the clinical setting and my clinical instructor loved it!"

- Samples of the self-assessment of generic abilities tool and written examination items are included in Appendix C as examples of additional pieces of evidence of learning.

Evaluating My Teaching

Peer Review/Classroom Observation

Formal classroom visitation occurs triennially. (Copies of their written reviews are found in Appendix F.) Academic Dean Vince Pelletier made the following comments after classroom observation:

> "Good use of real life examples to support objectives. Kept on target—yet very flexible when discussing different types of injuries." "Students appeared to be very comfortable asking and answering questions." "Excellent rapport with students. All of the students were attentive."

Comments noted by Academic Dean Polly Nash include:

> "Good variety . . . " "Good management skills." "Pacing was excellent."

Student Evaluations

The college provides a Student Evaluation of Instruction form for student use. Because PTA courses currently represent such a small sample, all student evaluation responses have been compiled together; future data will be delineated by course and semester to more accurately reflect teaching performance across the curriculum. Ratings are favorable for all diagnostic questions, with highest ratings relating to **commitment to create a climate of respect and foster ethnic and cultural awareness**. High ratings are also noted for items pertaining to instructor **enthusiasm** and instructor **accessibility**. The next table summarizes ratings on items that are linked to my philosophy statement regarding *creating ethnic and cultural awareness and a climate of respect for the attitudes and beliefs of other* *groups and individuals.* They are item 6, "The instructor encouraged students to express their ideas and opinions," and item 7, "The instructor treated students with courtesy and respect." Item 13, "The overall quality of instruction in this course was excellent," is also of value to me.

	COMBINED DATA SUMMARY FOR ALL SECTIONS	AVG. RATING OUT OF 4		
Item #	Statement	Fall 2007	Spring 2008	Fall 2008
1	Instructor presentations are well planned and organized.	3.7	3.5	3.7
2	The instructor clearly defined the objectives of this course.	3.8	3.5	3.8
3	The instructor clearly defined her expectations of me in this course.	3.7	2.8	3.8
4	The instructor displayed enthusiasm about the subject matter of this course.	3.9	3.8	3.9
5	The instructor spoke in clear, correct, and precise language.	3.9	3.8	3.7
6	The instructor encouraged students to express ideas and opinions.	3.9	3.9	3.8
7	The instructor treated students with courtesy and respect.	3.8	3.8	3.8
8	The examinations reflected the content and emphasis of this course.	3.8	3.5	4
9	The assigned homework, papers, or projects helped me learn from this subject.	3.7	3.5	3.7
10	The grading methods were fair and impartial.	3.8	3.7	3.9
11	The instructor returned examinations and/or assignments within a reasonable amount of time.	3.7	3.3	3.3
12	If you tried to contact the instructor outside of class, the instructor was generally accessible to give assistance.	3.9	3.6	4
13	The overall quality of instruction in this course was excellent.	3.8	3.6	3.7

Efforts to Improve Teaching

In addition to the college-generated evaluation form, I regularly implement an activity in which I solicit group feedback from the group regarding their preferences in the classroom. While some things are not negotiable, I have implemented student suggestions for current and future classes, including modifying project due dates, providing more case scenarios and open lab time, and increasing the time allotted for complicated content. The next table summarizes student responses for PTA 120 and PTA 122.

In PTA 120, I liked and want more . . .	I'd like less . . .	If I were teaching, I'd . . .
Handouts posted on D2L	D2L activity	Give study guides for exams
Case scenarios for practice	Comparative Religion activity format	Start documentation topic earlier in semester for more practice
D2L discussions	Professional Issues topics	List what students should know
More lab time	Death and Dying topic	
In PTA 122, I liked and want more . . .	I'd like less . . .	If I were teaching, I'd . . .
Lab time	Problems with temperature control in classroom	Move modality manual due date before the exam
Good balance of online and face-to-face activity		Add experiential lab for electrical current to "play"
Supplemental lab activities		Recommend a massage therapy textbook
Modality manual activity		Increase time spent on traction
PowerPoint handouts for every lecture		Spend more time on terminology for electrical current

Innovations in Teaching

My PTA courses are "enhanced": I utilize an online course management system to enhance content delivery by providing access to course materials and supplemental materials, promote

communication and collaboration, and utilize an online electronic grade book. The grade book provides students access to
their grades, which are automatically updated throughout the
semester; students have expressed appreciation for this tool, and
I find that it serves to motivate students. It also assists with early
identification of struggling students and provides opportunity for
intervention. I have also employed online activities to encourage
ethnic and cultural awareness, which include opportunities for
self-reflection, group projects, and discussion. (Samples of online
course assignments and activities are found in Appendix A and in
the cultural awareness activities in Appendix B.)

Curricular Revisions

I am heavily involved in development of the Physical Therapist
Assistant Program curriculum, which is based on state and professional standards and loosely modeled after Illinois Career and
Technical Education's Curriculum Revitalization Initiative (CRI). I
have created complementary learning units that are based on the
format utilized by the CRI. This model addresses student requests
for study guides and clarification of expectations. It also reflects a
process of acquiring knowledge to synthesis of knowledge as the
learner practices skills and then makes decisions regarding when
the skill may or may not be appropriate. (A unit sample based on
CRI is included in Appendix A and an example of a course outline
before and after revision in Appendix D.)

Teaching Conferences/Workshops Attended

I have participated in a variety of professional development activities, the most significant being Ethnic and Cultural Awareness
(Capella University) and the Federation of State Boards of
Physical Therapy Test Writing Workshop for Faculty. Both activities had direct impact on the courses I teach. Ethnic and Cultural
Awareness served to familiarize me with content and theory that
increased my own understanding and equipped me with tools and
strategies to utilize in the classroom. Samples of activities developed following completion of this activity are found in Appendix
B. The Test Writing Workshop helped me to align test items with
the format and degree of challenge students will encounter on the
state board licensure examination. I have implemented principles

of effective multiple-choice item writing and provide a sample of a written examination I prepared before and after the workshop in Appendix E. A list of additional professional activities I have participated in is included in Appendix G.

SHORT-TERM AND LONG-TERM TEACHING GOALS

Short-Term Goals (One to Two Years)
1. Seek written feedback from peer observers.
2. Review course methodologies and instructional materials of other instructors.
3. Observe other instructors, and provide written feedback.
4. Create written examinations that mirror PTA licensure examination and more accurately assess student learning.
5. Create hybrid course delivery for PHR 102 First Aid and Safety to be offered in spring 2009.

Long-Term Goals (Three to Five Years)
1. PTA Program Accreditation and Program Improvement.
2. Infuse/transform curriculum with multicultural perspectives.
3. Support campuswide teaching portfolio initiative.

APPENDICES

Appendix A: Course Materials
Appendix B: Ethnic and Cultural Awareness Activities
Appendix C: Evidence of Student Learning
Appendix D: Curriculum Revisions
Appendix E: Written Examination Revisions
Appendix F: Evaluating My Teaching
Appendix G: Professional Activities
Appendix H: Student Evaluation of Instruction
Appendix I: Evidence of Student Learning

CHAPTER THIRTY

PHYSICS

Michaela Burkardt

Department of Physics
New Mexico State University
Spring 2010

CONTENTS

STATEMENT OF TEACHING RESPONSIBILITIES

As a part-time faculty member, my primary responsibility is teaching introductory physics, mostly to nonmajors. About two-thirds of my students in the algebra-based courses have never taken any physics courses before, and many are timid about taking this required course. The courses I taught most recently are listed in the next table.

Course	Title	Role in Curriculum	Number of Students	Semester
Phys212	General Physics II	Algebra based, nonmajors, required	37–54	Spring 2008, Fall 2007
Phys213	Mechanics	Calculus based, physical science majors, required; dual credit	12	Fall 2008
Phys221	General Physics for Life Sciences I	Algebra based, life science majors, required	45–61	Fall 2008, Fall 2007, Fall 2006, Fall 2005
Phys222	General Physics for Life Sciences II	Algebra based, life science majors, required	28–43	Spring 2008, Spring 2007, Spring 2006, Spring 2005
Phys223	Supplemental Instruction to Phys221	Algebra based, life science majors, optional	9–22	Fall 2008, Fall 2007, Fall 2006, Fall 2005
Phys224	Supplemental Instruction to Phys222	Algebra based, life science majors, optional	10–20	Spring 2008, Spring 2007, Spring 2006, Spring 2005

TEACHING PHILOSOPHY

Whenever I begin working with new students, my first goal is to create some curiosity about physics and a classroom climate of mutual respect and trust. My students should become confident that they *can* learn physics, that it is worth learning, and that they will be more successful when we all work cooperatively.

Many of my life science students have said that they have difficulty with "stone-cold" math and science and need context for what they learn. I believe that students need to not just hear about physics, but see it in action and explore it hands-on. Therefore, I show lecture demonstrations in most of my classes or bring in simple, short experiments for group explorations. I often use household items for experiments to show students that physics is all around them in their lives. Outlooks to applications that they may encounter in their future careers also make the course content more relevant to the students.

The demonstrations were just plain EXCELLENT, and invaluable in terms of helping us get applicable situations for some kind of abstract ideas. (Phys222, spring05)

I want my teaching to be a positive learning experience for the students. I show my interest in them by asking about their future plans or fears and encourage them to give me feedback about their learning needs. Even in a class of fifty, my students are not just faces in the classroom, but personalities with their own background and learning styles. Since my students change every year, I need to adjust my teaching to each new group, always meeting them where they are and challenging them to the next step.

This is my favorite class—the challenge is fun. (Phys222, fall 2006)

When teaching physics, I emphasize concepts and challenge students to reason instead of "hunting for equations." I foster peer instruction and have used spontaneous small groups of students, as well as permanent learning teams in my courses. While students discuss concept tests, tutorial problems, or observations in class, many continue collaborations outside of class for reading questions or homework assignments.

My courses are structured for ongoing learning in and out of class. Frequent assignments ensure that students keep up with the (fast) pace of the course, and frequent formative assessment gives both students and me (as instructor) feedback about what learning has occurred. If I notice misconceptions, I inquire into the underlying assumptions and tend to confront students with them. Often I also find alternative ways to teach the not-yet-understood content.

> *She cares about teaching. She goes out of her way to create*
> *opportunities to learn, when she sees an obstacle or barrier.*
> *(Phys221, fall 2008)*

I want my students to be successful. They are my partners in learning, and therefore my instruction is student centered. I am open to constructive feedback and, when feasible, respond to student suggestions. I do provide academic challenge, but I also give support personally or through my teaching materials that help students achieve better understanding.

> *Dr. Burkardt is a great instructor & motivating me to excel*
> *not just in physics but all areas of education. (Phys222,*
> *spring 2008)*

I am passionate about physics, and I do love teaching. These two semesters are for many of my students the only time they are exposed to physics. This is my chance to share some of my enthusiasm with them, make them see the world with different eyes, and hopefully set a seed for a lifelong journey of scientific discovery.

> *Dr. Burkardt is quite simply the best teacher I have ever had*
> *in high school or college. She is amazing. She has actually*
> *made me consider changing my major to physics. She makes*
> *it so exciting. (Phys222, spring 2008)*

TEACHING STRATEGIES AND IMPLEMENTATION

Standards

A student should never be penalized for helping another student succeed. Therefore, my grading scales are absolute. Grades are earned with many varying assessments throughout the semester that are designed to give feedback.

Making Expectations Clear

I expect my students to read through textbook material before they come to class. Rather than just identifying the pages in the textbook, I give them reading assignments that introduce the purpose of this unit, define new terminology, direct to figures or examples in the book, and ask guiding questions that focus on important concepts. Several times throughout the semester, students are tested on their understanding after their reading and before classroom instruction.

Learning objectives are given for each class and for exams. I also provide example exam questions for practice, so that the style of exams is never a surprise, just the questions!

Providing Feedback

In classes of more than fifty students, giving meaningful and frequent feedback is challenging. I can still accomplish that, however, with the use of technology:

- During class, students have to analyze concept questions that they discuss with peers before submitting their answers using clickers (a classroom response system). Immediately afterward, a histogram of answers chosen is displayed. If the answers seem random, I engage the entire class in discussion, and the same question, or a related one, is posed again. This process makes students aware of misconceptions or mastery of the material just learned, and it also influences how much time I spend teaching this concept.
- Homework is mostly given online. Problem sets are randomized in terms of numerical values, so I can allow collaboration while still encouraging individual accountability. Once submitted, each problem is automatically and instantly graded, and students are allowed to resubmit until they get the answer correct.
- Learning materials such as reading assignments, lecture handouts, and solutions to homework and quizzes are distributed via a course Web site.
- Further optional "what-if" explorations via simulations or information about applications of physics are just one click away as links on the "class activity" Web page.

- An online grade book allows students to assess their success at all times.

Individualized feedback is given via paper tests or occasional paper homework. The questions include concept tests, numerical free-response problems, or short explanations. My feedback focuses on reasoning or problem-solving strategies and their documentation. I not only point out where mistakes have been made, but also acknowledge good explanations or improvements over time.

Need for Problem-Solving Practice

The initial approach of many students when confronted with a physics problem is "equation hunting" and "plug-and-chuck" using trial and error and little understanding. I discourage this approach by focusing on concept questions with no calculations or by giving implicit or too much information. Learning how to solve problems requires practice, just like you can learn to ride a bike only when you actually sit on one. Therefore, I spent class time working through examples or comprehensive problems with the entire class or have students work on team in class exercises (TICAs). I grade only one response for the team. This forces students to argue until they agree on one answer and it cuts down on my time grading. Examples of TICAs can be found in **Appendix B**.

To give students an opportunity to review problem-solving approaches outside class, I post worked-out examples or self-created online tutorials on the class Web site.

REPRESENTATIVE COURSE SYLLABI

With a standardized course syllabus, I give my students course information that includes my learning community vision, the encouraged forms of collaboration, strategies for success in physics, and evaluation detail. This helps set expectations and fosters a safe and supportive learning community. See representative course syllabi in **Appendix A**.

New Course Development, Materials, and Innovations

I developed new Physics for Life Sciences courses (Phys221 and Phys222) with the application of physics in life science laboratories and medicine in mind. While still introducing the standard content of an introductory general physics course, this course gives outlooks of how physics plays a role in medicine or is the basis of laboratory techniques. To supplement the textbook, I have written several handouts with interdisciplinary topics where the basic principles learned in my courses apply. Topics included jumping, the centrifuge, human hearing, blood circulation, electrophoresis, membrane potentials, or X-rays, and examples of these handouts can be found in **Appendix B**. By making physics more relevant to students who do not intend to major in this discipline, I increase their motivation.

The success of my informal weekly recitations several years ago encouraged me to pilot Supplemental Instruction (SI) as an optional one-credit course (Phys223 or Phys224). Between 25 and 40 percent of students in a Physics for Life Sciences course also enroll in the accompanying SI course that I teach myself. During SI sessions, students work cooperatively on tutorial-style questions and practice their problem-solving skills. The student evaluations for SI courses have consistently been outstanding, as can be seen in **Appendix D**.

Evidence of Student Learning

The physics department is using the nationally recognized Force Concept Inventory (FCI) to monitor student learning in introductory calculus-based courses. The FCI is given as pre- and posttest and consists of thirty cross-correlated multiple-choice conceptual questions about applications of force and motion and has been used nationally as a diagnostic tool for thousands of students. According to a study looking at the learning of six thousand students, published in 1998 by Hake, the normalized learning gain for traditional lecture style courses is 0.23 ± 0.04 and for active-learning style courses 0.48 ± 0.14. I am pleased that in fall 2008, the normalized learning gain in Phys213 was 0.62, which is comparable with the best results achieved nationally. For references, see **Appendix C**.

In fall 2007 the College of Arts and Sciences assessed all New Mexico Common Core courses for the objective, "Apply quantitative analysis to scientific problems." Using a rubric (primary trait analysis) I assessed the level of performance of forty-three students in Phys221 using the following criteria: "Understanding of problem," solution "strategy," use of "unit conversion and scientific notation," and "report" of the quantitative answer. Forty percent of the students scored as "exemplary," 40 percent as "acceptable," 20 percent as "marginal," and none as "beginning." The detailed report can be found in **Appendix C**.

As an indicator of student learning, I included some high, medium, and low student work on a representative exam, a list of corresponding learning objectives, and the equation sheet used in the exam in **Appendix C**.

EVALUATION OF TEACHING PERFORMANCE

Summative Student Evaluations

My student evaluations for the Physics for Life Sciences courses and their Supplemental Instruction courses have been consistently outstanding—highest in the department for service courses. I earn positive comments from my students about my enthusiasm, subject knowledge, willingness to help students learn, my attitude toward students, the organization of my courses, and my flexibility to adjust my teaching to students' learning styles. Student ratings for my teaching are shown in the next table.

Course	Phys221 (2005–2008)	Phys222 (2005–2008)	Phys223 (2005–2008)	Phys224 (2005–2008)	Phys212 (2007–2008)	Phys213 (2008)
Instructor's overall performance	A: 87.0% B: 10.4%	A: 90.2% B: 7.4%	A: 90.2% B: 7.8%	A: 100%	A: 61.8% B: 20.6%	A: 90.0% B: -
I would recommend this instructor (without reservations)	91.5% (83.1%)	100% (90.1%)	96.1% (88.2%)	100% (98.4%)	76.5% (61.8%)	90.0% (90.0%)

Course	Phys221 (2005– 2008)	Phys222 (2005– 2008)	Phys223 (2005– 2008)	Phys224 (2005– 2008)	Phys212 (2007– 2008)	Phys213 (2008)
Number of students responding	154	121	51	61	68	10
Response rate	81.1%	88.3%	91.1%	100%	81.0%	83.3%

Summaries of my evaluations for these courses can be found in **Appendix D**.

As can be seen from the summary table, my evaluations are more average for teaching the second semester of General Physics (Phys212). The difference is that I do not teach the entire two-semester sequence of General Physics myself, and students come with widely varying experiences from their first semester courses.

Formative Student Feedback Used for Improving Teaching

Observation of students approaching problems, student evaluations, questionnaires at midterm and at the end of the semester, as well as individual student comments, have been used to improve teaching. I believe in lifelong learning, and my teaching is no exception. The questionnaires have focused on helpfulness of teaching strategies, quality of the teaching material, clarity of evaluation standards, effectiveness of group work, and student-teacher relation, but also encouraged constructive suggestions. Sample questionnaires can be found in **Appendix D**.

I learned that each group of students is different in their preferred learning styles and their group dynamics. Repeating a recipe of success does not necessarily lead to success again. I strive to learn about my students' strengths and needs at the beginning of my first semester with them and adjust my teaching to suit their needs.

Often less-than-satisfactory outcomes on student exams inspire the creation of new examples or tutorials. I informally evaluate all student assessments by comparing learning outcomes with previous years to determine if a new teaching strategy resulted in greater learning.

Feedback from Colleagues

Stephen Kanim, associate professor in the Department of Physics and a respected *researcher* in physics education, called me (in 2006):

> *The epitome of a dedicated physics instructor.*

Michele Shuster, assistant professor of biology at NMSU, wrote in 2006:

> *The way in which she models the approaches to problem solving is, well, a model for the rest of us.*

David Smith, associate professor of chemistry, stated in 2006:

> *Given the evident rigor of her course materials, these end-user evaluations provide an important final certification of the overall quality of her instruction.*

The *promotion committee* of the physics department stated in 2006:

> *Her evaluations are so good that even those in the "worst" semesters would be the envy of any professor in the department teaching these types of courses. The best evaluations (those that she has been teaching recently) are almost unheard of in the current era. . . . Dr. Burkardt is an energetic leader of a sometimes neglected area in the Physics Department, the introductory algebra-based courses. We are grateful to have her teaching talent and organizational skills available to us.*

See more colleague comments in Appendix E.

Department Head's Appraisal

The department head's appraisal for years 2005–2007 have ranked me in the highest group (of five) for my teaching, course development, and service to the department. Using a new evaluation system, my teaching, outreach, and overall performance were rated as "exceeds expectations" for 2008—a special recognition, since I was the only faculty member in my department with this rating in the categories teaching and outreach.

Her discussion of teaching objectives in her annual report read like a text-book of good physics instruction. (DH Gary Kyle, 2005)

Dr. Burkardt is the top instructor in our department . . . (DH Tom Hearn, 2007)

See additional comments in Appendix E.

RECOGNITION OF TEACHING/AWARDS

My commitment to teaching has been recognized by my students, my colleagues, my department head, and the dean of the College of Arts and Sciences.

- In March 2007 I was the recipient of a NMSU Arts and Sciences Faculty Outstanding Achievement Award.
- In August 2007 I was promoted to college associate professor.

PROFESSIONAL DEVELOPMENT

To stay current in the use of technology in teaching, I took from fall 2007 through summer 2008 five graduate courses with the College of Extended Learning, for which I earned in summer 2008 a graduate certificate in online teaching and learning from New Mexico State University.

My major source for professional development has been the Teaching Academy at New Mexico State University (see Appendix F). During 2003–2008 I participated in more than 191 faculty training hours on topics like student learning, teaching paradigms, instructional design, and critical thinking. In 2009 I joined the Teaching Academy as coordinator of the PRIMOS project, funded by a U.S. Department of Education grant. My role has been to provide faculty development and lead a year-long cohort of STEM (science, technology, engineering, and math) faculty in advancing undergraduate teaching and learning in STEM fields both at New Mexico State University and Doña Ana Community College.

Service and Outreach

Even though service and outreach have not been part of my duties, I have been engaged in:

- Bringing hands-on science experiments to elementary school students and modeling inquiry-based teaching of science to elementary teachers (in second-, fourth-, and fifth-grade classrooms, until 2007) and middle school science teachers (SC²workshop, 2007).
- Lobbying for Phys213 and Phys214 and other science courses to be offered for dual credit—both as elective for high school graduation and college course work (2008).
- Serving on the district advisory council of Las Cruces Public Schools and several school advisory councils (2004–present).

A more comprehensive list of outreach and service activities as well as reflective letters from teachers can be found in **Appendix G**, Service and Outreach.

Appendices

A. Representative Course Syllabi
B. Sample Course Material
C. Evaluating Student Learning and Giving Feedback
D. Student Evaluations and Comments
E. Evaluations from Department Heads and Peers
F. Teaching Academy
G. Service and Outreach

CHAPTER THIRTY-ONE

PHYSIOLOGY AND DEVELOPMENTAL BIOLOGY

Michael D. Brown

Department of Physiology and Developmental Biology
Brigham Young University
Spring 2010

CONTENTS

1. Teaching Responsibilities
2. Teaching Philosophy
3. Teaching Strategies and Methods
4. Assessing Student Learning
5. Motivating and Inspiring Students
6. Evaluating My Teaching
7. Teaching Improvement
8. Goals
9. Appendices

TEACHING RESPONSIBILITIES

As a professional tract teaching faculty member, my primary responsibility is teaching undergraduate neuroscience and physiology courses (see the next table).

Course and Credits	Course Name	Role in Curriculum	Average # of Students	Frequency Taught
Neuro 205, 3 credits	Neurobiology	Required for majors, first neuroscience course for majors	70 students each section	1 section every other year
Neuro 360, 2 credits	Neuroanatomy	Required for majors, focuses on the functional anatomy of the brain and spinal cord	24 students each section	2 sections each fall and winter
Neuro 480, 3 credits	Advanced Neuroscience	Required for majors, capstone course for Neuroscience, PDBIO, and Biophysics majors	40 students each section	1 section each fall and winter
Neuro 481, 1 credit	Neuroscience Laboratory	Required for majors, capstone lab course	22 students each section	2 sections (cotaught) each fall and winter
PDBio 305, 4 credits	Human Physiology (with Lab)	Required course or elective for many majors (nursing, dietetics, exercise science, biology, etc.), covers the function of body organ systems	100 students each section	1 section each fall and winter

In addition to formal classroom teaching, I mentor several students each semester as teaching assistants. These students help write and grade quizzes and hold regular office hours and review sessions. I also work closely with graduate and honors undergraduate students. During the last three years, I have served on the graduate committees of three Ph.D. students and three M.S.

students and have advised four undergraduate honors students during the writing and defending of their honors theses. *Names of mentored students and feedback concerning their mentored experiences appear in Appendix A.*

I am the faculty advisor for 350 neuroscience majors. I assist these students in defining their career goals and in outlining a course of action to help them graduate from BYU in a timely manner and prepare them for their future careers.

TEACHING PHILOSOPHY

Learning is both an intellectual and spiritual endeavor. An excellent teacher provides an environment that allows both the intellectual and spiritual aspects of learning to flourish within his or her students. Such a teacher is thoroughly competent in his or her field and well versed and practiced in the most effective teaching styles and methods. He or she is a master at making difficult concepts clear in the minds of students and is absolutely committed to helping students not only understand, but wholly digest and apply the knowledge of the discipline being taught. The spiritual side of student learning is buoyed up by the teacher's genuine love, concern, trust, and respect for each and every student, as well as his or her own personal spiritual preparation.

An excellent student, in turn, works hard to develop and nourish the intellectual and spiritual aspects of his or her own learning. He or she commits to complete all readings, activities, and assignments to the best of his or her ability and to stretch his or her mind and thoughts beyond current capacity. The student comes to class each day with a hunger for new knowledge and leaves with a desire to teach others what has been learned. Such a student has absolute integrity and honor in life, including both academic and spiritual pursuits.

When an excellent teacher and an excellent student meet in the same classroom, both teacher and student are intellectually and spiritually edified. What occurs in that classroom is etched into the heart and mind of both teacher and student. In such a setting, students feel a genuine, personal connection with the discipline as they learn essential knowledge and skills that make their own life more rewarding and increase their ability to serve others around them throughout their life.

TEACHING STRATEGIES AND METHODS

Because students learn best when multiple learning modalities are used, I use a variety of teaching techniques, including the following:

- Study objectives and the course textbook. Prior to each class period, students complete study objective worksheets based on a specific reading assignment. In some classes, they are given a short quiz based on the material at the beginning of class. This encourages students to use the textbook in gaining a basic understanding of the material to be covered in the upcoming class. *Sample study objective worksheets are contained in Appendix B.*
- PowerPoint presentations and associated handouts. PowerPoint slides contain a minimum number of words and a maximum number of pictures and figures. Students take their own notes as we discuss the pictures and figures.
- Whiteboard drawings. Drawing clear pictures on the whiteboard with colored markers is an excellent way to get students involved during class. Because whiteboard drawings can be spontaneously modified, I am able to address students' questions as they arise.
- Blackboard online technology. Students can access detailed syllabi, study objectives, up-to-date grades, animations, handouts, and worksheets on the course Web site.
- Interactive visual aids. To assist students in their learning, I provide manipulatable three-dimensional organ and organ system models, short animations of molecular events, and interactive software programs.
- In-class involvement activities. Students are given short in-class involvement activities to complete individually or in small groups (two to three students). These include such things as completing worksheets, solving application problems, and examining medical case studies.
- Class presentations and discussions of current literature. In advanced classes, students critique recently published papers related to material covered in lecture and the textbook. Students learn to gather information from primary sources and apply their knowledge to topics that interest them.
- Relating science to life. In class, we talk about how science relates to real life (disease conditions, emotions, addictions,

sleep, motivation, and so forth). These asides break up the class into digestible segments, help students feel at ease, and allow science to "come to life."

Examples of class handouts and activities can be found in Appendix C.

Assessing Student Learning

To be an effective teacher, it is imperative to assess what students actually know and what they can do as a result of their classroom experiences. I assess student learning on an ongoing basis throughout each of my courses. Assessments are of both formal and informal nature and are listed below:

- Homework quizzes. In introductory courses (Neuro 205 and 360), students encounter a short quiz at the beginning of each class period. The purpose of these quizzes is to assess each student's understanding of the homework assignment and provide instant feedback to students so they know what information they need to have clarified during class.
- Active learning activities. In-class involvement activities are designed to assess student understanding and application of course material. Students get feedback from the instructor, teaching assistants, and each other as they work together to complete assignments.
- Exams. Student learning is formally evaluated on midterm exams and comprehensive final exams. These exams are based on readings, lectures, class activities, and knowledge and application of outlined study objectives. Exams contain a mixture of essay, short-answer, fill-in-the-blank, multiple-choice, matching, and true/false questions.
- Presentations and discussions. Advanced students demonstrate their learning on literature discussion days. A quiz covering the assigned papers is given at the beginning of class. Students then formally present their interpretations and evaluations of specific aspects of the papers to their classmates, answer questions, and lead a short discussion to gather others' ideas. Each student receives informal feedback from his or her peers and a formal grade from the instructor.

- Lab assessments. Assessment of student learning in lab (Neuro 481) is accomplished using lab practical exams, lab worksheet, and lab reports. Students are also given instruction and immediate feedback as they learn skills during lab time.

Please see Appendix D for examples of assessment tools and graded examples of student work.

MOTIVATING AND INSPIRING STUDENTS

The role of a teacher is not only to teach but to motivate and inspire students to perform to the best of their ability. To this end, I do the following:

- Share my own passion for physiology and neuroscience. Students report that my enthusiasm is contagious and that they "catch" the same desire to learn the subject.
- Express confidence and give encouragement. As often as appropriate, I express genuine praise and encouragement to my students in class, in e-mails, and in online announcements. If they do not do as well as I had hoped, I share my concern and try to help them discover how to perform better in the future. I give students individual attention before, during, and after class. Students report that my interest in their success motivates them to work hard.
- Provide a course organization to help students succeed. Detailed syllabi and study objectives are provided so that students know exactly what is expected in order to succeed. This "no surprises" approach allows students to focus on developing important skills and learning required content with confidence, knowing that they will be fairly evaluated on what they are learning. *Examples of course syllabi can be found in Appendix E.*

EVALUATING MY TEACHING

Student Evaluations

Student evaluations of my courses have been very positive. Average scores each semester have been well above the averages of my department (PDBio), college (Life Sciences), and the

SCALE: 1–8, WITH 8 BEING HIGH

	Neuro 360 Winter '08	Neuro 480 Winter '08	Neuro 481 Winter '08	PDBio 305 Winter '08	Neuro 205 Fall '08	Neuro 360 Fall '08	Neuro 480 Fall '08	Neuro 481 Fall '08	Average Scores
# of students	44	47	24	136	72	40	28	15	51
Overall course	7.0	7.7	7.2	7.2	7.3	7.6	7.7	6.7	7.3
Overall instructor	7.5	7.9	7.7	7.6	7.7	7.8	7.9	7.7	7.7
Amount learned	7.6	7.7	7.1	7.4	7.6	7.7	7.9	6.5	7.4
Intellectual skills developed	6.9	7.7	7.2	7.0	7.0	7.5	7.7	6.6	7.2
Integrates gospel into subject	6.9	7.7	7.7	7.4	7.4	7.3	7.6	7.5	7.4
Spiritually inspiring	7.0	7.7	7.7	7.5	7.4	7.5	7.7	7.5	7.5

university. Scores from representative categories are shown in the next table.

Complete student evaluations from each BYU course are shown in Appendix F.

Comments from students have noted that my courses are well organized, handouts and study objectives are helpful, students feel that I am an approachable and caring instructor, class activities are helpful to student learning, and that each course is very challenging yet fair. Former students who are now in graduate and professional programs report that the curriculum and study techniques they learned in my classes prepared them well for their programs. Three specific student comments (anonymous) are written below. *All student comments from each course I have taught during the last two years are shown in Appendix F.*

> One of the best classes I have ever taken—well structured, well taught, well organized, and a good textbook. The study objectives provided by the instructor were very useful in helping to sort out all of the information in the textbook. The handouts and in-class participation activities were great learning tools. The class was fun to attend and questions were always answered with consideration. (Neuro 205 student)

> [Although] this was one of the toughest courses I have taken at BYU, Dr. Brown instilled in me the desire to do better than I have in any other course at BYU. This course really helped me to learn how to learn. (Neuro 480 student)

> This [lab] course taught me a lot about microscopes and brain tissue. The course was well organized and we used our time learning valuable laboratory technique. One of the best, most hands-on classes I have taken at BYU. (Neuro 481 student)

What is most pleasing to me is that when students are asked how much they learned in my courses, they reported significant learning and that their intellectual skills increased greatly. They also reported that the gospel was related to the subjects of neuroscience and physiology and that they were spiritually inspired. These evaluations are rewarding to me because they verify that significant intellectual and spiritual learning is occurring in my courses.

Peer and Administrator Evaluations

During my time at BYU, my teaching has been evaluated by my department chairs (Dr. James Porter and Dr. William Winder), my faculty mentor (Dr. Ward Rhees), and faculty peers (Dr. Sterling Sudweeks, Dr. Scott Steffensen, and Dr. Edwin Lephart). Evaluations have included classroom visits and examination of course materials and policies. Two specific comments are written below. *Copies of all evaluations are included in Appendix G.*

> I was impressed with [Mike's] teaching ability, lecture organization, enthusiasm, and his ability to interact with and motivate students. He is undoubtedly one of the most outstanding teachers on the BYU campus. (Dr. Ward Rhees)

> Dr. Brown is clearly an excellent teacher. He is very conscientious about his preparations to teach, as evidenced by the excellent materials he has put together for his courses. The materials are of high quality, cover the significant topics relevant to the courses, and evidence demonstrates that they are well-utilized by the students in his courses. (Dr. Sterling Sudweeks)

TEACHING IMPROVEMENT

Course Revisions Based on Specific Feedback

Evaluation of formal and informal feedback from students has prompted changes in my course curriculum, teaching methodology, and assessment measures. As examples, comments from students have prompted me to do the following:

- Revise study objectives to clarify the expectations I have for student work and learning
- Provide more pictures and fewer words on student handouts
- Give more specific examples and analogies to help students understand difficult ideas

- Provide application-based practice questions to better prepare students for exams
- Revise policies for missed work due to excused absences
- Increase the availability of resources for group and individual studying outside of class

Feedback from faculty colleagues has led to the following specific changes in my courses:

- Increased rigor in presentation of details and applications in my 300/400-level courses
- Increased discussion of recently published primary research articles in Neuro 480
- Updated lecture topics and study objectives for all courses

Course Revisions Prompted by Evaluation of Student Learning

Careful evaluation of student grades on exams and quizzes, responses to questions in class, and performance on class activities also helps me to improve my teaching methods and materials. The following list summarizes some of the ways I have improved my courses since I have been at BYU. *For a more complete list, please see Appendix H.*

- More effective visual aids, class handouts, PowerPoint presentations, and active learning exercises have been added each semester.
- Animations, movie clips, and practical examples have been added to demonstrate difficult concepts and their applications.
- The Neuro 360 and 481 lab room has been remodeled and re-outfitted with the most up-to-date computer software, models, and microscopes.
- Electronic resources have been made more accessible to students by using Blackboard technology and by placing software programs on open access lab computers.
- Exam-stat reports are used to identify and revise problematic exam questions

New Courses, Materials, and Assignments

In the last five years, I have developed Neuro 360 (Neuroanatomy), a new course to BYU, and significantly redesigned Neuro 480 (Advanced Neuroscience) and Neuro 481 (Neuroscience Lab). I have also been heavily involved in designing the curriculum for the neuroscience major.

Staying Current in My Discipline and Participation in Meetings and Conferences

I am currently a member of the Society for Neuroscience, Faculty for Undergraduate Neuroscience, and the Human Anatomy and Physiology Society. These memberships not only help me to keep up with newly published methods, trends, and knowledge in my field, but they also allow me to share ideas with other faculty and with textbook publishers. I have attended the annual Society for Neuroscience meeting every year since coming to BYU. In 2007, I attended the Human Anatomy and Physiology annual meeting.

I attended the Teaching Professor Conference in 2005 and 2008. This two and a half-day conference for teaching professors in all disciplines focuses on important issues such as facilitating student learning, teaching large classes, faculty growth, technology in the classroom, and the scholarship of teaching and learning. After returning from each conference, I have implemented ideas that have improved my courses. As one example, I reevaluated all of my visual aids to make sure that they were large and simple enough to be seen from every seat in my classroom.

GOALS

I intend to provide students an outstanding learning experience in each course that I teach. Each course will reflect the most current knowledge and utilize the most effective teaching styles and techniques. To this end, during the next year, I will:

1. Evaluate the new edition of the current PDBio 305 text-book and competing textbooks from other publishers. I will

revise and update my PDBio 305 study objectives, lectures, PowerPoint slides, visual aids, and handouts to be compatible with the chosen textbook.

2. Keep current in neuroscience and physiology. I plan on attending the Society for Neuroscience annual meeting this year. I will continue to read current literature and share new discoveries and methods in my courses.

3. Include more active learning activities in classes. Students will be more active in class by solving application problems, analyzing clinical case studies, using interactive software programs, manipulating models, and giving class presentations.

APPENDICES

A. Mentored students
B. Course study objectives
C. Class handouts and activities
D. Assessment instruments and examples of student work
E. Course syllabi
F. Student evaluations
G. Peer and administrator evaluations
H. Course improvements

CHAPTER THIRTY-TWO

POLITICAL SCIENCE

Richard R. Johnson

Department of Political Science
Oklahoma City University
Spring 2010

CONTENTS

INTRODUCTION

My name is Richard Johnson, and I am a professor of political science who also serves as the chair of that department. I have taught full time for more than twenty years, nine at a state institution, and since 1997 at Oklahoma City University, and have had a consistent record of excellence in teaching and scholarship.

TEACHING RESPONSIBILITIES

I teach a 3/3 load, having a one-course release per semester because of the size of our department. Also, I contribute two to three courses per year to our classes in Singapore. I regularly offer courses in two General Education offerings (Governance in America, Comparative Politics), and teach upper-division courses in American politics as well as the Senior Capstone for our department (see the next table). Also, I advise about thirty students and three student organizations.

Courses taught: General Education courses are offered every semester; other offerings are in a two-year cycle.

Course Number/Title	Required or Elective	Enrollment
POLS 1003 Governance in America	Required	30–35
POLS 1013 Comparative Governments	Required: International students Elective: Domestic students	20–30
POLS 2413 Legislative Behavior	No major elective	10–12
POLS/HIST 2713 Regional Geography	No major elective	12–15
POLS 3213 State and Local Government	No major elective	10–15
POLS 3313 Modern Southeast Asia	No major elective	12–15
POLS 3503 Election Seminar	No major elective	12–15
POLS 4863	Major elective	6–10

TEACHING PHILOSOPHY

I see my role in terms of being the lead student in the classroom. I make important decisions on texts, readings, calendars, and set the framework for courses I teach. I have a responsibility for helping students master the basic principles and facts (especially in introductory classes), but also to challenge students through discussion, lecture, questions, writing, and review to reflect on issues pertinent to the course, critically evaluate issues, relate class experiences to real-world experiences, and prepare students to be discerning citizens in the larger community. In meeting these responsibilities, I stress communication as the key to achieving the best results.

I see teaching as central to how I define or see myself. I come from a family who in one way or another wanted to be teachers, and education was highly valued at home. In addition, some of the most influential individuals in my life were a couple of college professors without whose encouragement and mentoring I would not have even have thought I had the skills to teach at the university level. When I teach, advise, counsel, or just interact with students, I am doing what I most want to be doing in the world, and in some ways I hope that I am touching students' lives in some of the ways my life has been so influenced by key professors and others.

TEACHING OBJECTIVES/METHODS

Objectives and methods will vary by class. Many are tied into our departmental goals for which I am the primary author (Appendix 1).

I actually have a broad range of subjects that I teach, so context and pragmatism are important. In an introductory class, I may use comparisons, open-ended questions, written work outside of class that asks the student to critically reflect on the topic assigned, and, frankly, what is happening in the news. Many of the problems one has teaching introductory government classes include interest and applicability; part of my challenge is to create an environment where people can see the significance of the government and its actions to their lives and ask "why." I also include examples of good and bad research associated with the field of political science, as well as draw more broadly from social science areas to make or illustrate points.

Examples
- *Governance in America; Comparative Politics:* These courses are predominantly lectures interspersed with discussion of political events, outside readings, or assignments. As the class moves along, it does become more conversational. I lean more to the lecture more in the first half of the course, as many students do not have a good historic political or constitutional

background. I especially emphasize short papers that ask students to apply questions to real-world situations. Comparative Politics is much the same, but I place more emphasis on the comparative method and getting students out of preconceived notions of their country or other countries.

- *Upper Division:* In upper-division courses, the focus is less on the material that students need to master and more about importance and applicability. I may have a portion of the class where I give an overview of important concepts or points, but much of this may be driven by student inquiry ("Can you explain?" "I don't understand the relevance of what the author says"). I ask students to role-play, debate, analyze (usually written), review professional literature, or bring in people from the community with expertise on the subject at hand to further inform our discussion. In other words, I challenge students to grasp the material, apply concepts, critically evaluate material or statements, or put together concepts or ideas to come to a more insightful view of the subject. I am trying to engage the students in higher forms of learning. I also strive to challenge myself by engaging in new and different methods to stay current with my teaching. A recent example is using arts integration.

CURRICULAR REVISIONS

They sometimes are organic with the changing nature of texts or current events (especially in political science). Almost always, revisions come through discussions with colleagues about their methods, as I read and reflect on best practices, as I am involved in faculty developments projects, and as I discern the predominant types of learners I have in class. Some recent examples of curricular changes include:

- *Legislative Behavior:* required students to do two reviews from the professional literature, so that they were more aware of the research and big questions in this subfield.
- *Election Seminar:* students were assigned a final question on the impact of the elections on government policy. I found from previous sections that students did not always close the loop on the effects of elections on public policy.

- *Modern Southeast Asia:* took a standing course that I had taught previously and converted it to an arts-integrated course based on the theme of architecture.

Steps Taken to Evaluate/Improve Teaching

- I evaluate every fall and spring class that I teach and encourage and value student feedback. Comments, for instance, will give more valuable context to student concerns.
- I take part in faculty development programs as my schedule allows, such as the Teaching Portfolio workshop (Summer 2007), serving as a Priddy II Scholar (arts integration program) in 2007–08, and other programming through our Center for Excellence in Teaching and Learning.
- In completing my first edition of my teaching portfolio, one of the goals that I set for myself was to comment more fully on student papers. This goal came from attention to student evaluations and feedback. I have made a concerted effort to share more of my thoughts with students on their papers and provided a clearer grading rubric for papers; students have accordingly rated me higher in this area (See Evaluation of Teaching section).
- Reflect on best practices as presented in professional materials or conferences such as the Oklahoma Political Science Association (OPSA). OPSA typically has a panel on teaching within the discipline and includes varying perspectives and updates on practices.
- Working with colleagues in social science, where we teach several cross-listed courses. For instance I had discussions with colleagues teaching Contemporary Political Theory and Political Philosophy to encourage a greater focus on citizenship. This was an area found to be weak in our departmental assessment.

Evaluation of Teaching

Colleagues

Included are comments from peer reviewers from my last sexennial review. The observers were Dr. Curt Branch, a teaching partner from our Center for Excellence in Teaching and Learning, and Dr. Leo Werneke, a philosopher and my original dean at Oklahoma City University:

- In 2009 Dr. Branch stated: "In candor, I have been impressed with Dr. Johnson's conduct of general education requirements . . . his student evaluations are 'glowing.'"
- Dr. Werneke stated: "Not only is Dr. Johnson practicing a very effective pedagogy, he is also witness to the possibility of a truly civil discourse about controversial political issues. His student evaluations clearly indicate that students appreciate his work."

Student Evaluations

Some recent comments from students are listed after the numerical averages per question on our standard "TEVAL" form. In the next table, I include averages from some of the more important questions from classes in academic year 2007–2008. Scoring is on a 1–9 rating, 9 being high. Numbers of students in 1000-levels classes vary from twenty-four to thirty-five, and in upper-division classes the numbers vary from six to fourteen students. Please note the last category ("commenting on students' work") illustrates a goal met; former ratings were either side of 7.

Class	Overall Rating	Clear Goals	Preparation	Commenting on Students' Work
POLS 1113 Governance	8.1	8.4	8.6	8.0
POLS 1003 Governance	7.5	7.8	8.5	8.0
POLS 3213 State/Local	7.9	7.9	8.5	7.6
POLS 3203 S.E. Asia	8.6	8.6	8.6	8.0
POLS 4863 Senior Seminar	8.5	8.3	8.5	8.3

Some representative comments are listed below:

- *Senior Seminar* POLS 4863: "Dr. Johnson was very helpful and interested in what I was doing and made Senior Seminar very rewarding and beneficial."
- *Governance in America* POLS 1003: "Dr. Johnson is an outstanding teacher. Taking this class really helped me learn about government and current issues in the world."
- *Modern Southeast Asia:* "Overall this class is extremely successful in piquing our interest in the region. I feel a little more worldly for having taken this course!"
- *State and Local* POLS 3213: "I liked the discussion during class. Dr. Johnson encouraged independent thinking and opinions on issues. Good professor!"

By our standard measures, I have been consistently ranked in the exemplary range across an array of courses. I find students to be fair and candid and their suggestions helpful. For instance, in a previous edition of my teaching portfolio, the last measure in the table, "commenting on student work," was not as highly ranked. Through time and attention, I have responded to student input, and my evaluations give evidence of improvement. Further comments from colleagues can be found in *Appendix 3* and from students in *Appendix 4*.

STUDENT LEARNING

Departmental assessment also provides evidence of student learning. For instance, we include pre- and posttests for sections of Governance in America. For my sections, the scores from academic year 2007–2008 are presented in the next table; my duties the last couple of semesters have kept me from teaching introductory courses. Numbers are based on a maximum score of 25; displayed are the class averages. **I have typically had the highest improvement in class averages in my department**.

Fall 2007		*Spring 2008*	
Pretest	*Posttest*	*Pretest*	*Posttest*
11.6	17.6	11.5	17.4
11.6	16.6		

Another measure my department considers important is what our seniors do, especially those marked as having completed their program through Senior Seminar, which I teach. Based on the last three sections of the Senior Capstone course (2007–2009), students have graduated and engaged in important new areas. Specifically, eleven are in law school or have been accepted, four are accepted to master's programs, two are military, three are engaged in jobs in the political field, and three are taking some time off while considering graduate studies.

Three students whom I mentored have presented papers at conferences. A student in my first section of Modern Southeast Asia took a paper on Cambodia to a national Asia studies convention, won the student paper award, and went on to Columbia University for graduate studies. **In 2008, one of my advisees won the Undergraduate Best Paper Award from the Oklahoma Political Science Association for a paper he developed while doing an internship I supervised**; in 2006 another of my students was a finalist for this award.

I have included in *Appendix 5* several student testimonials. I would like to reference a note sent to me by a recent graduating senior:

> I just wanted to write you a short note to let you know how much I appreciate all that you have done for me. I greatly enjoyed your classes and teaching. If we could say one thing, we'd always know they would be interesting and a challenge. You really spoiled me. When you said you believe in good customer service I didn't fully believe you till I saw it, but you sure delivered. I could not have asked for a better, more genuinely caring advisor. Thanks for always being there for me no matter what I needed, even when it was just to talk. Undergrad would not have been the same without your leadership.

HONORS AND AWARDS

Previously, I was honored to receive the Oklahoma Political Science Association's Teacher of the Year Award. This is a competitive award based on student evaluations and scholarly merits.

Within the Oklahoma Political Science Association (OPSA), I have held numerous positions, including an editorial position in *Oklahoma Politics*, the yearly publication of the OPSA, and am one of only two political scientists in Oklahoma who serve as advisors to the national organization *Project Vote Smart*. The project follows state legislation across all fifty states. Since coming to OCU I have also become a member of *Phi Kappa Phi* and *Pi Sigma Alpha*, the national political science honor society. **I was recognized by our Center for the Excellence of Teaching and Learning as a Fellow of the Faculty Teaching Academy in 2008, one of the first group from our institution so honored.** In addition, I have authored scholarly papers and coauthored a text, *Oklahoma at the Crossroads*.

One of the most important opportunities that I have had at OCU is being chosen as a Priddy II Fellow. This program has three main functions. The first goal is to develop a cohesive learning community that will go through a number of exercises and exposures to different forms and ideas. Another is to help participants develop an arts-infused course. We spend considerable time looking at how the arts can enrich teaching across disciplines. Finally, we also spend substantial time studying the most recent educational literature. Without a doubt, the chance to examine the educational literature and activities has refreshed my ideas about teaching and challenged some of the more traditional ideas I had when it comes to education. I find this especially important as I would consider myself at midcareer.

Goals

Immediate Goals (One to Two Years)
- Develop a greater proficiency with rubrics and other measures of assessment. As teaching requires a multitude of methods, so does effective measurement of student accomplishments or learning.
- Experiment and further explore the themes of arts integration and civic engagement. I have taught one arts-integrated course and presented some materials on civic engagement.

Longer Term Goals (Two to Four Years)
- Stress a more interactive style of learning, especially in my introductory courses. We are seeing changes among students and their expectations, and interactive learning is judged to be more in line with the best practices in education literature.

- I would like to become more technology oriented in the class-room. This will have to be a gradual commitment given time constraints.
- Develop my skills as a more proficient administrator as a way to open up opportunities for my institution and my students.

APPENDICES

1. Departmental Objectives
2. Class Assignments/Sample Syllabi
3. Peer Evaluations
4. Student Evaluations
5. Student Testimonials

CHAPTER THIRTY-THREE

PSYCHOLOGY

Aaron Kozbelt

Department of Psychology
Brooklyn College of the City University of New York
Spring 2010

CONTENTS

CLASSROOM TEACHING RESPONSIBILITIES

At Brooklyn College, teaching demands are considerable. A full load is seven courses per academic year, though new faculty members are granted release time to pursue research. The Psychology Department is one of the largest at the college. Thus, there is continual high demand for many departmental courses, including those that I teach (see the next table for details).

Course Title	Course #	Typical Enrollment	# Times Taught	Undergraduate or Graduate	Required or Elective
Psychological Statistics	40.1	32	17	U	Required
Cognitive Psychology	57.1	40	7	U	Elective
Psychological Statistics	705	20	5	G	Required
Cognitive Psychology	738	12	1	G	Elective
Creativity and Cognition	801.03	10	2	G	Elective seminar
Neuroscience, Evolution, and Creativity*	801.06	8	1	G	Elective seminar

*Cotaught with Frank W. Grasso.

STUDENT MENTORING RESPONSIBILITIES

Besides my classroom teaching, I also have a number of other teaching-related responsibilities in the Psychology Department and at the college. Generally I mentor several Ph.D. students and master's students who focus on research in my areas of specialization: creativity and cognition, the psychology of the arts, and the psychology of humor. In addition, I have served on many master's and doctoral committees. I also typically have several undergraduates working in my lab as research assistants each semester; in all, I've supervised undergraduate research for about thirty-five student-semesters. Finally, I have mentored students in the CUNY B.A. program and supervised the year-long final projects of undergraduate students in the Honors College.

TEACHING PHILOSOPHY, GOALS, AND STRATEGIES

My teaching philosophy, goals, and strategies are tightly interconnected. My teaching methods are driven by my goals for what I would like students to learn. Typically I focus on two key learning goals: **1. Mastering the factual content of the course; 2. Being able to think critically about the content of the course and, more important, to engage in critical thinking in general. I work toward the first goal by carefully preparing discussion points and examples**. I also commit to this goal on the first day of the semester by announcing to students that they can expect me to come to class extremely well prepared for that day's material—and that I expect the same from them. I work toward the second goal by devising classroom examples and exam questions that force critical, dynamic reasoning about the course content rather than mere regurgitation **(see Appendices A and D)**.

My classroom style is largely lecture based, but my "lectures" are punctuated by questions to the class and, ideally, students' questions to me. I have a clear sense of the content I would like students to acquire in a particular class session, and I use a variety of methods to determine if students are learning that material. To some extent, I get this information via classroom interactions. For instance, I often provide a worked-out example of a statistics problem or cognitive psychological experiment and then vary the parameters of the problem or experiment and ask students to predict the result. By asking many variations on an initial question, I can show students the flexibility and the limits of the concepts and definitions under discussion, diagnose and reinforce students' understanding of the material by making explicit connections between different questions (that is, why they would yield similar or different answers), and also hint at the complexity of the relevant theoretical and empirical issues, which time does not usually permit us to completely cover in class. I also administer weekly quizzes in my courses (always consisting of ten true-false questions), which give a more objective assessment of student understanding.

Particularly in *Statistics*, it is extremely important to me that students learn to reason about quantitative situations, as this mode of thought is vital for understanding and is broadly transferable to many real-world problems. One method I have developed to encourage critical thinking is a set of multiple-choice questions that require students to actively compare and reason about the relations between statistical concepts rather than just the concepts themselves. I created these questions and have gradually evolved them over the last five years. They now comprise large swathes of the homework assignments and exams in both my undergraduate and graduate *Statistics* courses. **Appendix A** contains a sample of these kinds of questions, excerpted from my *Graduate Statistics* final exam.

It is also important for me to motivate students to be interested in and to work hard on subject matter that can seem daunting at first. I am most explicit about motivating students in my *Statistics* course, since most students enter the course with a great deal of apprehension and math phobia. On the first day of class, I try to honestly convey to students how much work the class will be by distributing a two-page handout on "How to do well in this class" (see **Appendix B**), in which I recommend very explicit strategies for mastering the material, not falling behind, and seeking outside help. This sets the expectation of a high standard right from the start and gives students the tools and tactics they need to meet those standards and to be successful in the course.

I also use various exercises to integrate the basic, abstract subject matter of my courses with students' personal experiences outside the classroom. Some examples:

- In my undergraduate *Cognitive Psychology* course, when we discuss memory and learning, I make explicit particular tactics and strategies that students can use for learning, retaining, and being able to transfer knowledge—indeed, I tell my students that this course is probably the only course at the college where the subject matter of the class is how to do well in the class! One example of this technique is teaching students the "method of loci"—a memory aid that allows people to memorize a large number of items (in order) rather easily by building on their preexisting knowledge of a familiar location. One exam question in the class always requires students to use the method of loci to memorize a list of twenty items, in order. Practicing the method and being forced to use it on an exam increases students' motivation and makes the experience of extending one's memory capacity a striking experience for many students— most of whom do very well on that exam question.
- Likewise, in my *Statistics* courses, I always have students find outside examples of graphs and other research to critique in

class. For instance, in an early lecture in the course on how to display data, we examine and discuss a number of very good and very poor graphs, evaluating their quality using a clear, simple rubric focusing on the graphs' truthfulness and aesthetics. I then have students look in the media and find examples of graphics that are meaningful to them and to provide a detailed critique and revision of the graph. I also tell students that if they have no criticisms of the graph, they must explain in excruciating detail, using the same rubric discussed in class, why the graph is perfect—thus, they will have a much easier time answering the question if they think critically about the graph. This is good motivation for students to think critically!

- Finally, the last homework assignment in my *Graduate Statistics* course always includes a question in which students must delve into the research literature (preferably in their area of specialization) and apply the principles and logic of null hypothesis testing to a statistical technique they have never encountered before. This kind of exercise forces students to abstract, generalize, and apply the most fundamental ideas of the course to an area they are motivated, as budding researchers, to understand.

CURRICULUM AND COURSE DEVELOPMENT

I have had the luxury of being able to focus on teaching a relatively small number of different courses numerous times and to learn from each experience, continually refining my courses. Many aspects of the courses, such as the exercises described in the preceding section, and methods of assessment described below, have evolved greatly from semester to semester. Over time I have also applied more of the language of learning goals and expectations to my course syllabi. **Appendix C** contains example syllabi from my undergraduate and graduate courses.

EVALUATION OF TEACHING

Formal Student Feedback

Besides observations and feedback from departmental colleagues, Brooklyn College faculty are evaluated by undergraduate students who evaluate faculty every fall semester via anonymous surveys. Results from the fall 2005 semester to the present are posted on the Brooklyn College Web site. It is widely held that the most representative and informative question on the survey is, *"How likely are you to recommend this instructor to a friend?"* Response options are "Very likely," "Somewhat likely," "Don't know," "Somewhat unlikely," and "Very unlikely." Data for this question for my two undergraduate courses are shown in the next table. (Note that the last three options have been combined; different sections of the 40.1 statistics course have also been pooled.) As can be seen, student feedback on my courses has generally been very positive; the other survey questions show comparable positive evaluations.

Semester	Course	Number of Respondents	Very Likely	Somewhat Likely	Other
Fall 2007	40.1	44	88.6%	4.5%	6.8%
Fall 2007	57.1	30	70.0%	23.3%	6.7%
Fall 2006	40.1	60	61.0%	25.4%	11.9%
Fall 2006	57.1	38	73.7%	18.4%	7.9%
Fall 2005	40.1	51	72.5%	21.6%	5.9%

Informal Student Feedback

Besides the quantitative aspect of student evaluations, I have received informal, qualitative feedback from a number of students. Among the comments I've received:

- "The class was very hard at the beginning, but it became easier when the topics were made more coherent." "Who ever thought statistics could be interesting or fun? You made it both." (Psychology 40.1: *Psychological Statistics*)
- "It was not an easy class but it was worth the work. I know a lot of cognitive psychology now." (Psychology 57.1: *Cognitive Psychology*)
- "Thank you for a great and an eye-opening semester after which I will never look at fellow *Homo sapiens* the same way. Thank you for your suggestions during the presentations; they helped me focus and better the paper." (Psychology 801.06: *Neuroscience, Evolution, and Creativity*)

Classroom Observations by Other Faculty

At Brooklyn College, each faculty member is scheduled to be observed teaching by another faculty member in his or her department once per year. Afterward, the instructor and observer talk about how the class went, identify strengths and weaknesses of the instructor, and discuss pedagogy more generally. The resulting evaluation is signed by both faculty members and becomes part of the instructor's personnel file, figuring into tenure and promotion decisions. I have found this process to be extremely interesting and valuable, both as an observer and as a subject of observation. As an observer, I have engaged in a number of fruitful discussions with other faculty members and learned a great deal about how to engage students in the classroom. As a subject of observation, I have gotten positive reviews from my colleagues. Some excerpts:

- "A very well organized presentation of a difficult topic (power) using a binomial test example. Students were generally attentive, with relevant questions. Appears to have a good rapport with the class." (Psychology 40.1: *Psychological Statistics*, Fall 2007)
- "The instructor delivered a well organized and thoughtful lecture on creativity and decision making. A wealth of ideas was introduced and discussed with reference to a highly complex topic such as creativity, but the general theme of describing this process as fundamentally no different from other forms of cognition was made salient. The question posed for the study of decision making was whether people make decisions in rational or irrational ways, but the delivery of this information set the curious student wanting to know the answer forthcoming in the next class. Overall, his was a wonderful class and delivered in a lively, exciting way." (Psychology 57.1: *Cognitive Psychology*, Fall 2006)

EVIDENCE OF STUDENT LEARNING

Teaching *Statistics* and *Cognitive Psychology* has made the issues of outcome assessment and student learning very salient, since *Statistics* deals with how to analyze empirical data and *Cognitive*

Psychology is concerned with processes of learning, memory, and problem solving, which are central to any education. As I frequently teach these particular classes, I have continually tried to develop them—not only in terms of content and presentation style, but also in developing efficient assessment tools to determine the extent to which my learning goals for my courses are actually being met. For instance, for most of my time as a statistics instructor, I have given a surprise diagnostic quiz early on in the class, usually during the second class meeting. For several years, I gave a fifteen-item quiz inherited from a senior faculty member that covered basic mathematical reading of the sort that would be useful for the *Statistics* class. Scores on this quiz were moderately predictive of students' final grades in the course, but I was not entirely pleased with the instrument, since it tapped general mathematical ability rather than the specific content of the course, which is what I was much more interested in (and which seemed more amenable to improvement via instruction).

Last year in my undergraduate *Statistics* course, I implemented a new assessment strategy, an explicit pretest-posttest design, to evaluate student learning. The instrument was a twenty-item true-false test (see **Appendix D**). The questions deal with content knowledge of the subject of statistics and are drawn randomly from a large pool of questions that feed into weekly ten-item true-false quizzes (each of which counts for 2 percent of the final course grade). The pretest takes less than ten minutes to administer at the start of the semester; it does not contribute to the student's grade in the course. The posttest is a different set of twenty true-false questions, drawn from the same population of questions, and is built into the final examination. The results of the pretest-posttest comparison were very encouraging. *For the fifty students for whom I had complete data, the average pretest score was 10.7 (equivalent to guessing), and the average posttest score was 15.6—a large and statistically reliable improvement.*

I was very pleased with this set of results—first, from the standpoint of verifying student learning, and, second, from the standpoint of being able to efficiently (and, I hope, meaningfully) assess the extent to which learning goals are being met.

STUDENT ACCOMPLISHMENTS

In addition to the assessment of in-class learning goals that are most characteristic of undergraduate courses, I also naturally have a vested interest in the real-world accomplishments of my students (graduate and undergraduate), as they pertain to and reflect my mentoring. As my own research program has grown, the opportunities for publishing papers and doing conference presentations in conjunction with my students have increased dramatically. I have been fortunate to have outstanding graduate and undergraduate students, and so far I have had reasonable success in mentoring them. While most of my publications are solo authored, I have published four papers in peer-reviewed journals with students as coauthors, and another three such papers have been submitted and are under revision. I have also copresented nine papers or posters at conferences—including several national and international conferences—with students. (See **Appendix E** for a list of publications and presentations coauthored by students I have mentored.)

PROFESSIONAL OUTREACH AT BROOKLYN COLLEGE

My activities contributing to improved teaching at Brooklyn College are not limited to instructing students in my own courses. Over the last five years, I have also organized and run faculty workshops on the cognitive science of teaching and learning, most of which have been organized by the Office of the Provost or Associate Provost. I often ran several workshops per year, each usually attended by ten to twenty faculty members. In these workshops, I gave a series of mini-lectures on topics relevant to understanding how humans (including Brooklyn College students) learn and how we might use this knowledge to teach better. The topics included the importance of background knowledge in the formation and retention of new memories, how to increase the likelihood of transfer of what has been learned in one problem setting into a new problem setting, and the value of metacognition—that is, reflecting on one's own thinking—in problem solving. These topics were transparently linked to how to improve one's teaching, based on emerging knowledge from cognitive science about how the mind works. In these workshops, my mini-lectures were followed by group discussion on how faculty have already implemented or could implement this knowledge to improve instruction. (See **Appendix F** for example outlines of my presentations at such seminars.)

I was also a cofounder and co-organizer of the Brooklyn College Cognitive Science Colloquium from 2003 to 2006. Supported by the Provost's Office, this series brought to campus renowned outside speakers from a variety of disciplines constituting the cognitive sciences. Notably, one well-attended talk was given by cognitive psychologist Dan Willingham of the University of Virginia, who writes regularly on these topics for *American Educator* and who spoke about the impact of cognitive science on education at the colloquium. (**Appendix G** includes the announcement advertising Professor Willingham's talk.)

Finally, I note that I am also the coordinator for the Psychology Department's ongoing efforts at outcome assessment as the college prepares for Middle States reaccreditation. I have coordinated several intensive departmental workshops on designing efficient and effective outcome assessment measures and using the feedback to improve teaching (see **Appendix H** for an outline of one such session). I have also worked with the Psychology Department faculty on refining a longer-range vision for assessment vis-à-vis the broader undergraduate Psychology curriculum.

FUTURE GOALS

So far, I have learned a great deal about teaching, particularly in my time at Brooklyn College. Generally speaking, I believe I am on the right track and that I am already an effective instructor. I am most pleased with having been able to continually develop classes like *Statistics* and *Cognitive Psychology*, which are often seen by students as daunting or dry, and make them engaging for students by forcing them to think hard and critically about the course concepts. I am also pleased that I have been able to develop an extremely efficient assessment instrument in my *Statistics* course, which has clearly demonstrated student learning.

In the coming year, my goal is to extend the pretest-posttest assessment methodology to all of my courses (undergraduate and graduate). In the coming three to five years, I would like to develop new courses, especially undergraduate special topic seminars on creativity and the psychology of the arts, which will build on the techniques and pedagogical principles that I have begun to understand.

APPENDICES

- Appendix A: Example Multiple-Choice Questions in Statistics
- Appendix B: "How to Do Well" Handout in Statistics
- Appendix C: Course Syllabi: Statistics, Cognitive Psychology
- Appendix D: Example True-False Questions in Statistics
- Appendix E: Publications and Presentations Coauthored by Students I Have Mentored
- Appendix F: Example Handouts for Faculty Workshops on Teaching and Learning
- Appendix G: Announcement for Cognitive Science Colloquium—Dan Willingham Talk
- Appendix H: Materials for Psychology Department Outcome Assessment Retreat

CHAPTER THIRTY-FOUR

SOCIAL AND BEHAVIORAL SCIENCES

Kristine De Welde

Department of Social and Behavioral Sciences
Florida Gulf Coast University
Spring 2010

CONTENTS

Teaching Philosophy
Teaching Responsibilities and Experience
Course Design
Student Assessments
Feedback from Colleagues
Teaching Honors and Awards
Scholarship of Teaching and Learning and Related Activities
Teaching Improvement Activities
Current Teaching and Pedagogical Goals
Appendices

TEACHING PHILOSOPHY

My fundamental goal as an instructor is to engage students in the world around them using *critical thinking*, so that they are able to articulate their thoughts in a structured and coherent fashion. Doing so offers them confidence to contribute to their communities (campus, local, national, global) in significant ways.

Teaching students to think independently and problem-solve is imperative. One way in which this can be accomplished is by presenting students with current and thought-provoking material. *I encourage student engagement with current events, using a sociological lens to interpret what is happening.* This is evidenced, for example, by my use of "experiential exams," which require students to go out into the world, make observations, and analytically decipher what they've seen via course concepts, theories, and ideas (see syllabi, **Appendix A**).

Helping students develop the capacity to ask difficult questions of the world is pivotal. Collaborative work sessions and semistructured discussions are useful for developing this skill. I find that developing questions around the course material, such as assigned readings, and then encouraging students to work out answers, individually and collectively, helps them better understand the material. They tend to have ownership of the material and their emergent knowledge since they have invested time and energy developing ideas.

I try to displace my own authority in the classroom so that students become part of a learning *process*, where they are not simply passive recipients of knowledge. I provide an ***active learning*** environment. I do not rely solely on "academic" writings to help students learn sociology. I use fiction, poetry, songs, art, and personal statements. Furthermore, the ability to see how individuals are connected to a larger whole, also known as the ***sociological imagination,*** is put into practice in my classes by using simulations, speakers, videos, experiential assignments, and readings that compel students to reach beyond their personal experiences. I try to empower my students so that they see themselves as agents capable of social change.

The culmination of critical thinking and the sociological imagination leads naturally to questions of ***civic engagement.*** That is, if students are aware of and thinking seriously about their world and their place within it, they will often find themselves compelled to "do something." I regularly provide a service-learning component in my classes for students to become engaged citizens of their communities. The lessons offered through civic engagement are profound and lasting, and reinforce the need for both critical thought and difficult questions.

By structuring my courses around strategic questions and by demonstrating to students that they are capable of developing complex responses to their world, I believe that I encourage them to question the world they live in, while fostering their confidence to find informed answers to their questions. My varied pedagogical techniques, commitment to diversified material, and opportunities for engagement are a testament to my faith in the merits of teaching sociology.

TEACHING RESPONSIBILITIES AND EXPERIENCE

Although I have been at FGCU for only a few years, I have a much broader repertoire of teaching. I have had the opportunity to teach a wide variety of courses at a large research university (University of Colorado-Boulder), a small, private liberal arts college (Flagler College), a large, private university (University of Denver), and finally at Florida Gulf Coast University. Teaching has been the cornerstone of my academic career. The following tables outline my teaching experience. Table 1 illustrates courses I have taught at FGCU. Table 2 illustrates courses I have taught at other institutions.

COURSE DESIGN

The manner in which I design my courses reflects serious consideration of my teaching philosophy. For example, my course requirements are carefully organized around meeting my goals of critical thinking, participatory learning, and civic engagement. I utilize short answer, essays, response papers, collaborative learning groups, and research papers to make certain that students have the freedom to engage with the material in ways that are interesting to them. Examples of these can be found in my course syllabi (**Appendix A**).

The opportunity to teach the same courses over many years has been a unique learning experience as I have revised the curricula based on student feedback, current research, and my own reflective process. For example, students often comment on their appreciation of **guest speakers**; and although they are difficult to coordinate, I consistently work to bring in more speakers

TABLE 1. COURSES TAUGHT AT FGCU (2007–2010)

Course (Enrollment)	Course Description
Introduction to Sociology SYG 2000 (25–180)	An introduction to the fundamental concepts in the field of sociology, the main social institutions of human society, the primary theoretical paradigms, and some illustrations of sociological research. EMPHASIS: Social structure, inequality, social change
Sex, Gender & Society SYG 2200 (15–35)	This course explores analytically the role of gender as a primary force in organizing our society, as well as how it impacts our everyday interactions. We will also examine how gender, coupled with race, class, sexual orientation, and disability, stratifies American society. EMPHASIS: Gender, race, and class stratification
Sociology of Sex Roles and Gender SYD 3800 (30)	This course considers sex roles and gender from sociological and social constructionist perspectives. We focus on the concepts of intersectionality and agency in the context of gender using a global focus that connects individual experiences with society. We also examine the relationship between power and privilege, which underpins social inequalities that are inevitably gendered (and raced, and classed). EMPHASIS: Power, agency, and resistance in a global context
The Family SYO 3120 (35)	This course examines marriage, families, and their variations from a sociological perspective. The goal of the course is to increase students' understanding of the social, historical, and cultural forces that shape definitions and meanings of family life in contemporary U.S. society. EMPHASIS: Variety of family forms, family as a social institution

TABLE 1   (*continued*)

Course (Enrollment)	Course Description
Hurricane Katrina: Unpacking a Catastrophe ISS 2011 (HONORS) (25)	This course explores the challenges posed by the Hurricane Katrina disaster, including local and federal responses, and future directions of the Gulf Coast. In this course students will familiarize themselves with the most current research on Katrina and its aftermath in an effort to understand the importance of social scientists in unpacking the vulnerabilities of marginalized communities. We grapple with the question of whether Katrina offers lessons learned or lessons lost. EMPHASIS: Environmental justice, inequality, social movements
Sociology of Food SYG 3930 (30)	This course is designed as an introduction to the field of sociology of food. In this course we explore current issues of food production, distribution, and consumption from a sociological perspective. We consider the relationships between inequality, poverty, food insecurity, and food production; food movements; and the patterns of food consumption as related to "choice," culture, class, and identity. EMPHASIS: Food insecurity, inequality, food movements
Issues in Culture & Society: Interdisciplinary Gender Perspectives IDS 3301 (60)	This course examines gender from an interdisciplinary perspective, as we investigate the biological, sociological, historical, and performative forces that affect sex and gender. We will attempt to increase awareness and appreciation of different views concerning sex and gender in relation to one's gender, age, sexual orientation, and religious, racial, and/or ethnic background. This course is team-taught, with the four professors in this class presenting particular

TABLE 1   (*continued*)

Course (Enrollment)	Course Description
	perspectives from their own individual disciplines of biology, sociology, history, and performance/performativity. EMPHASIS: Gender, intersectionality, interdisciplinary approach
Ethnographic/Qualitative Methods Forthcoming fall 2009	This course allows students to develop their own independent research project using qualitative methods. Through the design, implementation, and analysis of an ethnographic study, students will learn about research ethics, methods, data analysis, and dissemination of original ideas. EMPHASIS: Developing independent research skills
Development of Sociological Thought/ Sociological Theory Forthcoming spring 2010	This course requires students to think theoretically. Students will read and understand theoretical explanations of social phenomena as written from the viewpoints of several social theorists from the 1800s through the present day. The course requires that students understand and explain social phenomena from a variety of theoretical perspectives. EMPHASIS: Historical and contemporary sociological and social theories

TABLE 2.   COURSES TAUGHT AT OTHER INSTITUTIONS

Course (Relevant Institution)	Course Description
Women and Violence (University of Denver)	This course explores how the very private nature of gendered violence (most prominently violence *against* women) has its roots in social conditions. We examine how the social categories of gender, race, class, sexual orientation, and physical ability

TABLE 2 (*continued*)

Course (Relevant Institution)	Course Description
	intersect to produce complex social problems related to men, women, and violence. EMPHASIS: The gendered aspects of violence against women
Community Involvement (Flagler College)	This is a service-learning course premised on understanding our changing communities, civic duty and participation, the role of the individual and her/his community in a global society, and the power of the individual to enact change. EMPHASIS: Social change, civic engagement, applied sociology

from the community who could make appropriate connections between the course material and the "real world." Because of outside experts or community leaders I have hosted in my classes, many students have become involved in outreach programs, fundraising efforts, and internships.

My course design is adaptive to student feedback, innovative pedagogy, and **new technologies**. For example, in my current *Sociology of Food* course, my students are posting weekly blogs to their own blogging sites, which we established in the first week of classes. They are required to read each other's blogs and comment on them such that it is not just me, the professor, reading their reflections and insights, but a true (virtual) learning community has emerged as they read each others' ideas and learn from each other. And they are simultaneously learning a contemporary and cutting-edge skill.

One of the most important responsibilities my students have is to engage in classroom **discussion**. I use readings and/or videos seen in class as the basis for these discussions. Though I always have specific questions that I put forward, I try to allow for discussions to meet student needs. By crafting questions around an issue, students often develop basic theoretical ideas on their own. I also strive to incorporate group exercises in my courses, often placing students in consistent "affinity groups" or changing "collaborative learning groups." I may, for example, provide a set of questions for students to consider together and then discuss with the larger class.

In my classes typically students write **response papers** throughout the course that bring together readings, videos, discussions, and their own learning. This helps them remain engaged in the course, and it helps me determine whether they can apply the material, and whether the pace of the course should be adapted. Depending on the course, papers may be short, informal responses; they may be more structured around specific questions for students to answer; or they may involve experiential learning. I provide extensive written feedback on these and generally give students opportunities to revise them and further develop their arguments.

Application of course materials to students' daily lives is one key way to assess their ability to take course concepts beyond the classroom. I use **experiential exams** or assignments that require students to apply what they are learning to a mundane scenario, such as watching a movie, visiting a toy store, or watching people in public settings. They learn to appreciate how a critical analysis of their surroundings can aid in developing independent thought, being more compassionate toward others, realizing social justice, or being engaged citizens.

In courses that focus on the integration of materials from various sources (such as in *Ethnographic Methods*), much of the course is structured around the development of either a **comprehensive course paper** or research report. I give students freedom to choose topics that are of personal interest to them and to develop the papers alongside relevant course materials.

Regularly, I offer a (sometimes optional) "track" for **service-learning**. Students are required to fulfill a certain number of hours at their service site, which they can choose from a list of providers with which I have made arrangements (for example, a local women's shelter, council on aging, environmental youth group, county health department, local food bank). Students also are required to maintain a portfolio of various reflections over the course of the term where they demonstrate their understandings of course material in relation to their service work. Different ways of incorporating service-learning into a class depend on many factors such as class size, topics being covered, and the balance with other assignments. I find that courses with a service-learning component are the most rewarding for both students and myself. A fine example of this was by a group of my *Sociology of Sex Roles and Gender* students who planned, created, and carried out a local version of "The National Clothesline Project." This is a powerful visual representation of hand-painted T-shirts in honor of victims of sexual abuse and violence. This was a tremendous success, and we now do this every year!

STUDENT ASSESSMENTS

Throughout my years of teaching, my student evaluations have been very good. The next five tables feature the most recent course I have taught at FGCU (mean student ratings on a 5-point scale).

INTRODUCTION TO SOCIOLOGY—SYG 2000

	Fall 2007 *N = 35*	*Fall 2007* *N = 32*	*Spring 2008* *N = 95*
Overall assessment of instructor	4.8	4.9	4.8
Stimulation of interest in course	4.7	4.9	4.8
Communication of ideas	4.8	4.8	4.8
Problem solving or creative thought required	4.8	4.9	4.7
I learned a great deal	4.8	4.8	4.8
Encourages student participation	4.8	4.9	4.8

INTRODUCTION TO GENDER STUDIES—SYG 2200

	Fall 2007 N = 37	Fall 2007 N = 37	Fall 2008 N = 38	Fall 2008 N = 35
Overall assessment of instructor	4.7	4.6	4.4	4.7
Stimulation of interest in course	4.8	4.7	4.6	4.7
Communication of ideas	4.6	4.6	4.6	4.8
Problem solving or creative thought required	4.6	4.7	4.4	4.8
I learned a great deal	4.8	4.6	4.5	4.9
Encourages student participation	4.9	4.7	4.6	4.8

THE FAMILY—SYO 3120 (ONLINE)

	Spring 2008 N = 13
Overall assessment of instructor	4.6
Stimulation of interest in course	4.6
Communication of ideas	4.6
Problem solving or creative thought required	4.8
I learned a great deal	4.6
Encourages student participation	4.8

SOCIOLOGY OF SEX ROLES AND GENDER—SYD 3800

	Spring 2008 N = 20
Overall assessment of instructor	5.0
Stimulation of interest in course	5.0
Communication of ideas	4.9
Problem solving or creative thought required	4.8
I learned a great deal	4.9
Encourages student participation	5.0

INTERDISCIPLINARY SOCIAL SCIENCES: HURRICANE KATRINA:
UNPACKING A CATASTROPHE (HONORS)

	Fall 2008 N = 26
Overall assessment of instructor	4.6
Stimulation of interest in course	4.6
Communication of ideas	4.5
Problem solving or creative thought required	4.7
I learned a great deal	4.6
Encourages student participation	4.7

Comments from students demonstrate that they have positive learning experiences in my courses (see **Appendix B**) and that I achieve my primary goals of engaging students in critical thinking. For example, a student in Introduction to Sociology wrote this on his/her course evaluation:

*This class has taught me to **think critically** about what I take for granted. We have examined norms, values, ideas, socialization, gender, etc. and each discussion has enlightened me to the inequalities that I had no idea even existed. **I have begun to examine my own behavior in order to stop the perpetuation of prejudice, racism, stereotypes, etc. and feel like I am a better person because of it**. Because of this class, I will be pursuing a minor in Sociology! (Spring 2008, emphasis added)*

A student in Sociology of Sex Roles and Gender reflected on the challenging material in the course and the respectful environment we created:

*This course required a great deal of open-mindedness and the presentation of the material as well as **the class as a whole was cooperative in making the class a perfect environment to discuss any idea** without the fear of being rejected and beat on for thinking outside the norms, even **though the class material presents this challenge**. (Spring 2008, emphasis added)*

A student in Introduction to Gender Studies remarked on my excitement for teaching:

*This class really helped me to better understand gender in our society. Dr. De Welde was a great teacher who was very **passionate** about the subject. I talk about this class a lot outside of class. (Fall 2007, emphasis added)*

FEEDBACK FROM COLLEAGUES

Although student opinions are invaluable, it is equally important for instructors/professors to receive feedback from their colleagues. In the last year, a senior colleague in Sociology at FGCU attended my large (180) Introduction to Sociology course and had this to say about my teaching:

> *Kris De Welde is one of the best teachers I have ever observed. Whether in a small group setting or a large lecture hall, her unique quality is the ability to generate curiosity among her audience. I think this is because she is truly excited about Sociology and that energy shines through. (Prof. J. Manley)*

I am currently team-teaching a class with three other professors in an Interdisciplinary Gender Perspectives course representing sociology, biology, history, and performativity studies. My senior colleague in biology included this in her evaluation of my teaching:

> *I have had the honor of teaching with Dr. De Welde this past semester. I am struck by her enthusiasm for the subject, her intelligence, and her passion for teaching. Dr. De Welde sets high standards and expects students to meet them, but her joy in the subject and her skill in leading a class make the students gladly want to follow wherever she goes. She not only expertly teaches the material, but guides the students to delve deeper and to critically evaluate information that they may have previously taken for granted. Truly, she is one of our best! (Prof. M. Rosenthal)*

TEACHING AWARDS AND HONORS

Although I have been at FGCU for a few years, I am hopeful that my history of excellence in teaching will be reflected in recognition from students and colleagues. For instance, at Flagler College, I was nominated by students for the prestigious **"Who's Who of America's Teachers"** (2006). Earlier in my career, I received the Betsy Moen **Walk the Talk** award (2002), which recognizes excellence in feminist scholarship, teaching, and activism.

I have applied for and received two service-learning grants at previous institutions and a more recent curriculum innovation grant from FGCU's Center for Environmental and Sustainability Education. An example of how I have used these funds is through the Sociology of Food course. I teach this as a service-learning course that addresses local and global food insecurity, with an emphasis on the "politics of choice." Students work with local organizations such as ECHO Farms and the Harry Chapin Food Bank, as well as a national organization, Feeding America (formerly Second Harvest). In group projects funded by the grant I received, students host campus events to raise awareness about FGCU's food/environmental practices with respect to humane and sustainable food systems and global hunger/poverty.

SCHOLARSHIP OF TEACHING AND LEARNING AND RELATED ACTIVITIES

Throughout my career, I have participated in the Scholarship of Teaching and Learning (SoTL) as a means to improve my teaching. I have read religiously the teaching journal in my discipline, *Teaching Sociology*, published in it (see **Appendix F**), and reviewed manuscripts for it. I have received several service-learning and teaching enhancement grants. Furthermore, I regularly have presented papers and led workshops on service-learning and innovative pedagogy. I am committed to improving my teaching by engaging in communities of teacher-scholars who have the same passion and drive that I have for my life's work.

In my complementary work as researcher, I have studied science, technology, engineering, and math (STEM) education innovations and am involved in a book project on resistance to classroom innovations in STEM. In 2008 I wrote a grant proposal to the National Science Foundation with a colleague in the College of Business to study innovations in distributed (online) teaching and learning (this was not funded). See **Appendix E** for an executive summary of this proposal.

My professional presentations and publications on teaching and learning are focused on pedagogical innovations, or on the profession. Recent examples include:

- Kay Valentine and Kris De Welde, "All Teached Out? A Workshop on Teaching Challenges and Coping Strategies." Sociologists for Women in Society Summer Meetings, San Francisco. 2009.

- "Resistance in Sustaining Pedagogical Innovations: Lessons for Sociology from STEM Innovators." Annual meeting of the American Sociological Association, Boston. 2008. (Paper accepted, but I could not attend)
- "Embracing a Service Learning Perspective." DU Public Good Conference: The Theory and Practice of Public Good Work, Denver. 2007.
- "Bridges in Service-Learning: Creating Interdisciplinary Opportunities for Students." Presented at the annual meeting of the Southern Sociological Society, SWS session, New Orleans, LA. 2006.
- "How to Engage Your Students in the Community with Service Learning." Flagler College Faculty Symposium, St. Augustine, FL. 2005.
- "'I'm Glad I'm Not Gay!': Heterosexual Students' Emotional Experience in the College Classroom with a 'Coming Out' Assignment." *Teaching Sociology, 31*(1), 73–84. Coauthor: Eleanor Hubbard. 2003.
- "Reconstructing Gender Instructor Manual/Test Bank, 3rd edition." Accompaniment manual to *Reconstructing Gender: A Multicultural Anthology*, 3rd edition. McGraw-Hill Publishers. Coauthored with Estelle Disch. 2002.

TEACHING IMPROVEMENT ACTIVITIES

Continuing my education as a professor is paramount in meeting my goals and maintaining high levels of student learning. I believe that continuous professional curiosity and development are necessary to maintain one's knowledge, interest, and vitality in teaching. I have attended numerous conferences, workshops, and seminars on my profession, which include the following:

- Association of American Colleges and Universities Engaging Departments Institute. The purpose of the institute is to support the development of leadership within and across departments for strengthening and assessing students' liberal learning (aacu.org). 2009.
- Peter Seldin's Teaching Portfolio workshop. Sponsored by the College of Arts and Sciences, Florida Gulf Coast University. 2009.

- "Teachers Are Made, Not Born," a full-day workshop on the scholarship of teaching and learning in sociology. Sponsored by the American Sociological Association, SoTL section. Annual meeting of the American Sociological Association, Boston. 2008.
- "Interdisciplinary Studies Summer Intensive," workshop on teaching the Interdisciplinary Studies core civic engagement course. Sponsored by the College of Arts and Sciences, FGCU. 2008.
- "Angel: Getting Started." Sponsored by ELearning Department, FGCU. 2007.

CURRENT TEACHING AND PEDAGOGICAL GOALS

My goal is to continuously improve my teaching by setting clear, attainable goals. My current goals include short-term goals such as implementing grading rubrics for student papers, as well as long-term goals such as increasing my research and publications on teaching:

1. Invite two senior colleagues in the next year to observe and assess my classroom teaching. I would like written and verbal feedback from them.
2. Over the next few years, I would like to work as a mentor with select students on independent research projects that will eventually be submitted for presentation and/or publication.
3. Based on student feedback, verbal and written, in course evaluations, I feel it has become important for me to clarify my grading criteria on writing assignments and offer more structure on how I grade student work. I have implemented a handful of different grading rubrics to accomplish this goal. I began this in fall 2008 and will be collecting student feedback on the different tools in order to standardize the rubric for specific assignments. I hope to distribute a standardized rubric to students in the 2009–2010 academic year.
4. I would like to develop two scholarly papers for publication over the next two years. For example, as an effort to assess the effectiveness of blogging on student learning, I would like to collect data on students' experiences with blogging in the

Sociology of Food course, and a handful of future courses in which I will adopt this assignment. Subsequently, my goal is to write an article for publication based on the use of this innovative technology and pedagogical strategy.

APPENDICES

A. Representative Course Syllabi
B. Student Comments
C. Letters from Student
D. Letters from Colleagues
E. Executive Summary of National Science Foundation Proposal
F. Teaching Sociology article: "I'm Glad I'm Not Gay!"

Chapter Thirty-Five

Social Work

Amanda Evans

Division of Social Work
Florida Gulf Coast University
Spring 2010

Contents

Teaching Responsibilities

I teach two classes per semester (fall and spring) in both the graduate and undergraduate programs in the Division of Social Work. I also teach a summer elective on either the subject of death and dying or interrelational violence. In addition to classroom teaching, I provide advising, field education liaison, and site visits to nine or ten graduate students per semester, which is credited as a course in my teaching assignment.

The next table is representative of my teaching recurrent teaching responsibilities.

Course Name	Course #	Role in Curriculum[a]	Student Class Size
Practice I	SOW 6305	R, G	15
Practice II	SOW6306	R, G	15
Psychopathology	SOW 6124	R, G	26
Advanced Practice Seminar	SOW 6369	R, G	26
Field Education	SOW 6537 and 6555	R, G	10
Death and Dying	SOW 6931	E, U, G	30

[a]R = Required course. E = Elective course. U = Undergraduate. G = Graduate.

TEACHING PHILOSOPHY

My philosophy of teaching is grounded in the belief that my role as an educator is to facilitate the acquisition of new knowledge and skills related to professional practice. To that end, I believe:

- Knowledge and skills are acquired over time, not all at once.
- All students have strengths and personal knowledge that they bring into the learning experience.
- That the teacher and student are in partnership in the learning process and that there is reciprocity in the sharing of knowledge.
- Respect for the opinions and viewpoint of students fosters trust and models professional conduct.
- That my students are my future colleagues.

I believe that the foundation skills of competent practice are highly developed communications skills, both written and verbal, and the ability to think critically about problems. Therefore, I regard:

- The ability to speak and write well as core skills for student learning.

- Critical thinking as the foundation of problem-solving skills.
- My role as an educator to be directly related to developing course activities where students can demonstrate verbal, written, and critical thinking skills.
- Students as scholars who must take on the responsibility to explore, analyze, and integrate their educational opportunities for competent practice.

Teaching Objectives, Strategies, and Methods

Teaching Objectives

The following teaching objectives guide my teaching methods in all classes:

1. *Facilitate educational opportunities that supply new knowledge and skills to students on topics related to professional practice.* This is accomplished in each class by assigned readings, lectures, and guest speakers. I also try and incorporate interaction with community practitioners and agency visits when possible. (Weekly reading assignments and topics related to new knowledge and skills can be found in Appendix A. Projects that evaluate student learning are found in Appendix C.)

2. *Advance students' writing and verbal communication skills to a level appropriate to professional practice.* I use both written and oral evaluative tools in my classes to measure student communication skill. On the undergraduate level, I work with students to supply the fundamental skills of writing a scholarly paper and how to speak in front of peers and in small groups. On the entry level of graduate school, I use written papers to assess the students' writing abilities. I expect basic grammar and formatting skills at the beginning of the program and demonstration of professional scholarly writing by graduation. I meet with students individually if concerns are noted and they are referred to the university writing lab for assistance. The ability to communicate orally is an essential skill in social work practice, so every course I teach requires some form of spoken presentation. (Detailed information on verbal and written assignments can be found in Appendix B.)

3. *Develop students' capability to think critically about problems related to human behavior and society.* Each course I teach requires students to examine their existing values and bias in order to understand how they approach human behavior and problems. In each class, assignments are generated so students may demonstrate the ability to recognize differing viewpoints, cultural influences, and the use of research, evidence, and analysis to deal with problems within the assignments. (Activities related to critical thinking can be found in Appendix B.)

Teaching Methods and Strategies

I utilize a variety of teaching methods in the classroom, including lecture, experiential activities, active class discussion, and role play. I assume that students enter class prepared by completing the assigned reading for the week and review that information via question and discussion either on the Web or in the classroom. I reinforce the learning from their reading by providing additional activities or lectures relevant to the topic for that week. I utilize a variety of methods to accommodate different learning styles that include direct practice activities (kinesthetic), video and PowerPoint (visual), and discussion and lecture (auditory).

The following courses are representative of how my teaching methods reflect my teaching objectives of advancing knowledge and skills related to professional practice, communication skills, and critical thinking.

SOW 6305 Practice I

Acquisition of basic counseling skills and understanding values and ethics in social work practice are the goals of this foundation year course. I utilize lecture, weekly readings, and classroom discussion to deliver the content for this course. Because it introduces students to concepts related to engaging, assessing, and intervening in client issues, I also use a significant amount of experiential activities such as role play. (A sample of experiential activities can be found in Appendix B.)

SOW 6306 Practice II

Building on the content introduced in Practice I, students begin to explore the role of theory and intervention effectiveness in their direct practice with clients. We discuss the evolution of major psychological theories and evaluate research related to the effectiveness of the related interventions for various populations of clients. (See Appendix A for a copy of the syllabus with course agenda. A sample of experiential activities can be found in Appendix B.)

SOW 6124 Psychopathology

The content for Psychopathology is entirely related to diagnosing mental illness according to the DSM IV-TR [*Diagnostic and Statistical Manual of Mental Disorders*, 4th edition, text revision] and related research. I have revised this course to be taught back in the classroom, as opposed to online, as a result of student and alumni feedback related to clinical licensure. This course requires advanced critical thinking skills for assessing and diagnosing mental illness. Course content is delivered via classroom discussions, PowerPoint, videos, and weekly readings. Graduate students must complete this course in their Concentration year. (The course content and weekly agenda can be found in Appendix A. Case study assignments that help measure students' competence in the diagnostic process and examples are found in Appendix B. A film analysis project and a final examination are found in Appendix C.)

EVALUATION OF TEACHING

Florida Gulf Coast University utilizes the Student Assessment of Instruction (SAI) for standardized measurement of faculty teaching. I rely heavily on student evaluations for courses that I teach for the first time, as well as those that I have taught for years. I strongly encourage students to be candid in their evaluations and to provide suggestions as to how the course could improve when taught again. I find the comments to be very useful in helping me determine what the students perceived was beneficial and what opportunities there may be for course improvement. I view course development as an ongoing process, and constructive criticism related to course improvement is encouraged. The reciprocal nature of course evaluation reflects my teaching philosophy and reinforces the collaboration between learner and instructor in the classroom. I feel this interactive process facilitates adult learning and fosters trust. I am gratified with the very positive assessments from students as shown in the next table: 5 = Excellent, 4 = Very Good, 3 = Good, 2 = Fair, 1 = Poor.

Course Name	Course #	Overall Assessment of Instructor
Practice I	SOW 6305	5.0
Practice II	SOW 6306	5.0
Psychopathology	SOW 6124	4.6

The following samples of anonymous written comments from the student evaluations help validate my perception of my teaching objectives, especially facilitating new learning and critical thinking.

- Dr. Evans is my career role model. (Practice I, Fall 08)
- I could listen to her lecture all day. (Psychopathology, Fall 08)
- I thoroughly enjoyed the class with Dr. Evans and learned more than I expected. (Psychopathology, Fall 08)
- It was great to not only learn from the textbook but to see the material in action at work. (Psychopathology, Fall 08)
- Dr. Evans is a great professor and shows much concern about her students. She is entertaining and really knows this topic. (Practice II, Spring 08)
- Dr. Evans tied everything together very well using lecture, assignments, and discussion. (Psychopathology, Fall 08)

The complete evaluation forms with all comments can be found in Appendix D. In addition to the standardized evaluation forms, I periodically ask students to evaluate a course and a textbook. I do this to determine if they perceive the text directly related to the defined course objectives and to determine if the course objectives were reflected in the classroom activities, discussions, and assignments. I also receive communication from students and alumni related to how their education prepared them for direct practice. These can be found in Appendix E.

TEACHING IMPROVEMENT ACTIVITIES

Although my teaching evaluations are consistently very good to excellent, I know that there are new and different skills and techniques that I can apply to the classroom. Therefore, to ensure that I would take the time to explore new techniques, I began building specific teaching goals and objectives into my annual professional development plan (PDP). A detailed narrative of these activities can be found in Appendix F. The next table reflects the teaching improvement activities I have explored and implemented.

Year	Activities
2008–2009	Maintain an average of 4.0 on my student assessments of instruction.
	Request a peer review of teaching one time each semester (fall/spring).
	Complete teaching portfolio for submission with self-evaluation due by March 21, 2009.
	Review library material on critical thinking.
	Find at least one resource to improve online teaching interaction with students.
	Conduct site visits and review documentation for all M.S.W. advisees. Meet with students regarding career goals and educational concerns.
	Develop student action plans related to educational concerns as needed.

FUTURE TEACHING GOALS

Short-Term Goals: Two Years

- **Enhance** my experiential learning activities skills to offer more creative ways to learn in the classroom. I am strongest in the area of lecturing and facilitating group discussions. I would like to have more small group and hands-on types of activities to draw on.
- **Explore** the research related to creative ways to evaluate learning. I feel I may have become too dependent on

students' writing papers. While I feel strongly that writing skills are essential for a competent professional, I feel that for some classes, they do not measure what I wish to know.

- **Write** teaching goals and objectives into my PDP annually. This has been successful and encourages me to keep the goals in the forefront of my mind during the year.
- **Improve** my skills related to the Socratic method, especially in the advanced clinical courses. I feel this would benefit the students' ability to think critically as well as keep the courses from becoming rote.

Long-Term Goals: Three to Four Years

In the future, I am interested in becoming a dean. Toward this end, I would like to begin exploring the scope of that position and skills that are necessary, and determine if I need to enhance my current knowledge to better qualify me to compete for a dean position.

APPENDICES

- Appendix A: Representative Course Syllabi
- Appendix B: Sample Assignments
- Appendix C: Course Projects
- Appendix D: Student Learning
- Appendix E: Student Evaluations
- Appendix F: Teaching Improvement
- Appendix G: Student/Alumni Feedback
- Appendix H: Presentations and Publications on Teaching

CHAPTER THIRTY-SIX

THEATER

Amy E. Hughes

Department of Theater
Brooklyn College
Spring 2009

CONTENTS

1. TEACHING RESPONSIBILITIES

I teach undergraduate courses in theater history, as well as graduate courses in theater history, critical theory, historiography, and research methods. Outside the classroom, I invest considerable time and energy in student advisement, particularly in regard to professional development. As program head of the M.F.A. in dramaturgy and theater criticism, I supervise and support nine to ten students completing internships, practical projects, and independent study courses for credit; and during the spring semester, I direct four or five degree candidates completing master's theses. Occasionally, I also work with students in the department's other M.F.A. and M.A. programs who seek help and guidance regarding conference participation, scholarly publication, and teaching.

2. Teaching Philosophy

At the heart of my teaching philosophy are two fundamental values. First, I believe that the teacher should serve as a *facilitator* rather than lecturer, because students learn best when they engage the material in active and constructive ways. Second, I endeavor to transform the classroom into a creative, experimental lab— ideally, a **collaboratory**. As chief facilitator, I emphasize that all of us (including me) are involved in a collective effort to help each other learn. This approach necessitates flexibility and innovation on my part, as well as considerable trial and error; the exercises and activities that I coordinate in class sometimes succeed and sometimes do not. But every experiment plays a crucial role in my own learning process as a teacher.

Methods and Strategies

To meet the two objectives inherent in my teaching philosophy— to be a cheerleader rather than a dictator and to foster collective creativity—I ask students to grapple with the content using four general methods of engagement: writing, speaking, doing, and playing. Using this multifaceted approach, I try to account for the myriad learning styles that exist within the diverse community in my classroom.

I believe in the power of *writing to learn,* **so I integrate low- and high-stakes writing into my courses**. This is a fundamental tenet of Writing Across the Curriculum (WAC) and Writing in the Disciplines (WID) pedagogy. For example, I require undergraduates to free-write at the beginning of every class, offering an impulsive response to a prompt based on the assigned reading. This exercise allows them to identify themes and questions central to the day's topic; it also enables me to assess their progress and provide feedback regularly.

Formal writing assignments are staged, requiring a proposal or abstract, one or two drafts, and a final draft. I offer guidance throughout the writing process and often devote one class to peer review so that students can learn from each other's work. In addition, I use online resources, such as Blackboard and PBWiki .com, to facilitate peer review and collaborative composition. (A recent assignment using wiki technology is in Appendix A.)

Finally, because research indicates that cramming for tests usually results in temporary retention, I allow students to bring to the final exam a four-page handwritten "knowledge index" charting the material covered during the semester. I encourage each student to think of this master document—which may be structured in whatever manner facilitates his or her unique understanding of the course content—as a resource he or she may consult long after our time together is over.

Because some individuals learn through *speaking*, I invite students to solidify their knowledge and teach each other by talking formally and informally in class. As a result, I rely heavily on collaborative pedagogical techniques requiring teamwork and conversation in small teams. During every session, students solve problems in groups and report back to the entire class. In formal "exam teams," they discuss key concepts on a daily basis and, at the end of the semester, help each other study for the final; teams earn bonuses if all members in a group earn a B+ or better on the exam. Students also collaborate on formal presentations and projects for credit. (A handout in Appendix A details a presentation assignment in my undergraduate theater history course.)

I regularly incorporate practice, or *doing*, in my teaching. I insist that students *do history* by researching and analyzing primary sources, or *do theory* by proposing and articulating their own theories regarding audience reception, dramatic structure, or theatrical production. We perform excerpts from assigned plays in class—sometimes extemporaneously, other times with advance preparation. Or I ask students to share ideas about how a theatrical text might have been staged at a particular historical moment or how it can be adapted and realized in present-day practice.

I also believe that we learn by *playing*—and the double meaning of that word, invoking both acting and games, accurately reflects how play informs our work. I find that students participate in the learning process much more actively when the classroom welcomes exploration and even friendly competition. Inspired by the Reacting to the Past pedagogy initiative developed by Mark C. Carnes at Barnard College, I invite students to immerse themselves in the cultural details of a specific era through role-play, or "games," during which they engage in passionate, in-character debates in class. (One exercise that I developed, based on the controversy over Pierre Corneille's *Le Cid* in 1637, is in Appendix A.) Instead of a traditional midterm exam, I emcee a trivia game in the style of *Jeopardy!* and the winning team receives a bonus on the final. I have found that students appreciate the opportunity to assess their progress this way rather than through the potentially punitive mechanism of a test.

Mentoring and Advisement

Providing excellent mentoring and advisement is central to a college's mission and strategic plan, and I take this aspect of my teaching very seriously. Because Brooklyn College is a public institution serving an incredibly diverse community, our students lead intense and busy lives, and I take pride in making myself available in whatever way is most convenient for them: in-person meetings, phone conferences, e-mail, even text messaging. I help undergraduates with writing, time management, and other challenges, and I occasionally counsel them about internships, graduate programs, and career opportunities as well.

As program head of the M.F.A. in dramaturgy and theater criticism—which trains promising individuals for careers as production dramaturgs, literary managers, theater-in-education administrators, theater critics, and teachers—I mentor nine to ten students during two years of study in a curriculum that combines academic course work, hands-on experience in campus productions, professional internships, and a thesis project. (A list of my advisees during 2008–2009 is in Appendix B.) As needed, I also offer support and advice to graduate students pursuing advanced degrees in directing, design/technical theater, performing arts management, and theater history/criticism in the Department of Theater.

Pedagogical Transparency

Because I view the educational process as a partnership between teacher and student, I believe that open and honest communication about why I make particular instructional choices helps students to fully and faithfully participate. In each syllabus, I detail the historiographic approach I have chosen for the course (including its strengths and weaknesses), our objectives for the semester, activities and assignments I will use to assess student learning, pertinent departmental and college policies (accessibility, attendance, late work, plagiarism, and so forth), and the complete reading schedule. In other words, I make my expectations as transparent as possible. (Appendix C includes representative examples of course syllabi.)

I also ensure transparency by deploying a formative assessment of my teaching at the midpoint of the semester. I ask students to write an anonymous statement discussing what they appreciate in the course and what they would suggest, add, or alter. Rather than keeping this feedback to myself, at our next meeting I summarize some of the major themes in their responses, both positive and critical. This exercise not only enables me to make adjustments before the term is over, but also affords me the opportunity to articulate the theories behind my practice— why I require daily free-writing, for instance, or why we engage in collaborative work. I believe these conversations help students to take ownership of the learning process and know that their opinions matter to me and to each other.

3. STUDENT AND PEER ASSESSMENT OF TEACHING

Assessment provided by students and peers plays an important role in my ongoing development and growth as a teacher. Table 1 highlights questions on Brooklyn College's student evaluation instrument related to the key objectives of my teaching philosophy: to be clear about my expectations and pedagogical approach (organization), to provide generous advisement and support to students (availability), to create an inclusive environment that

TABLE 1.   PERCENTAGE OF STUDENTS WHO GAVE HIGHEST POSSIBLE SCORE
IN THE CATEGORY: 5 FOR "EXCELLENT" ON A 1 TO 5 SCALE

Question	My Score	Dept. Average
Instructor's ability to organize ideas and materials for class	83%	60%
Instructor's availability to students outside of class	79%	60%
Instructor's openness to students' comments, questions, and viewpoints concerning class topics	86%	74%
Instructor's ability to encourage independent thinking	76%	63%

respects diverse points of view (openness), and to encourage students to think independently and creatively. The table shows the percentage of students who responded to these questions with the highest score—5 on a 1-to-5 scale indicating "Excellent"—alongside the departmental average. (Scores are rounded to the nearest whole percentage point and reflect feedback from both undergraduates and graduates.) See Appendix D for the full report.

I have also benefited from generous, helpful, and positive evaluations from colleagues. For the past three years, I have received the highest possible mark ("Outstanding") in all categories. Following is a brief excerpt from my first annual evaluation, written by my department chair:

> This semester, I have observed in the undergraduate students an excitement never before witnessed. . . . Ms. Hughes has transformed the students' perception of theater history, has made it come alive, and has given them a true understanding of how the history of their art form gives foundation to their work in the present. I commend her for her efforts, and for her superb skills in inspiring our students.

Appendix E includes additional excerpts from annual reviews and teaching observation reports.

4. EVIDENCE OF STUDENT LEARNING

One of the greatest rewards of teaching is seeing students apply what they have learned. Appendix F, which features a paper submitted for a role-playing exercise in History of the Western Theater II, exemplifies how I employ games to inspire students' creativity. To show how I use staged assignments to improve writing skills, Appendix F also includes the first and final drafts of a paper written by an undergraduate in conjunction with a group project. (Consult Appendix A for complete descriptions of these assignments.)

On the graduate level, evidence of student learning manifests not only in assignments submitted to fulfill course requirements, but also in successful internship and job placements, papers accepted at conferences, and a 100 percent graduation rate. Appendix G lists master's theses I have directed over the past two years, and Appendix H provides a list of professional arts organizations that have accepted my M.F.A. students for internships or full-time employment.

5. SCHOLARSHIP ON TEACHING AND PROFESSIONAL OUTREACH

I consider the application of pedagogical theory and method to be one of my main research and professional interests. I currently serve on the executive board for the Roberta S. Matthews Center for Teaching at Brooklyn College. I also coauthored an article about the advantages of including communication-intensive activities in Introduction to Theatre courses that was published by the peer-reviewed journal *Theatre Topics*. (A copy of this article, "Community Through Discourse: Reconceptualizing Introduction to Theatre," is in Appendix I.)

At conferences and workshops, I exchange ideas with other professors, reflect on my own teaching, and learn new techniques to use in the classroom. Over the past several years, I have presented papers, participated in panels, and led seminars on a variety of pedagogical topics (see Appendix J). I also completed an intensive four-day workshop at Brooklyn College on developing teaching portfolios and mentoring colleagues through the process. (A copy of my certificate of completion is in Appendix K.)

In addition, I regularly attend the annual Reacting to the Past Institute at Barnard College, where I learn innovative ways to employ role play to spark students' interest in history and literature. Thus far, I have received instruction for modules set in ancient Athens after the Peloponnesian War, Revolutionary France, China during the Wanli succession crisis, and England during the ascendancy of Charles Darwin's theory of evolution.

6. Short- and Long-Term Goals

This year I will develop and teach a course within Brooklyn College's Core Curriculum based on and inspired by Reacting to the Past. I am deeply invested in the college's mission to provide undergraduates with a solid education in the liberal arts, and I look forward to teaching within the general education context. I will also continue improving the courses I routinely teach in history, theatrical theory, and historiography; in particular, I hope to use formative assessment to help me strike an even better balance between the goals I set as instructor and the suggestions made by students.

Over the next **one to two years**, I would like to identify ways to mentor graduate students in the Department of Theater who wish to deepen their knowledge about pedagogical method through independent study or teaching apprenticeships. In addition, I hope to invest more time and energy in academic conferences and workshops related to instruction and learning.

Within **five years**, I plan to develop at least one article about teaching for scholarly publication, perhaps coauthored with a graduate student or TA. I also hope to be increasingly involved in college-wide committees or initiatives focusing on teaching. Some possibilities include (1) supporting new faculty members seeking to enhance their practice through reflection and experimentation, (2) participating in committees or advisory bodies related to the college's curriculum, and (3) attending professional development seminars and sharing what I learn with my colleagues on campus.

7. Appendices

Appendix A: Sample assignments (Wiki Project, Primary Source Project, *Le Cid* Debate)

Appendix B: MFA advisees during 2008–2009

Appendix C: Sample syllabi

Appendix D: Student evaluation reports (including departmental averages)

Appendix E: Annual evaluations and peer observations of teaching

Appendix F: Student papers

Appendix G: List of MFA theses advised (last two years)

Appendix H: Students placed in internships and full-time positions (last two years)

Appendix I: Published article: "Community Through Discourse," *Theatre Topics*

Appendix J: Presentations and workshops given at professional conferences

Appendix K: Certificate of completion for Teaching Portfolio Workshop

REFERENCES

Armstrong, P., Stanton, K., & Mannheimer, K. L. (2005). How would you teach this class? *Chronicle of Higher Education.* Retrieved from http://chronicle.com/article/How-Would-You-Teach-This-Cl/45011

Barrett, H. (n.d.). *Electronic teaching portfolios.* Retrieved from www.electronicportfolios.com/portfolios/site99.html

Barrett, H. (2000). *Electronic portfolios = multimedia development + portfolio development: The electronic portfolio development process.* Retrieved from http://electronicportfolios.com/portfolios/aahe2000.html

Barrett, H. (2005, October 16). *Online ePortfolio research—elementary version* [Web log post]. Retrieved from http://electronicportfolios.org/blog/2005/10/online-eportfolio-research-elementary.html

Barrett, H. (2009, October 16). *Limitations of portfolios* [Web log post]. Retrieved from http://electronicportfolios.org/blog/2009_10_01_eportfolios_archive.html

Batson, T. (2002). The electronic portfolio boom: What's it all about? *Syllabus, 16*(5). Retrieved from http://campustechnology.com/articles/39299

Boyer, E. L. (1990). *Scholarship reconsidered: Priorities of the professoriate.* Princeton, NJ: Carnegie Foundation for the Advancement of Teaching.

Devanas, M. (2006). Teaching portfolios. In P. Seldin & Associates, *Evaluating faculty performance: A practical guide to assessing teaching, research, and service* (pp. 111–130). Bolton, MA: Anker.

Glassick, C. E., Huber, M. T., & Maeroff, G. I. (1997). *Scholarship assessed: Evaluation of the professoriate.* San Francisco: Jossey-Bass.

Greenberg, G. (2004). The digital convergence: Extending the portfolio model. *EDUCAUSE Review, 39*(4). Retrieved from www.educause.edu/apps/er/erm04/erm0441.asp

Kilbane, C. R., & Milman, N. B. (2003). *The digital teaching portfolio handbook: A how-to guide for educators.* Needham Heights, MA: Allyn & Bacon.

LaGuardia Community College. (2007). *LaGuardia program assessment description*. Retrieved from www.eportfolio.lagcc.cuny.edu/documents/tutorials/Other_PDF/Assessment_Tutorial112807.pdf

Lorenzo, G., & Ittelson, J. (2005). An overview of e-portfolios. *EDUCAUSE Learning Initiative*. Retrieved from www.educause.edu/ir/library/pdf/ELI3001.pdf

Miller, J. E. (2005, September). *Teaching portfolios for faculty and graduate teaching assistants*. Paper presented at the International College Teaching Methods and Styles Conference, Reno, NV.

Mills, M., & Hyle, A. E. (1999). Faculty evaluation: A prickly pair. *Higher Education, 38*(3), 351–371.

Mues, F., & Sorcinelli, M. D. (2000). *Preparing a teaching portfolio*. Amherst: University of Massachusetts, Center for Teaching.

Ouellett, M. L. (2007). Your teaching portfolio: Strategies for initiating and documenting growth and development. *Journal of Management Education, 31*(3), 421–433.

Piernik-Yoder, B. (2009). Facilitating scholarship of teaching through electronic course portfolios [PowerPoint presentation]. *EDUCAUSE Learning Initiative*. Retrieved from http://net.educause.edu/ir/library/powerpoint/ELIWEB0911.ppt

Rate, N. (2009, November 11). *ePortoflios and mLearning Part 1* [Web log post]. Retrieved from http://nickrate.com/2009/11/11/eportfolios-and-mlearning-part-1/

Reese, M., & Levy, R. (2009). Assessing the future: E-portfolio trends, uses, and options in higher education. *EDUCAUSE Center for Applied Research*. Retrieved from http://portfolio.project.mnscu.edu/vertical/Sites/%7B0D936A3C-B3B2-48B8-838C-F5A3B3E0AF6C%7D/uploads/%7B2231316D-EFA9-4A6D-B382-734A350E4510%7D.pdf

Reynolds, C., Labissiere, Y., & Haack, P. (2004). Developing reflective practice in teaching assistants through electronic portfolios. *Journal of Faculty Development, 20*(1), 37–44.

Seldin, P. (1991). *The teaching portfolio: A practical guide to improved performance and promotion/tenure decisions*. Bolton, MA: Anker.

Seldin, P. (1997). *The teaching portfolio: A practical guide to improved performance and promotion/tenure decisions* (2nd ed.). Bolton, MA: Anker.

Seldin, P. (2002, March). *Guidelines for evaluating the teaching portfolio*. Faculty seminar presented at Pace University, Pleasantville, NY.

Seldin, P. (2004). *The teaching portfolio: A practical guide to improved performance and promotion/tenure decisions* (3rd ed.). Bolton, MA: Anker.

Seldin, P. (2010, February). *Evaluating the teaching portfolio*. Roundtable discussion at the American Council on Education Department Leadership Program, San Diego, CA.

Seldin, P., & Associates. (1993). *Successful use of teaching portfolios.* Bolton, MA: Anker.

Seldin, P., & Miller, J. E. (2009). *The academic portfolio: A practical guide to documenting teaching, research, and service.* San Francisco: Jossey-Bass.

Sorcinelli, M. D. (1993). *Teaching portfolio.* Amherst: University of Massachusetts, Faculty Senate Committee on Teaching Evaluation and Improvement and the Center for Teaching.

Sorcinelli, M. D., & Ouellett, M. (1998). *Teaching documentation program.* Amherst: University of Massachusetts, Center for Teaching.

Sorcinelli, M. D., & Ouellett, M. (2002). *Teaching documentation program* (2nd ed.). Amherst: University of Massachusetts, Center for Teaching.

University of Texas at El Paso, Center for Effective Teaching and Learning. (n.d.). *Introduction to teaching portfolios: An overview of the purpose of portfolios in evaluating teaching and their format.* Retrieved from http://sunconference.utep.edu/CETaL/resources/portfolios/intro.htm

Zubizarreta, J. (2004). Checklist for the evaluation of teaching portfolios. In P. Seldin, *The teaching portfolio: A practical guide to improved performance and promotion/tenure decisions* (3rd ed., p. 34). Bolton, MA: Anker.

Zubizarreta, J. (2006). The professional portfolio: Expanding the value of portfolio development. In P. Seldin & Associates, *Evaluating faculty performance: A practical guide to assessing teaching, research, and service* (pp. 201–216). Bolton, MA: Anker.

INDEX